D0935738

THE CHAGRES

ALSO BY JOHN EASTER MINTER

Parachute Troops, U. S. A.

RIVERS OF AMERICA BOOKS

already published are:

KENNEBEC by Robert P. Tristram Coffin
UPPER MISSISSIPPI (New Revised Edition, 1944)
by Walter Havighurst
SUWANNEE RIVER by Cecile Hulse Matschat
POWDER RIVER by Struthers Burt
THE JAMES (New Revised Edition, 1945) by Blair Niles
THE HUDSON by Carl Carmer
THE SACRAMENTO by Julian Dana
THE WABASH by William E. Wilson
THE ARKANSAS by Clyde Brion Davis
THE DELAWARE by Harry Emerson Wildes
THE ILLINOIS by James Gray
THE KAW by Floyd Benjamin Streeter
THE BRANDYWINE by Henry Seidel Canby
THE CHARLES by Arthur Bernon Tourtellot
THE KENTUCKY by T. D. Clark
THE SANGAMON by Edgar Lee Masters
THE ALLEGHENY by Frederick Way, Jr.
THE WISCONSIN by August Derleth
LOWER MISSISSIPPI by Hodding Carter
THE ST. LAWRENCE by Henry Beston
THE CHICAGO by Harry Hansen
TWIN RIVERS: *The Raritan and the Passaic,*
by Harry Emerson Wildes
THE HUMBOLDT by Dale L. Morgan
THE ST. JOHNS by Branch Cabell and A. J. Hanna
RIVERS OF THE EASTERN SHORE by Hulbert Footner
THE MISSOURI by Stanley Vestal
THE SALINAS by Anne B. Fisher
THE SHENANDOAH by Chard Powers Smith
THE COLORADO by Frank Waters
THE TENNESSEE: THE OLD RIVER, *Frontier to Secession*
by Donald Davidson
THE CONNECTICUT by Walter Hard
THE EVERGLADES by Marjory Stoneman Douglas
THE TENNESSEE: THE NEW RIVER, *Civil War to TVA,*
by Donald Davidson
THE CHAGRES: RIVER OF WESTWARD PASSAGE
by John Easter Minter
SONGS OF THE RIVERS OF AMERICA, edited by Carl Carmer

Rivers

OF AMERICA

EDITED BY

Hervey Allen AND *Carl Carmer*

AS PLANNED AND STARTED BY

Constance Lindsay Skinner

ASSOCIATE EDITOR · JEAN CRAWFORD

ART EDITOR · FAITH BALL

The Chagres:

RIVER OF WESTWARD PASSAGE

BY

John Easter Minter

ILLUSTRATED BY

William Wellons

RINEHART & COMPANY, INC.

NEW YORK · TORONTO

PRINTED IN THE UNITED STATES OF AMERICA
BY THE HADDON CRAFTSMEN, INC., SCRANTON, PA.
DESIGNED BY STEFAN SALTER

TO THISTER

WHO HELPED ME SEE IT THROUGH

Contents

Foreword

I FIRST saw the Chagres in July, 1941, when I arrived in the Panama Canal Zone as a junior officer of a unit of U.S. Army parachute troops. Washington had abandoned its pretense of neutrality; our mission was to reconnoiter the airfields and the capitals of Latin America and lay plans so that we could, at a moment's notice, fly to the aid of any New World government that might be threatened by an Axis uprising.

Those were busy days for me, and they got even busier when the fury descended on Pearl Harbor, for the Panama Canal logically expected to be the next target. What with digging foxholes and oiling machine guns, I had no time for probing into what I knew would make a great story—the story of the Chagres, River of Westward Passage.

It was in the following May, only a few miles from Chagres water, that a freak accident made me a minor celebrity. There had been a rumor (as usual) of an enemy task force approaching the Bay of Panama, and we had been ordered to establish a line of resistance against approach to the canal by land. As we bailed out over the jungle, I was struck in mid-air by one of our own transports; the impact tore off the wingtip of the plane, but my parachute was not damaged; it brought me safely to the ground. Nine days later I regained consciousness under an oxygen tent in Gorgas Hospital.

My survival astounded the medics, for I had suffered twenty-seven fractures, a punctured lung, and a paralyzed leg. (I learned later that they advised my commanding officer to prepare my life-insurance claim, and that rehearsals for a military funeral had been held.) When, after thirteen months of patching, I left the hospital on crutches, my friends congratulated me for "robbing the undertaker." I was, they assured me, "living on borrowed time."

I could think of no better way to spend my borrowed time than to search out the biography of the River of Westward Passage.

Even if mankind had not yet succeeded in building the canal that raises the Chagres to its present pre-eminence, its story would still be one of the best, among all the stories of the world's rivers, to tell. Its central theme is man's battle against the rocks, his challenge of nature's greatest hindrance to world commerce. The offshoots are men's battles against one another. Naturally, the fighting makes livelier reading than the peace, however victorious, that follows it.

Here is a story without parallel in this world. It has been acted out and told by explorers and exploiters, soldiers, sailors, and airmen, clergymen and physicians, engineers and traders, statesmen and scientists, adventurers, crackpots, bandits, and bums, of many colors and creeds, each accenting his own concept of the important things. With all its facets the story fills thousands of volumes, and thousands more could be written on what has been left untouched.

I have written about what I liked best; there has been no other criterion. I hope that the reader will find the result well enough integrated to satisfy his sense of history and well enough decorated to satisfy his taste for entertainment. I have approached the task with a feeling of respect, and sometimes of awe, for the towering conflicts and climaxes. If the story of the Westward Passage does not burn itself into the mind and heart of the reader, the fault will lie with the telling.

J. E. M.

BIRD'S-EYE VIEW

I: RIVER OF GOLD

The Chagres has never gone anywhere, but it has seen just about everything. It has seen more gold, for instance, than have all the other rivers of the world combined. Its valley contained so much gold at the beginning of its recorded history that the Spaniards called Panama "Castilla del Oro"—Golden Castile. By the time this supply had run low, Peru was discovered; then across the Chagres the Dons drained the fabulous wealth of the Incas, which was enough to match all the gold in the commercial channels of Europe. Later the Yankees shipped out via the isthmus virtually all the gold that was mined in the California days of '49, which amounted to more than a billion and a half dollars. Today the Chagres carries the bulk of the world's trade goods—an even more potent form of gold—across the hump from one to the other of the two great oceans.

Our river's first sights were volcanic eruptions, for it was born during an era of terrestrial upheaval. Soon afterward it watched the migrations of Mongoloid tribes into South America. Aeons later, its waters bore the landing boats, and its shores felt the slippered feet, of gentle Christopher Columbus, as he probed the eastern shore of the American continent in search of his chimerical Westward Passage to the Orient. It saw Vasco Núñez de Balboa as he slashed through the jungle, his brain afire with stories of a land to southward where the paupers wore breastplates of gold, and it mirrored his image as he finally gained a mountaintop above its banks for the first white man's sight of the blue Pacific. Soon afterward its banks felt the tread of the lesser Conquistadors, as they walked first in wonderment and then in crazy lust when the natives showed them their dazzling piles of yellow metal.

Its crocodiles churned the water to foam as they fought over the bodies, brown ones and white ones, cast there after the battles between invader and native patriot. Its banks guided Francis Drake and Henry Morgan as they led their Pyrate bands through the jungle to fall upon the bulging treasure houses of the Spanish king. Its waters reflected to the night sky of the New World the strange voodoo rites, the bloody orgies of darkest Africa, brought across the Atlantic in hellish slave ships by unwilling immigrants.

It carried the bungo boats in which adventurers from young America and old Europe raced toward California and her gold, and closed quietly over the bodies of those who drew too late. It watched the labor and the life of colonies of Chinese, Hindustanis, and Malaysians, with their strange dress and their strange rites of obeisance to Oriental gods, who had been lured to the Chagres country with promises of a month's wages every day; then it saw them die, almost to a man, of jungle fevers. Finally, after thousands of lives and millions of dollars had been spent, its banks quivered with the passing of the world's first transcontinental railroad trains.

It looked on while Count Ferdinand de Lesseps spent money and lives until he had almost bankrupted the French nation without achieving an interocean waterway.

Then, as Panama broke her political ties with Colombia, our river furnished a face-saving obstacle to the troops who had come from Bogota to quell the revolt. (The army had to sail away homeward, unbloodied, in a comic-opera denouement: the soldiers could not persuade a hard-headed Yanqui passenger agent to extend credit for their railroad tickets to the proposed scene of battle.)

It helped (and hindered) the American sanitary workers as they transformed the isthmus from the vilest pesthole in the world to the garden spot of the tropics. Then, when George Washington Goethals had finished his locks and ditches and dams, the Chagres sent its waters plunging in, to grow into the lakes, to surge through the turbines, to fill the locks, to raise and lower the ships, to shrink the world by half.

The Chagres is the world's most valuable river.

It is, whether you base your evaluation on a narrow dollars-and-cents tabulation of material services rendered, either in the total of ships and cargoes carried or in time and money saved by obviating the voyage around Cape Horn, or whether you weigh its broader, higher import as a prime weapon in the race-old, unending battle to make of the world a better place to live.

Its value by either scale rests on the fact that it is the river that operates the Panama Canal—feeds its lakes, fills its locks, generates its electric power, even furnishes its army of workers with their drinking water and with excellent game fishing for their holiday sport. It is the bloodstream of the world's greatest transport and communications center and the fount of power for the greatest machine that mankind ever built.

II: RECONNAISSANCE

In the fastness of the rugged Cordillera, half a mile above the level of the sea, the Chagres becomes a river as a thousand streamlets unite in hard trap rock. The heading basin, as bare and clean as an enameled bathtub, pours its sky-pure water over a worn but unstained lip of gray crust, to splatter a few feet below into a curving limestone trough. Here begins a watercourse through primeval jungle, now between sheer dolomite cliffs, now over swirling rapids, now across broad sábanas, now down picturesque stairstep falls, always under withering sun, refreshing moon, or pelting rain.

Within the space of fifty river miles the bed drops to an altitude of less than three hundred feet; this precipitous rate of descent gives the current a normal speed of seven miles per hour. By the time it passes the Chico outpost, where it sees its first human habitation, our river has been augmented by six major tributaries: Chagrescito, Esperanza, Piedras, Limpio, Mariposa, Chico.

Along the next few miles it sees on its banks a few bohíos—the open huts with high-pitched roofs of dried palm leaves, in which Indian families live much as they have lived for ages past. Time was when huts such as these extended from here down to the river's mouth, solitary ones and in clusters large and small, seldom more than an arrow's flight between. For the Chagres valley always has been a good provider: plenty of fish and game, fertile land which produces abundantly with little or no cultivation, equitable climate.

Around the great bend below Chico the river's speed diminishes, as it meets and mingles with its own stilled waters which have been impounded by Madden Dam. Long before the deep, narrow channel spreads into the expanse of the upper man-made lake, with its 22 square miles of surface 240 feet above sea level, there is no noticeable current.

Into Madden Lake the Chagres delivers eighty billion cubic feet of water each year.

Chico Station consists of a tiny frame bungalow which the Panama Canal hydrographers maintain for the observation of the river's unpredictable stages. Above it the country is without doubt virgin to human settlement; it is too rugged to invite habitation, even by the most primitive of peoples. The possibility of occupation by forgotten races of the past may be dismissed, for in early times it was less eroded, and hence even more rugged, than it is today. There is virtually no level ground except for the playas along the river, and on one of these a house would stand only until the next flash flood.

Seldom have men ventured more than a few miles above Chico. A few small expeditions, which have included scientists, hydrographers, engineers, timber cruisers, prospectors, surveyors, and writers, have pushed all the way to the headwaters by cayuco; it takes weeks, because of the swift current and the necessity of frequent portages around mile-long rapids. So it may be said that a narrow strip of land to either side of the river has been explored. The remaining two hundred square miles of the uppermost valley have never known the gaze of man, except from the air.

No one has ever found any sign of human habitation, present or past, within sight of the banks above the Chico outpost. This answers as well for the unexplored backlands, for if there are people they live close to water. The legend of a tribe of savage Indians, shooting poisoned darts and suffering no stranger to ascend above a certain point on the river, is baseless.

In every direction the explorer sees only the abundant life of the forest which has not been sullied by Man. The green hills roll endlessly away. There are a few broad, deeply ridged sábanas, where bedrock is too near the surface to allow trees to grow, and occasionally a great knoll whose covering of soil is too thin to support anything more than short grass. And everywhere the naked rock juts up, in splotches of gray above the green.

Here are all the animals of the American jungle. Crocodiles bask on the playas. Boa constrictors twine in the branches overhead. The bushmaster, the fer-de-lance, other venomous snakes, and many more which are harmless, slither along the moist ground. Scorpions and tarantulas race and hide among the rocks. Lizards, from the size of a housefly to the five-foot length often attained by the iguanas, nibble the foliage. Tapirs and peccaries scramble through the clusters of stately hardwoods. Giant sloths inch along the spreading limbs, head down. Monkeys and marmosets chatter in the coconut palms. Birds of rainbow plumage scream and trill as they dart overhead. Ant bears probe the man-high emmet hills with their long, sticky tongues. Along the banks the cormorants dive into the coursing, crystal-clear water for catfish, shad, trout, bass, mancholo, and babu. Unseen pumas and black panthers watch it all from their lairs, waiting for night to fall.

This world is theirs, as it has been from the beginning. It is the unexplored upper valley of the Chagres, the fierce, mysterious land beyond the neatly painted white house which the U.S. government has built at the Chico junction. Here are a thousand stories that will never be written.

The river's course is half run before it enters a theater which shows the doings of mankind.

Before Madden Dam was completed in 1934, the Chagres flowed on unhampered past the destined damsite at Alhajuela, slowing its speed a bit as the bed broadened and the rate of fall became gentler. More tributaries joined it; gradually it grew into the mightiest river of the isthmus. But today the pent-up waters of Madden Lake have flooded the junctions of the Bonito, Fea, Indio, Tranquilla, Pequeni, Puente, and Azote Caballo, so that now each one flows independently into the upper reservoir.

Through the vents of Madden Dam the waters of the upper Chagres basin flow only at the will of the canal engineers. Controlled release from this reserve generates electric power, ameliorates sudden floods which formerly swirled directly into the lower lake, and maintains the summit level of the world's most important water highway which crosses the isthmus 155 feet below.

The Chagres, before the canal builders came, wound on to the Caribbean Sea, collecting as it went the waters of its lower tributaries: Madroñal, Limon, Gatuncillo, Caño, Bailemono, Frijoles, Frijolito, Gigante, Trinidad, Gatún. But nowadays the dam at Gatún, two decades older than the one at Alhajuela, again holds back our river's waters, piling them up to flood all these junctions except the first two. From a natural bed which at the lower dam has dropped almost to sea level, the impounded stream mounts behind the earthen barrier to a height of 85 feet. This time it spreads into a lake with a surface area of 164 square miles, which was the largest artificial body of water in the world until Boulder Dam created Lake Mead in 1936. Into the lower basin the Chagres system delivers another eighty billion cubic feet of water, in addition to the annual supply from Madden Lake.

The dam at Gatún is a vast, gently sloping ramp which rises athwart the Chagres bed some seven miles inland from its natural mouth. Its three flights of locks connect with a sea-level trench, through which the ships and the Chagres waters make their way into Limón Bay.

At Dos Bocas, nineteen miles above Gamboa, the Chagres bed turns with a sweeping bend from southwest to west, and near Gamboa turns farther to join the route of the canal. Here begins another breath-taking masterpiece of Yankee ingenuity: the Chagres waters divide, and flow in two diametrical directions—to the right, northwesterly, into Gatún Lake, and to the left, southeastward, into the world's only man-made canyon, the nine-mile gorge which is called Culebra Cut.

Along this latter-day channel the Chagres flows through matchless grandeur across the continental divide; it is the only river ever to do such a seemingly impossible thing. At Pedro Miguel its waters feed through the single flight of locks down into tiny Miraflores Lake on the Pacific slope. Then, as the ships steam on into the double-flight locks at Miraflores town, the Chagres waters—

diluted now by those of the similarly imprisoned Río Grande—find their way into a sea-level ditch which carries them into the blue Pacific. Our river is the only one ever to flow at the same time into two oceans.

At Gatún the waters plunge again into turbines and turn the generators whose power operates the Panama Canal—swings the ponderous gates, works the pumps, drives the electric mules, lights the towns. For our river is the lifeblood as well as the highway of the greatest machine that man has ever built.

The excess water tumbles down a concave spillway, at which fishing for tarpon is unexcelled. From there the Chagres flows in its natural bed for its last few miles before reaching the sea, through its old mouth between the native village of Chagres and the imposing ruins of the castle of San Lorenzo, just as it did in the centuries before man solved the problem of the great interocean gateway. The mouth is 120 pre-dam river miles, or about 50 miles airline, from the uncharted headwaters.

Here we are only nine degrees north of the equator. As the sun wavers between Cancer and Capricorn, carrying with it an ascending current of warm, moist air, it brings its rain belt across the Chagres valley. In February, March, and April, while the sun is far to the south, there is little or no rain. During January and May, the months of solar movement, rains are moderate. Then from June through December, while the sun is far to the north and directly overhead, the rains come. No place on the globe receives a higher concentration of rainfall. At Porto Bello, 29 November 1911, the all-time world record was set:

2.48 inches in 5 minutes. The valley has an average yearly precipitation of 130 inches.

Cloudbursts upon the mountains often last for three days, creating torrents on the river which surge downstream in great waves. In its narrower canyons the water climbs fifty feet in three hours, and subsides as rapidly. During the wet months the river's normal stage is ten feet higher than in the dry. In each rainy season the Chagres delivers an average of twenty freshets; great floods run in cycles of three to ten years. There have been times when the canal engineers opened all vents and then stood by helpless as the lake level continued to rise.

The ridge which delimits the Chagres watershed runs eastward from Gatún and climbs the rolling foothills into the Cerranía del Brujo. The divide of this range it follows, at a few miles inland from the Caribbean and roughly parallel to its shore line, with an average elevation of two thousand feet. It skirts the still-higher headwaters basin and joins the continental divide near Cerro Azúl, a 3,000-foot hump on the crest between the Chagres and Pacora valleys.

For fifty miles along the northeastern rim of the bowl the dreamy Caribbean Sea is visible, spreading northward from the jagged coast with its once-glorious cities of Nombre de Díos and Porto Bello. Just off shore to the east are the thousand and one gemlike islands and islets of San Blas, set each one inside a frame of white sand.

Across Cerro Bruja the rim climbs to a height of four thousand feet; here the far Pacific is visible on the one hand and the nearby Atlantic on the other. Eastward of this highest point in the Cerranía, the atmosphere begins to thicken with moisture as air currents from over the two oceans, at different temperatures, meet and mingle at the heart of the doldrums. From here across the heading basin spreads an almost continuous bajareque—"low rich." Wetter than a fog, thicker than a drizzle, yet gentler than a rain, it feeds the streamlets of the Chagres fount and keeps our river flowing broad even during the dry months, when other streams of the isthmus shrink to a trickle. Through this ever-present moisture the sun rarely penetrates. The seacoast to the north, less than ten miles distant, is seldom visible from the ridge.

At Cerro Azúl the rim of the bowl bends westward, joins the continental divide, and follows it across the higher axis of the majestic Cordillera de Panama. Here it looks down upon the plains and jungles that lead to the old and new capitals of Panama, and out over Balboa's great South Sea. At Culebra Pass the rim dips into the broad man-made chasm and moves across its floor, 45 feet beneath the surface of the Chagres waters and within 40 feet of the mean level of the sea.

Still westward and higher now, until the rim curves gently northward, leaving the continental divide to skirt the headwaters of the Trinidad and the lesser western tributaries before it slopes gently down to meet its starting point at the lower dam. The Chagres basin embraces an area of some thirteen hundred square miles, and covers almost three-fourths of the Yanqui strip across the Isthmus of Panama. This bowl, ever since the dams were built, has stood one-sixth filled with Chagres water.

As a watershed for a great river, the area is tiny; many a county in the United States is larger. From an altitude of fifteen thousand feet the entire bowl is visible; the great lower lake, with its many feeders converging from all directions, looks somewhat like a blue-black octopus nestling in a crevasse of green moss-covered rock, its tentacles twined into the cracks of the surface. Then, as our plane spirals downward, the features take on recognizable shape:

Skirting Gatún Lake and crossing its northeastern lobe runs the relocated track of the Panama Railroad. Still farther to the east stretches the transisthmian Boyd-Roosevelt Highway (completed 1943), crossing the broad crest of Madden Dam. In the center of the larger lake rises the incomparable island of Barro Colorado. Along the shores of the spreading Chagres waters stand the model towns, the vast airports, the busy wharves and drydocks, the untold fortifications of the Panama Canal.

Across Gatún Lake the sea-borne commerce of the world shuttles from one to the other of Earth's greatest oceans. And beneath the plying keels of the ships, deep under the captive Chagres waters, lie the sites of Carib villages, Spanish ventas, French construction towns, American labor barracks, much of the original route of the Panama Railroad, miles of the ancient highways across which the Dons drained the unbelievable wealth of Peru and western Mexico. Extending northward and southward from the lakes to their Atlantic and Pacific terminals run the old and new water, rail, and trailway routes which have spanned the strategic Chagres valley.

This is the Chagres Theater, the stage across which our story unfolds.

BOOK ONE

LINK WITH THE AGES

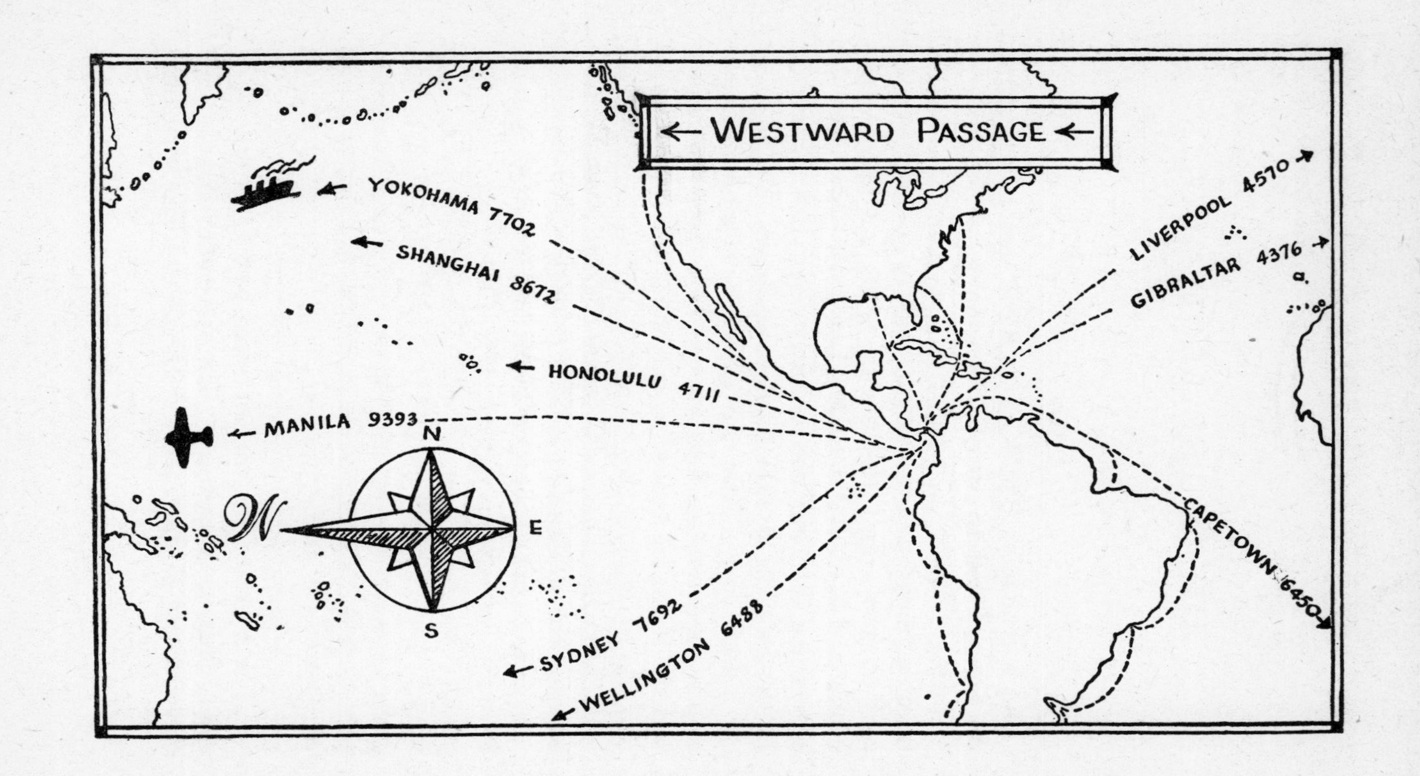
← WESTWARD PASSAGE ←
YOKOHAMA 7702
SHANGHAI 8672
HONOLULU 4711
MANILA 9393
SYDNEY 7692
WELLINGTON 6488
LIVERPOOL 4570
GIBRALTAR 4376
CAPETOWN 6450
N
E
S
W

III: IN THE BEGINNING

THE tear-shaped, liquid infant Earth, newly born from the Sun's exploding crust, hurtled through space, cooling, shrinking. Gravity balanced with momentum to brake its headlong flight; it began to spin, and the still-molten mass mushed into a ball. But the tip of its tail had already cooled and hardened, so that it could not spread into the new shape. It held itself intact, rising like a wen on Earth's face, the world's greatest mountain.

Faster spun Earth; the gathering centrifuge began to tear the mountain from its bed, and for a time Earth had the shape of a bowling pin. Finally it broke apart, and the great mountain streaked away in its turn until it reached its own balanced distance. There it settled itself into an orbit as Earth's moon.

This rupture, in which Earth lost a fortieth part of its mass, brought on the greatest disturbances that our planet has ever experienced. The portion that had stretched out toward the node snapped back, shaking the globe to its core and splitting its one great land mass from pole to pole. The umbilicus gaped for millions of years, an open cavity in Earth's face, with Vesuvius and Etna —wounds even today unhealed—rising in its center.

Earth cooled, its vapors condensed, the water level rose. Then, quite recently, the sea broke through the thinnest spot in the crater, at Gibraltar, filling it to form the Mediterranean Sea and father the story of Noah's flood.

A longitudinal fissure opened into the cavity that now holds the Atlantic Ocean, shifting almost a third part of the original land mass to westward. The break followed a great structural fault which by chance meandered, at the hairline midriff of the new continent, for five hundred miles along a serpentine line only fifty miles inland from the brink of the rising waters.

By this slight margin did the Great Hand that sundered the original land mass decree the Isthmus of Panama. A waver of the pen as it sketched a random line, a few more grains of sand for the western tip of Africa, and there would have been no thread of firmament across the dark face of the deep between the two vast islands which are the Americas. The merest trifle to the Great Hand, to man it presented a massive feature of Earth's surface, the greatest geographical obstacle to world trade, as yet far beyond his puny power to efface.

With no Isthmus of Panama there would have been no Chagres River, no canal, perhaps no human beings on the whole extent of South America when the white man's vanguard stumbled upon it at the turn of the fifteenth century. Then Columbus would have found his Westward Passage to Cathay; the Spaniards would have seen no natives bedecked in gold; the colonization might have been by builders rather than adventurers . . .

But only the Great Hand that ordained it could write of what differences this tiny jog of the pen has made in the story of Man.

The Isthmus of Panama bends eastward at North America's southernmost tip, curving down, up, down, voluptuously, in the shape of one of the ancient Oriental symbols of life, which is appropriate in view of its tropical fecundity. Below it spreads the expanse of South America, looking very like a pear hanging from its stem. And as the stem carries life to the fruit, just so did the isthmus carry to South America its first infusion of humankind: descendants of the Mongoloid peoples who had migrated ages before from Asia to North America, via Bering Strait.

Along this land bridge at its narrowest segment flowed the mighty Chagres. Our kindly river gave food and drink to the ancestors of all the aborigines of South America, while the first tribes wandered, bivouacked, fought, and wandered, on their way to find the great Magdalena, then the greater Orinoco, and then the matchless Amazon, some of them to people the jungles of Brazil and the plains of the Argentine and others to build the empire of the Incas.

Here at the isthmus the two great oceans, together comprising more than half of the world's surface, come nearest to each other except at the poles. Here, alongside the Chagres, the great mountain range that is the backbone of the American continents—called the Rockies to the north and the Andes to the south—ebbs to the paltry height of three hundred feet, even discounting Man's hollowing-out of Culebra Pass. It is the junction of continent and continent, of sea and sea, of North and South, of East and West. It is the meeting place of the old and the new.

It is the pivot of the World.

This neck of land has been thrust now far above and now far below the level it has chanced to find for the current geological era. In times which were recent, as the geologist looks at time, it has shrunk below the surface of the sea, so that the waters of the oceans mingled. Then, as volcanoes blasted the sky and the earth crust groaned and split, the land rose, higher, higher, until the waters were parted, and higher, until the bridge was more than two hundred miles wide. In that era the Pan-American mountain range had no wasplike waist; its ridgeline marched down through the sign of Cancer at altitudes which approached those in Chile and Wyoming. Then the Chagres River flowed for another six hundred miles before it reached the sea, carrying off melted snow and ice from lofty heights in addition to the seepage from the endless tepid rainfall of the lowlands, which even then was filtering through the leaf mold and making the Chagres valley into a tropical Eden.

The Dawn Man was roaming over Eurasia when the isthmus shuddered and settled again into the sea. A descendant of his had begun to convey ideas by cutting stylized pictures in stone when our river's mountains rose once more from the deep. Probably some of its first people already were spreading over the younger continent, for Columbus heard from every Carib tribe a legend of a strait—always in the direction of the Chagres. When the geologist says that the Isthmus of Panama is new land, he does not mean that there was a time when the ocean floor was smooth under the strait. The land is new because it is covered deep in volcanic soil, which built its level again up above the surface of the sea.

There have been no active volcanoes in the Chagres country since Pliocene time, but at least two new cones have risen from the earth's surface elsewhere in central America within the past decade. Volcanism in the region is not dead, but sleeping, and its sleep is fitful. Minor quakes in Panama are common; major ones are rare, for the top land is already volcanic ash; it contains no unbroken stratum of adamant rock to resist unbalancing pressure until the eventual crack and readjustment brings upheaval.

The mountains of the Chagres country, although aligned with the range that divides America from Alaska to Cape Horn, are not blood relatives of the Andes and the Rockies. They are Antillean, with axes transverse to the axes of their fellows to the north and south.

Some geologists say that the almost inundated ranges whose higher peaks are the islands of the Caribbean Sea intersect the two land masses at the isthmus, perhaps were forced above the water level in some massive pinching-together of the continents. Many a visitor merely says: "They don't look like any other mountains I ever saw." For these round-topped, steep-sided rocks were formed not by folding under lateral pressure, as were the Rockies and Andes, but by volcanic intrusion. The "peak in Darien" was not strictly a peak; it was a dome.

The Cordillera de Panama carries the continental divide as it skirts the southern rim of the Chagres basin. As on the continents above and below, the divide here runs three times as far from the Atlantic as from the Pacific. Small rivers and nameless creeks drain the Pacific slope, which is so narrow where it passes opposite the Chagres bowl that it offers no chance for a large stream to develop.

Curving north and west from the backbone range is the Cordillera de San Blas, whose crest delimits those sides of the Chagres basin. A western spur, the Cerranía del Brujo, closes the circuit.

Through this watershed the Chagres flows westward into the Atlantic, which is as difficult to visualize as the fact that the Atlantic entrance of the Panama Canal is 27 miles west of the longitude of the Pacific entrance.

IV: WHITE TUYRA NOT YET COME

DOWN the isthmus of Central America roamed the high-cheeked Asiatics, at about the time their cousins in India were putting out the first feeble roots of the world's oldest recognizable racial culture. Veering eastward with the curving land, they funneled across the narrow neck commanded by the Chagres, followed the beaches of Darién until they reached what is now called Colombia, and from there fanned out again to spread, mile by random mile, across the broad expanse of South America.

There were many racial groups among these first nomads. In time they settled down and consolidated themselves, perhaps unwittingly, into well-articulated segments, with the Chagres valley as one of the principal frontiers. Centuries passed, and the differentials widened. Toward Mexico the peoples grew taller and broader, with highly evolved facial features; they developed the high order of intelligence that generated the Aztec and Maya civilizations. In the other direction, toward the Amazon country (Paria), there appeared a small-statured simian type, comparatively inferior in mentality, known as the Carib; it was quite distinct from the racial divisions farther to the south, which emerged as the peoples of Peru and the Argentine.

As an ethnic boundary, the Chagres valley was the scene of many a violent irruption from one direction or the other, with accompanying substitutions in its inhabitants. But there appears to have been no important reamalgamation along the dividing line toward a blended frontier type, and the Caribs seem to have dominated the valley except for brief periods. The subgroup that held the border most of the time called itself the Ku-hnah, or Cuna (sometimes Cuna-Cuna), which signified People; to the Cunas themselves the word carried no sense of racial division, and meant simply Man as distinguished from Beast. They comprised in turn a number of smaller tribal elements: Coiba (Cueva), Guaymi, Cocoli, Borabi, Valiente, and many others, some of the lesser ones occupying no greater territory than a single village.

To say that their culture was more primitive than that of their pyramid-building neighbors to westward, or that of their city-planning cousins to the southeast, does not mean that the society that grew up in our valley was simple. There was as much dogma about the mysteries of existence, as much ritualism connected with life's milestones, as is found in the most advanced civilizations of the world. The Cuna culture was merely of a lower order than that of the Aztecs (who charted the heavens with an accuracy that rivaled the ancient Egyptians), or of the Mayans (whose way of counting by twenties was in some respects superior to our own decimal system), or of the Incas (whose golden sewers suggested the Cloaca Maxima of ancient Rome). Their customs varied, of course, from village to village and from generation to generation. But the Spanish archives, the Smithsonian reports, and other archaeological studies show a fairly consistent pattern of distinctive folkways during the times before the coming of the white man.

Expectant mothers did not venture into water that came much higher than the knees, for fear of drowning their children. As the hour of birth drew near, the father went into confinement along with the mother, and was expected to match her discomfort groan for groan. Immediately after the delivery, the mother was carried by the midwives to the river and immersed up to her chin, to receive her first bath in months. There she stayed until she regained enough strength to swim around a bit; she was then deemed to be fully restored after her ordeal.

The attainment of puberty involved complex ceremonies:

Following a girl's first menstruation, the women of the village carried her to a river playa, stripped off her single saronglike garment, laid her on the ground, and piled sand over her body until her head alone remained uncovered. Then one of them gathered her long hair at the back of her neck, another gripped it a finger's width away, and a third began to saw the strand between their fists with an obsidian knife. While the cutting went on, others drew a wide black line down the ridge of her nose with greased charcoal; this was the only cosmetic, used by all women but forbidden to children.

With the hair bobbing completed, the women fell to dipping water from the Chagres and pouring it over the neophyte; thus they washed the sand from her body while she rose to a sitting and finally to a standing position and stood naked before the tribe, a marriageable woman, fingering the ends of her hair which thereafter would be worn at this shoulder length. She then received gifts of jewelry, adult clothing, and ornaments, and so could begin immediately to cast her dusky eyes over the eligible young men of the tribe.

The ceremonies attendant upon reaching manhood were initiated by the youth himself, whenever he felt that the time had come. The crowning stipulation was that he trek alone for a full day's journey into the hills, select a suitable guayacan tree, fell it with his own hands, carry the trunk unaided down to the banks of the Chagres, and there carve from it a worthy cayuco, which he must navigate safely downstream through the frequent rapids to his village. There a committee of old men inspected his boat. If it failed to meet with their approval, or if the youth was known to be inexcusably inept with the bow and arrow, or the blowgun, or any other of the requisite arts, they broke up his cayuco. He was then encouraged by them to correct his weak points and try again. But if he passed muster, they stood his boat up against a tree, and he was thereupon qualified to be chased by any girl of the village whose hair had been cut, and who was so disposed.

After a successful pursuit (which for the sake of respectability had to be prolonged by the bashful groom for a while at least, no matter how willing he might be), the bride led her quarry to her father's hut. There the families and their friends, in holiday attire, picked up the couple and laid them side by side in a newly woven hammock. The attendants swung the hammock gently, chanting "Boo-EE! Boo-EE! (Marriage!)" during the consummation of the courtship.

If a young man happened to prefer someone else, he could flee so earnestly that the huntress would not fail to perceive his intent to evade her. (No doubt she made face-saving remarks when she returned from the woods to the village empty-handed; or perhaps she appeared with an armful of mangoes, as though fruit gathering had been her purpose all along.) But if he was undecided, he could submit to the capture and the rest of the ritual, and the next morning climb out of the girl's hammock and leave the hut, saying only "Boo-EE, pah!" He was then free to be chased by another girl, even if the spurned one had acquired a pregnancy. Only when he returned for a second night in the hammock with her was the contract considered closed; that made him a member of her family, subject to the orders of his father-in-law so long as the old man should live.

At planting time the men spent their daylight hours standing motionless on the rock ledges which jutted out over the running water, with bows drawn and arrows sighted straight down, letting fly whenever a fish happened to swim underneath. They carried each day's catch to the high priest, who sprinkled every fish with a few drops of the blood of an enemy tribesman and thus made it ready to be placed in the ground with the grains of maize in fit condition to bring forth an abundant crop.

The women did the actual planting, as they did everything else of drudgery in this utopian valley. But there was, each season, a select group of the most beautiful ones who were excused from this labor. Instead, their responsibility was to languish in the hammocks of the chieftain and his hierarchy of medicine men, who lay with them constantly during every hour of the seeding so as to invoke the highest possible degree of fertility for the crops. A woman who returned from this ritual to her hut pregnant was considered doubly honored, and her husband was expected to feel great distinction that his woman should be the bearer of the veriest symbol of the tribe's prosperity. The ones chosen for these rites received wrought-gold supports for their breasts, which no other women of the tribe were allowed to wear.

As with most primitive peoples, disease was attributed to a tuyra—an evil spirit, usually the soul of an animal which the sufferer had brought down either by arrow, trap, or blowdart. Hence, as a precaution, huntsmen made it a rule to beg forgiveness of the dead bodies of the animals they had killed, or to plead to them that the killing had been an accident. Should sickness come on despite these efforts at appeasement, the medicine men brought grotesque semihuman statues, carved from tree trunks, and placed them around the ailing one's hammock, to frighten the tuyra away. They also administered potions concocted from crocodile's blood and other savory ingredients.

When such remedies seemed to have failed, and death was believed to be imminent, the chief's own bearers were summoned. They lashed the dying man's hammock to long poles supported on their shoulders, and jogged off along a special path which led to an area beyond sight or shout of the village or any of the usual trails. There they swung the hammock between two trees, tucked a four-day supply of food and water in beside the sick one, and left him alone under the watchful gaze of the zopilotes—the black-and-white vultures of the American tropics. If the abandoned one could somehow recover his strength and return to the village under his own power, he was welcomed with shouts of joy. Otherwise, the tribe would know when they saw the zopilotes circling in the distant sky that the struggle for life had been lost. Days later, after the birds and the ants had cleaned the bones thoroughly, the bearers returned and carried hammock and contents back to the village for burial. Into the masonry crypt also went a supply of food and a jug of wine, in addition to a full-sized skeleton of gold, which would serve the departed one better than would his own ordinary bones in the Happy Valley.

Before the braves took the warpath, the priests made big medicine in wholesale lots by disemboweling captured enemy tribesmen, sickly slaves, and the tribe's own lepers, lunatics, and other hopeless defectives on their altars. In grave emergencies, such as prolonged drought or scarcity of game, they also sacrificed some of their fairest boys and girls, after giving the doomed ones several days of feasting and lavish entertainment.

Advice as to whether and when they should make war was obtained from a grandfather crocodile, which was kept inside a high circular wall of packed mud on the riverbank. Only the high priest and his chosen heir apparent were permitted to go near the enclosure; they alone carried to the reptile his rations, which consisted largely of the flesh of sacrificial victims. When the tribe was in need of his guidance, one of the attendants stood guard outside the wall while the other placed a ladder against it and climbed up. On reaching the top, he lifted the ladder over, placed it against the inner side, and climbed down out of sight. After a protracted conference, he reappeared and conveyed to the waiting elders of the tribe the counsel of the oracle.

This crocodile, the people were told, was purest white in color, and was possessed of immortality as well as an all-pervading wisdom concerning the affairs of men. (Possibly the first one to be thus impounded was an albino; thereafter it was unnecessary for the priests to find young albinos to be smuggled in as replacements, since no one ever saw inside the wall except the caretakers; indeed, there was no necessity for a living animal at all, except as a means of disposal of the great quantities of flesh that were thrown in.) There was a legend, which was well known to the natives of the valley long before they ever saw a European, that this saurian Sibyl had warned repeatedly of the coming of a new kind of devil from across the sea, a white tuyra who would bring these people endless misery.

Nowadays, the San Blas Islands that dot the Chagres coast are the idyllic habitat of a tribe whose ancestors fled from the mainland during the rule of Pedrarias the Cruel. The San Blas (Sambellas) Indians, as they now call themselves, are the purest racial stock and the most independent people to be found anywhere in the world; they are kept so by the stringency of an oath which each San Blas man takes over the dead body of his father, to kill his women and himself rather than accept miscegenation or political involvement.

Visitors of either sex are received with cordiality, but are not allowed to remain ashore after sundown. When a San Blas woman bears a child whose features are not unmistakably orthodox, both are put to death; the men are taught that contact with alien women is physically revolting as well as morally degrading. The Republic of Panama holds titular sovereignty over the islands, but the people decline to pay taxes or to acknowledge allegiance in any way. Government agents, schoolteachers, missionaries, physicians, and tourists alike are firmly escorted to their boats at dusk, with a warm invitation to return another day.

This fanatic isolationism holds their material progress

virtually at a standstill; life for them differs hardly at all from the way it has been for centuries past. But they are not backward commercially; their distinctive handicraft brings fancy prices in the shops of Colon and Panama, and most of them have fat accounts in the banks of both cities.

The armchair sociologists in the bars and clubs of the Isthmus will tell you that this attitude on the part of the San Blas tribe stems directly from a deep-seated distrust of all foreigners, resulting from the sixteenth-century persecutions of Pedrarias. But the San Blas chieftains, many of whom have traveled extensively over the world, chuckle indulgently at this popular theory. The tribal policy is based, they reply, not on a futile hatred for a man who has been dead for four hundred years, but on a mature perception by its leaders of the present state of the world.

"Competition for worldly goods brings progress—as you call it—but it also brings a war every generation," said an island patriarch who had attended Yale. "Peoples everywhere are slaves to the amassing and the protection of that very wealth that they somehow think means independence rather than slavery. The safest course, particularly during this transitional period of history when the nations are struggling against the inevitable world-state, is to live so simply that no other people can envy you."

That entails considerable sacrifice, grandfather.

"Granted. But for the complexities we avoid, the struggles we evade, and the freedom we enjoy, the price we pay is small."

V: ELUSIVE STRAIT

THE first European to set eyes on our river was Christopher Columbus of Genoa, the Admiral of the Ocean Sea. It was on or about 31 October 1502.

Two years earlier Rodrigo de Bastidas, a wealthy notary from Triana, had sailed from Cadiz to explore the littoral of Tierra Firme from the mouth of the Orinoco. He entered the eastern rim of the Chagres arena by passing to westward the point which Columbus later was to designate as Nombre de Dios. By that time his two vessels were crowded with captured Caribs and chests of gold; but however profitable he was finding the venture, he had to abandon it in the vicinity of Porto Bello; the finger-sized teredo worm of American tropical waters was riddling the hulls of his ships.

With Bastidas was a ship chandler named Amerigo Vespucci, a compatriot of his friend and customer Cristoforo Colombo. (Why the new continent should have been given his name, instead of Columbus', is hard to understand.) And among the ordinary seamen was a frontier migrant named Vasco Núñez de Balboa.

From the Chagres coast Bastidas turned northward and raced against the fast-working teredo to Santo Domingo, where both his ships sank as soon as they were unloaded. There, at the then capital of all Spain's possessions in the New World, he filed the charts of his exploration and handed over to the viceroy the royal quinto—the king's fifth of the slaves and treasure.

While Bastidas was there his friend Columbus arrived from Cádiz, with four dilapidated caravels of 50 to 70 tons, on his fourth and last voyage to the Indies. To man his *Capitana, Santiago de Palos, Gallego,* and *Biscayna* he had 135 jailbirds and ne'er-do-wells, the scum of the squalid ports of Southern Europe, for these were all that he could get. His objective was the same as it had been on the previous three: discovery of the legendary Westward Passage to Cathay. Columbus had with him two men who spoke Arabic, and letters of introduction addressed "To the Exalted Potentates of the Orient" (followed by blank spaces which Columbus was to fill in when he learned their names), signed by the Spanish king and queen.

After studying Bastidas' charts Columbus adjusted his plans. He would sail westward until he encountered the mainland, and from there would probe the curving coast to the southeast until he reached Bastidas' westernmost point. Somewhere along there he hoped to find the fulfillment of his original dream, which had led to his discovery of a New World.

His course from Santo Domingo would have carried him to Yucatán. But in the Gulf of Honduras he encountered a native chieftain, Guimba, sailing the sea in Cleopatrian state on a palm-shaded raft, with a corps of attendants and paddlers. The cacique, not without misgivings, came aboard the flagship and conversed with el Almirante, through native interpreters who had joined the expedition in Santo Domingo.

By sailing for several days to the southeast, Guimba said, Columbus would find "a narrow place between two great waters," and then, another ten days on the other side, the country of Ciguare. The people of that country wore crowns and bracelets of gold, and used golden household utensils. They also, as the chieftain warmed to his subject, wore golden armor, carried swords and crossbows, rode on horses, and sailed in great ships such as this one, armed with golden cannon!

At least that is what Columbus understood him to say, according to his report to the Spanish monarchs. The statements as to abundant gold were true of Peru, as Pizarro was to verify thirty years later, and the directions were correct for reaching there. But Guimba certainly had never seen a horse, and he could hardly have seen a cannon before climbing aboard Columbus' caravel.

Here was an instance of the admiral's notorious tendency to twist an informer's words into what he wanted to hear. No doubt he took the excited man about the ship, showing him a cannon and asking whether he knew what it was, pointing to an engraving of a mounted man-at-arms and asking if he had ever seen such a thing, and getting to each question an enthusiastic nod. The witness may have meant simply that he liked those things very much; or he may have claimed to be familiar with them so as not to appear ignorant and inferior to his host.

The important thing, at any rate, was the Westward Passage, and the native had told of a narrow place between two seas. Perhaps it never occurred to Columbus that this ambiguous phrase might mean an isthmus rather than his strait. He dismissed Guimba with a handful of trinkets and changed his course to southeast.

The country of Ciguare must be an Asiatic province of the Great Khan. And Guimba was a minor potentate of Tartary; Marco Polo's descriptions verified it. This meant that the geographers had overestimated the size of the globe. The greatest discoverer died without learning that his new calculation of the equatorial circumference, made to conform to this theory, was incorrect.

The squadron stopped frequently along the coast of Tierra Firme before reaching the Chagres, everywhere hearing of a land farther to the east where gold was abundant. Across this land flowed a great river; the name which the natives gave for it sounded, to Columbus' over-anxious ears, like Ganges.

At all these visits the natives had been friendly until the last one, some twenty leagues to the west, where the sailors had grown bold in their liberties with the Indian women. A brawl had followed; several natives had been killed, and the caravels had sailed away in an atmosphere of hostility.

Apparently the jungle telegraph had outsped the ships, for as the fleet entered the mouth of the great river the natives gathered on both banks by the hundreds, brandishing their clubs and wooden swords, pounding their drums, winding their conch shells, shouting, wading out into the water and splashing it toward the caravels.

Columbus ordered down a longboat and sent the Haitian interpreters ashore. After protracted argument the natives agreed to a tentative truce, and then the admiral himself landed with a chest full of hawk's bells and other trinkets. In a few minutes the childlike brown people had forgotten their anger. Soon each one was absorbed in a toy, while the chest overflowed with golden ornaments.

Columbus strolled along the riverbank, noting that it was infested with crocodiles such as he had seen on the banks of the Nile. Later he entered the feature on his charts as the River of Crocodiles, and for many years this remained its only name among the Europeans.

Columbus had heard that the Ganges was inhabited by such reptiles; he felt sure that he was on the eastern side of the peninsula of India. Through the interpreters the natives told him that a great sea lay only a few suns to the south; this, he supposed, would be the Indian Ocean.

On the bank of the river, a short journey inland, was a hill from which the great water could be seen, the natives assured him. Come, and they would show the way. So Columbus assembled a party and prepared to set out upstream in one of the longboats. But after much sign-language gesticulation among the interpreters and the native guides, Columbus gathered that the promised vista was several days removed. It would be folly to leave his crews among these natives for so long a time, and in the event of an outbreak of hostilities he would be bottled up in the river. It was the rainy season; there might come a torrent at any moment, followed by a flash flood; then the logs and the crocodiles in the river would become a hazard. Anyway, they could not now be far from the strait; doubtless they could sail around this arm of land in less time than it would take to cross it. So he abandoned the project, and left to Balboa the discovery of the Pacific Ocean.

That night, to avoid another nasty incident, Columbus ordered that all hands stay on board. The record contains no hint that this order was not obeyed, but the next morning the Indians for some reason had relapsed into the same hostility which they had shown when the squadron first appeared. As the longboats approached the bank, the natives waded out and began to belabor the sailors with their wooden weapons.

They had laid aside their bows and arrows, with which they might have done serious damage; evidently they wished only to impress on their callers the idea that they were overstaying their welcome. Clad as they were in armor, the crewmen were taking no punishment; they fought back good-naturedly.

Columbus decided to regain prestige by inspiring awe. He ordered a cannon fired without ball. As the terrified natives ran helter-skelter for the jungle, the men leaped ashore and ran calling after them, at which they dropped their weapons and returned, docile enough, to resume the trading that had overcome their rancor of the day before.

Next morning the squadron set sail and crossed the bar of the river to continue eastward. Columbus had hardly lost sight of his anchorage when he saw an arm of water which extended far into the land. He was elated. Surely this was his strait.

He told the helmsman to hold close to the shore, and fell upon his knees in a prayer of thanks. After years of struggle and hardship, he was at last entering the Westward Passage.

A few hours later the squadron was entering the open sea again, after probing what is now called Limón Bay. Sadly Columbus entered on his charts the Bay of the Ships, for it seemed big enough to hold all the navios of the world. English seamen later would mistranslate the designation into Navy Bay.

Almost immediately the squadron turned into another recession; once again the hopes of the admiral soared. But it was another bay. There were gold deposits about it which the natives worked regularly, the interpreters learned from people along the shore, so Columbus charted the Bay of the Mines.

In midafternoon they came upon an excellent harbor, surrounded by open and elevated country, thickly populated and covered with orchards and vegetable gardens. Promptly Columbus christened it Porto Bello—Port Beautiful.

Here he remained for a week while a storm raged on the open sea. At first the natives were timid and somewhat hostile when the interpreters chased them down and insisted on holding conversations. Then, when they saw the variety of fascinating trinkets, they swarmed out in their cayucos and surrounded the caravels, offering fruit, vegetables, and bolls of cotton in trade.

Of gold they had little, only the leaders and their women wearing any at all. None of it would they trade. Columbus learned that all they did possess had come through barter with neighboring tribes who controlled the sources.

The squadron sailed from Porto Bello with only seven leagues of unprobed coast remaining between them and Bastidas' westernmost point. The ships crept along with Columbus constantly on the quarterdeck, where he divided his time between kneeling in prayer and searching the coast with his eyes for an inlet which might turn out to be his Westward Passage.

Finally he crossed the longitude charted by Bastidas, still with no sign of a strait. He entered the point on his charts as Nombre de Dios.

Columbus made many geographical designations which reflected his feelings at the time; here was an example. Off Honduras months before, the first feature he encountered after his meeting with Guimba was a cape which he titled Gracias á Dios—Thanks to God, for he was at last, he thought, on course to find the breach in Tierra Firme that would let him through to the Orient. Now the dream had vanished. Frantically he checked his charts against those of Bastidas, making adjustment for the widest possible error. But there it was: Tierra Firme had been probed, and there was no Strait of Columbus. Name of God!

Gracias á Dios was a shout of enthusiasm, of great expectations, as he sailed toward discovery of what would be the world's most important geographical feature. Nombre de Dios was a moan of lament, a reverent curse of disappointment.

The ships were rotten. Every day they sprang new leaks as the teredo ate through the uncoppered wood. Men sprawled on the open decks, racked with the jungle's fevers. Still Columbus held to his eastward course, determined to pursue his forlorn hope a few desperate leagues farther.

But now the wind changed and mounted, driving the squadron back to Punta de Manzanillo, where it took refuge in a small harbor protected by three tiny islands. Here the natives were friendly, but short of gold like those at nearby Porto Bello. They had their land under diligent cultivation, and produce was so abundant that Columbus christened the place Port of Provisions. For two weeks he remained, taking timely advantage of the storm at sea to repair the crazed vessels.

Then they sailed on, and a league to the east entered another small harbor, where the natives crowded the shore, waving their golden ornaments overhead as an invitation to stop and barter. Certainly Bastidas had reached this point, for the Indians seemed to know what commodity interested such visitors most.

But Columbus knew that his time was short, as more of his fever-weakened seamen had to be assigned to plugging leaks and bailing water from the holds. So he went on without pausing, only to have the wind change again and blow him back toward Porto Bello. Higher swelled the wind, and the squadron took refuge in a small harbor which Columbus named the Cabinet. There was room for his four ships only, and the vessels were crowded so close to the shore that the men could leap from the decks to the land. The party sent to inspect the harbor had misrepresented it to their commander, and once inside Columbus saw why: there was a large village, with unusually pretty women and plentiful gold. He would have moved out, but the weather was worsening, he could not take the chance.

Columbus pleaded with his men to let the native women alone. Their earlier misconduct, he assured them, had led Providence to harass the expedition with this contrary weather. Again, in this place they had no safe refuge: the ships were as accessible to the land as was the land to the ships. He promised the severest punishment to anyone who went ashore without permission.

But it was no use. The men knew their gentle admiral. He would reward their disobedience by praying for their immortal souls instead of having them strung up by the thumbs and flogged. So they slipped ashore that night to fraternize with the natives in their huts.

They were received with abundant hospitality, including all the chicha copah they wished to drink. This led to brawling among themselves and with their hosts, and finally to such open liberties with the women that the braves fell upon them to drive them out. In the drunken riot that ensued, several natives and two sailors were killed.

In the middle of the night the miscreants roused Columbus, told their side of the story, and urged him to send an armed group ashore in retaliation. He refused, observing that they had got no more and probably a bit less than they deserved.

At daybreak Columbus found the natives crowding the shore, yelling and brandishing their weapons. He saw that they might at any moment grow bold enough to leap on board, and with their numbers this could end only with a massacre of the crews. He would have sailed away, but for the storm. Seeing no hope of regaining the natives' good will, he decided to strike fear into their hearts. He ordered cannon fired without ball.

These natives must have learned from those who lived at the mouth of the Crocodile River that the strange visitors could make thunder and lightning, but that it did no harm. Instead of fleeing in terror, they intensified their demonstration and began to hurl rocks onto the decks. Columbus reluctantly ordered that a ball be fired into their midst. It killed several, and the mob quickly dispersed.

The elements raged on for a week, but there was no more trouble with the sailors. Seemingly they had not realized before that a native could kill a white man. They kept to the ships by night, and by day they held within easy sight and call of the ships to do their strictly business bartering.

Satisfied at last that there was no strait, Columbus decided to leave a settlement somewhere along this golden coast. Under his agreement with the Spanish crown he was entitled to the viceroyalty of all lands that he charted, and a tenth of all the revenue produced by them, the grant descending forever to his heirs in royal fashion. To establish a colony would preclude arguments and counter-claims by his fellow explorers, who by now were driving stakes all around the Caribbean arm of his Ocean Sea.

So the squadron sailed on 5 December to westward from El Retrete, and that afternoon put in at Porto Bello. Here would be an ideal site for his colony, except that it was too far from the sources of gold. Then Columbus bethought himself of an island that he had skirted in probing Navy Bay. At the time all eyes had been fixed on the mainland, and no one remembered any details of the island. But it was perfectly situated, both for gold and for protection.

Next morning the squadron set sail for the bay, but again the wind changed and began to beat the ships back. For three months Columbus had prayed for such a wind, and now that he had reversed his course it came. Soon it grew into a gale, and shifted about so that it was impossible to navigate. He sought to put back into the harbor, but just as he tacked toward it a wind of hurricane force struck and carried the squadron out to sea.

For nine days then the elements raged, in a storm which Columbus described as "the worst that has ever been seen." Crazy winds tossed the little ships about, now across Navy Bay, now past the mouth of the Chagres, now off Porto Bello. During all this time the crews slept little, and Columbus hardly at all; he had to fight night and day with all his skill to keep the squadron from being piled up on the coast or hopelessly dispersed.

The sea, wrote Columbus, "boiled like a cauldron" and "ran in mountainous waves." By night the swells seemed to be vast billows of flame, due to a belt of the tiny phosphorescent animals which frequent the Caribbean. For hours on end the sky "glowed as a furnace" with continuous play of lightning, and all the while came "not rain, but a second deluge." The crews were drenched and almost drowned in their open vessels. Bail, bail, bail. Make sail, warp, shorten, furl, and strike. Weary and sleepless, certain that an evil spirit had seized them, they began to confess their sins to one another.

Then, confirming their fears, came an apparition: the boiling sea boiled up in the distance, forming a thin, wavery cone of water which grew and grew until it flared out again into the livid sky. Few of the men had ever seen such a thing, and when it headed straight for the ships they were sure that the vengeance of God was upon them for their sins. They clamored for the gold to be cast into the sea, as a measure of atonement.

But steadfast Columbus, lashed to the rail of the quarterdeck, forbade it. He swept the dripping mat of his long white hair from his beatific face and ordered that each man recite any passages from the Scriptures that he happened to know. Then he renewed aloud his fervent prayers to the God who, he believed, had selected him to win a fortune through his discoveries and use it to recover the Holy Land from the infidel. When the waterspout was almost upon them it veered suddenly and passed harmlessly by; this cemented in every heart a conviction of the efficacy of prayer and holy quotations.

Then the storm subsided, and the men found that the fresh provisions they had taken on at Porto Bello were rotten. And their hardtack had been soaked; it was so wormy that they were obliged to eat it with their eyes closed.

There followed two days of deathlike calm, under a searing sun, with the ships in full sight of the Chagres coast but unable to stir toward it. Little wonder that Columbus lettered on his charts, across the mouth of his River of Crocodiles, another meaningful designation: Coast of Mockery.

Around the helpless vessels congregated a horde of sharks. The sailors saw in this another ill omen, for they believed that these man-eaters, like vultures, received prescience of death. But they were glad enough to catch the ravenous monsters, using hooks baited with strips of cloth, to eke out their miserable fare.

Finally the air stirred, and the battered fleet sailed at last into Navy Bay. Columbus inspected his island and found another disappointment. It was low and swampy, densely overgrown, covered with crocodiles, alive with flying and crawling insects; its fetid odors carried with the wind far out over the water. Prominent in the vegetation was a tree that Columbus had never seen before, the manzanillo. The natives, said the interpreters, used its poisonous juice for dipping the points of their arrows and darts.

Columbus charted the Island of Manzanillo, and sailed for the last time from Navy Bay, hardly dreaming that four centuries later an English-speaking people, of the New World that he never knew he had discovered, would come into that bay and cut an artificial Westward Passage in belated fulfillment of his boyhood dream. Nor that on that pestilential island which he had rejected for his settlement would rise two beautiful cities, which would bear the two names of the great Italian discoverer in their Spanish form: *Cristobal* and *Colon.*

To eastward for three leagues sailed the tiny fleet, and into the mouth of the River of Crocodiles for the second time. It was Christmas Day, 1502. This time the natives unexplainedly withdrew into the jungle, leaving the sailors to help themselves to the ample stores of food.

Within three days the labor of repairing, cleaning, and watering was done, but Columbus, after consulting his astrological charts, refused to set sail under the sign of Saturn. There the squadron stood until the third day of the new year; then it sailed, still eastward, onward and out of the Chagres Theater, toward an ill-fated attempt at a settlement on the River Belén. . . .

Four months later the squadron sailed dejectedly back across the mouth of the Chagres and Navy Bay, driven to sea after severe losses in a battle with the Indians of the Belén region. Once more it entered the harbor of Porto Bello, and held there overnight. Next morning three of the worm-riddled ships limped northward across the Caribbean toward Española. The fourth, the hopelessly crazed *Biscayna,* had been abandoned in the harbor, where it sank within an hour after bailing ceased.

It was six years before the Chagres country saw another white man.

BOOK TWO

GOLDEN KINGDOM

. . . I cannot forbear to commend the patient virtue of the Spaniards; we seldom or never find that any nation hath endured so many misadventures and miseries as the Spaniards have done in their Indian discoveries; yet persisting in their enterprises with an invincible constancy, they have annexed to their kingdom so many goodly provinces, as bury the remembrance of all dangers past.

Tempest and shipwrecks, famine, overthrows, mutinies, heat and cold, pestilence and all manner of diseases, both old and new . . . extreme poverty, and want of all things needful, have been the enemies wherewith every one of their most noble discoveries, at one time or other, hath encountered. Many . . . have spent their labors, their wealth, and their lives, in search of a golden kingdom . . .

SIR WALTER RALEIGH
History of the World

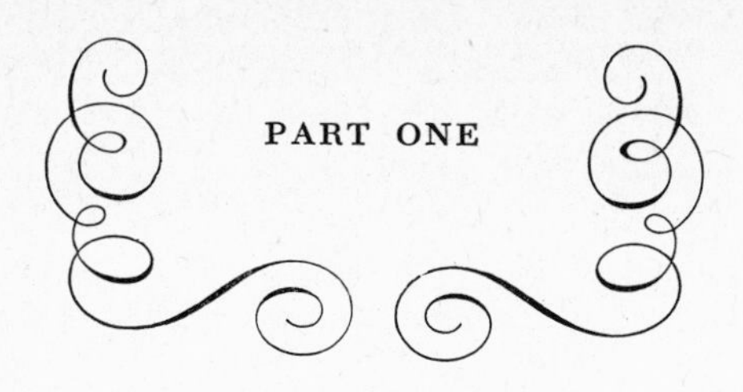

PART ONE

The Conquistadors

VI: LOYAL REBEL

COLUMBUS had driven a hard bargain with King Ferdinand—too hard for his own good. His remaining years were blighted with imprisonments, trials, suits at law, and haggling over the crown's failure to fulfill the agreement. After the great discoverer died in 1506 his son Diego carried on the battle.

These complications served to delay until 1509 the colonization of the American mainland, which Columbus had tentatively called Tierra Firme in the hope that the king would insist on christening it Colombia. The king had refused to appoint anyone as his viceroy there, since the outcome of the pending litigation might nullify his action. Finally he bought peace by naming Diego viceroy of the island of Haiti, called Española by the Spaniards.

With his hand at last free, the king found that he had two favored candidates for the job of settling the mainland, so he divided the territory at the Gulf of Urabá. The eastern half he allotted to Alonso de Ojeda, who had coasted the Chagres country as an officer of Columbus' squadron. The western half, with the Chagres as its heart, went to Diego de Nicuesa, whose only claims to distinction were his noble birth, his long service as carver at the royal table, and a famous dancing mare which he had trained to entertain the Spanish court.

It was a flip of a coin that decided which of them would become governor of Castilla del Oro—Golden Castile, as Columbus had titled the unbroken coast that had broken his heart. The concessions were for four years, with the appointees paying to the crown the usual quinto of all revenues. Each viceroy obligated himself to build for the crown two fortresses in his domain.

Early in 1509 there was much ado in Santo Domingo, the capital of Española and at that time of the whole of Spanish America, as the two colonization parties made ready to sail.

In charge of recruiting for Ojeda was Martín Fernández de Enciso, one of a group of lawyers whom the king had just sent out from well-regulated old Spain in the hope of leavening some of the lawlessness that is typical of every frontier. Among the volunteers who had gathered at the audiencia he found Vasco Núñez de Balboa, a vagrant frontiersman whose attempt at operating an Española farm had bankrupted him. Enciso rejected Balboa, quoting a law that no man could remove from a province while he owed money there.

Nicuesa sailed 20 November 1509, with seven ships, eight hundred men, and six horses, for the western part of the isthmus, while Enciso took a smaller group and headed for the Gulf of Urabá. Ojeda's party steered for the coast of what is now Venezuela.

Nicuesa's plan was to reoccupy the site of Belén, which Columbus had abandoned, and found a second city at Porto Bello. Accordingly, when the squadron sighted the mouth of the Chagres, half of it turned west and the other half turned east. The governor himself led the Porto Bello group.

The party received a cordial welcome from the natives when it appeared in the Port Beautiful. (Sure enough, there on the beach was the rusty anchor of the scuttled *Biscayna,* just as Gregório, a member of the party who was a veteran of Columbus' voyage, had predicted.) The natives crowded around them as they came ashore, shouting and clapping. But when they realized that the newcomers were there not to trade but to take over their village, they withdrew and quietly vanished into the jungle.

Nicuesa, who had just come out from old Spain, assumed that the Indians were abandoning their town without argument. He set his men to work felling trees and building houses. The veterans in his party warned him that the natives would not submit to this expropriation without a fight, but Nicuesa laughed at them.

"Surely they all know by this time that it is useless to resist us," he reasoned.

On the second night the outposts gave the alarm. The villagers, vastly reinforced by braves from neighboring towns, had surrounded them. The colonists seized their weapons just in time to avoid being massacred while they slept, and in the battle that followed some twenty Spaniards were killed. The attacks continued until dawn, when Nicuesa gave the order to withdraw to the ships.

It was Nicuesa's first experience with mortal combat. Unnerved by the sight of his wounded men sprawling on the decks, he decided to build his city on an uninhabited site. His squadron sailed eastward a few leagues and came upon a likely spot. The distracted Nicuesa, relieved to see a place where there were no savage Indians, shouted:

"We will stop here, en Nombre de Dios."

Some historians cite this as the origin of the town's name, assuming that it was a prayerful remark. But the point had already been so charted by Columbus, and it is hardly possible that Nicuesa was without copies of the discoverer's charts. So it is more likely that Nicuesa was using the proper designation, with no more thought of prayer than if a motorist looked at his road map and said "Let's camp here, by the head of the St. John." Or he may have been a punster.

There, where Columbus had realized that there was no Westward Passage, the colonists built the first successful European city on the American mainland.

But their own occupation of it was ill starred. After the settlers had settled, Nicuesa sent a ship westward to Belén to get news of his other party. Back it came, loaded with feverish, half-starved soldiers. They had landed and found the remains of Columbus' colony, they related; they had set to work restoring it, but when their food supply ran out the Indians had refused to sell them more at any price. They could not put to sea without food, and so were reduced to a diet of crocodile meat. Scores had died, and the survivors had resigned themselves to death;

they had ceased even to mount guard. The second attempt to establish an outpost at the mouth of the Belén had ended in disaster.

The survivors joined the Nombre de Dios contingent and for a while the town struggled along, with the Chagres fevers taking a steady toll.

Enciso's detachment also had adventures.

As soon as the squadron was on the open sea, up popped Balboa from a barrel on deck which Enciso had thought to contain flour. The legal eagle looked up the law on stowaways, and was about to put Balboa ashore on an uninhabited island when the latter dropped a remark about having been with Bastidas on his Tierra Firme exploration in 1500. So? This fellow might prove valuable; Enciso thumbed through his book and found another law, under which he signed the uninvited passenger as a member of the colonization party.

When the Spaniards landed they were cordially received by the chieftain Careta. Bastidas had kidnaped scores of his subjects nine years before, but the old patriarch seemed willing to forgive the injury. Enciso asked, through his Haitian interpreters, that Careta gather his people to hear an important announcement; always meticulous in his adherence to the letter of the law, Enciso meant to carry out strictly the colonization procedure as specified by the Council of the Indies.

When the tribe was duly assembled, Enciso introduced himself as the legally authorized agent of the properly appointed governor of this land. Then he cleared his throat and read to the wondering aborigines an interminable manifesto, couched in full-dress legal phraseology.

The interpreters labored to keep abreast of him in their sign language while he elaborated the articles of faith of the Roman Catholic Church and explained its organization, emphasizing the pope's claim of supremacy over all the kingdoms of the world. He notified them that Pope Alexander VI had granted all these lands to Spain; then he outlined in endless detail the organization of the Spanish government. Finally he announced that the pope had directed him to convey to the inhabitants his order that they embrace the Catholic religion and submit to the Spanish crown.

If they complied, he assured them, all would be well. But if they refused, "Then I will employ my power against you, and make war upon you in all ways and places that I am able to, and will subject you to the yoke and obedience of the Church and of his Majesty, and will take your women and children and make of them slaves, and as such I will sell them and dispose of them as his Majesty may order; and I will seize your property, and do you all the damage and evil that I can, as is deserved by vassals who do not obey or wish to receive their lord and who resist and oppose him."

Careta gesticulated rapidly to the interpreters in reply, condensing the matter to its essence:

"You say: there is only one God; He governs heaven and earth; He is lord of all. This much may be so. Then you say: your king want this country; he ask heap big Medicine Man; Medicine Man give your king this country. Those two must be somewhat crazy; this country belongs to somebody else."

This demurrer, with its unquestionable legal merit, must have appealed to Enciso's sense of logic, for he quoted it in *Suma de Geografia* (Seville, 1519). What counterplea he made, if any, is not recorded. But Enciso immediately invoked the authority he had just claimed, and requisitioned the village.

Careta's capital was several leagues inland; this was only a seacoast hamlet which the chieftain operated to supply his inland domain with fish. So he gave the order to withdraw.

The party set to work building Antigua (not to be confused with another Antigua, the ancient capital of Guatemala), the second successful settlement on the American mainland, and Enciso set to work drawing up reams of regulations to govern it. He appointed the other lawyers to the key jobs in the city's administration, and they took delight in enforcing his orders and exacting stiff penalties for the slightest infractions.

When Enciso sailed for Santo Domingo to replenish supplies, he selected another lawyer to take charge during his absence. Things went on as before. The men of Antigua grew sick of hearing about what was lawful and what wasn't.

Then, as the old-timers had expected, Careta and his braves attacked to recover the expropriated village. There seemed to be no juridical remedies; Balboa found Enciso's lawyers prostrate with fear, so he took command. Under Balboa the battle was won and the colony was saved from extinction. When Enciso returned he found Balboa running things in Antigua. Enraged at this usurpation of authority from his legal appointee, he put Balboa in irons—"to teach him respect for the law."

But soon there was another Indian attack, and the frightened Enciso had to release Balboa and give him command. Balboa again defeated the natives handily, and then announced that he wanted volunteers for an expedition into the valley of the River of Crocodiles. Object: gold.

But Enciso, now that the emergency had abated, was ready to take charge again. Balboa's confinement would be remitted, of course, in consideration of his services to the common weal; but under the law . . .

Balboa had heard enough of the law from Enciso. He told him to go to hell. Then he addressed the assembled colonists: those who preferred to follow Balboa should then and there stand with him, and those who preferred Enciso should take his side. All but the handful of lawyers gathered around Balboa.

It was the first rumbling of democracy in the New World.

But this was mutiny, raged Enciso, hastily riffling his book. Under the law, he could execute any man who thus revolted against legally designated authority. Balboa placed his hand on his sword and invited Enciso to try it. Enciso called upon his faithful few, in the name of the law, to seize the rebels.

Balboa and his men drew their swords and stood ready.

The opposition made no move.

Enciso consulted the index, but could find nothing appropriate to quote in such a case. So Balboa had it his own way.

Shortly afterward a dispatch boat arrived from Nombre de Dios, with news that a plague (probably cholera) had reduced the garrison to sixty half-starved and fever-ridden men. Governor Nicuesa needed help. Balboa loaded the boat with provisions and sent it back, with a messenger to explain the situation and to invite Nicuesa to come to Antigua and confirm his de facto government.

In a few days Nicuesa came, weak and feverish, but loudly denouncing Balboa instead of thanking him for his aid. He would have Balboa's head for this insubordination.

Violence, even when it contained no small element of self-preservation, was beyond the honorable rebel. But his hotheaded lieutenants, without his knowledge, placed Nicuesa and a few followers in a leaky boat and set them adrift in the Caribbean, with a little food and water to give them a sporting chance. It was 1 March 1511. They were never seen again.

Years later, on a tree on the coast of Cuba, was found this carved legend:

"Here perished the wretched Nicuesa."

Thus ended the career of the first European ruler of the Chagres country.

Balboa should have dealt similarly with Enciso; if he had, Pedrarias would not have scourged the Golden Castile, and Balboa instead of Pizarro would have conquered Peru; it would have saved three million American aborigines from extermination and millions more from heartless torture. But Balboa foolishly allowed his rival to assemble his followers and depart in one of the ships lying in the harbor. Enciso set sail for Spain, to report directly to his duly constituted Majesty on the strictly illegal goings-on in his Castle of Gold . . .

VII: CONTINENTAL BEACHHEAD

BALBOA'S situation was not so precarious as a similar one would be today. Enciso would be several months crossing the Atlantic; he might even be lost at sea. Once there, the king might not believe him. And if he did, it would take more months to outfit an expedition and still more months for it to cross the ocean. Balboa had plenty of time.

So he began a long-range campaign to build local prestige. He wrote a letter to Diego Colon at Santo Domingo recounting what had happened, and with it sent a hefty pouch of gold nuggets. Back by returning messenger came the viceroy's approval of such resourcefulness in a perplexing situation, and his commission for Balboa to act as his representative in Golden Castile pending instructions from the king. Also, as Balboa had hoped while filling Diego's pouch with gold, he promised to send to the king by the next ship a letter supporting Balboa's actions. This might help to counteract the expected accusations by Enciso.

Then Balboa set to work organizing the numerous tribes of his domain into a close-knit political unit.

His formula was beautifully simple. He sent his native interpreters out as intelligence men, to circulate among the various tribes, extol his virtues, and report to him on intertribal rivalries. When he found two caciques at odds, he allied himself with the stronger to conquer the weaker. In this way the tribes that accepted his leadership gradually enslaved and absorbed those which refused it.

He required his men to deal honestly with the natives. They had to make fair trades, and keep their bargains. No native woman could be casado—"housed"—by a Spaniard without her own and her tribe's consent. Rapidly Balboa developed a situation unique in all the New World: in his territory a European could leave the protecting walls of the cities and safely venture far into the jungle, alone and unarmed, even by night.

For a while he had trouble with Careta. The old man seemed to be harboring a grudge for the invasion of his village and his subsequent defeats in war. He eventually made a solemn treaty of alliance, over a pipe of peace, but even then he always found an excuse not to meet his quotas of gold and food.

Finally Balboa led a company of soldiers to Careta's village to ask why the agreed quantity of maize had not been received. Careta was very sorry; what with a war against a neighboring tribe, and an epidemic of calentura, and a poor crop season, and one thing and another, he had been unable to lay by any grain at all. Balboa's intelligence men knew better, but the Spaniards bowed out. That night they returned and attacked the village. After a stubborn battle, in which Careta lost many braves and Balboa a few of his soldiers, the town was taken and all the survivors captured.

The victors found ample food stores. This exposure of Careta's lie, to a sworn friend and ally, humbled the chieftain more than did the defeat. How had Balboa known that he was lying? Big medicine. And the Indian had complete respect for big medicine. As the two leaders conferred in the cacique's house after the surrender, Careta remarked:

"I am a fool to oppose a man who can look at me and tell what I think."

Then, touching Balboa's razor-sharp Toledo blade, he added, "And I am a fool to oppose a man who possesses a weapon such as this, which can in one stroke cleave a man in twain."

Obviously Careta had seen the light, and was ready to mend his ways. But since he had lied to Balboa, and had been caught, he had no right to expect that Balboa would accept his unsupported word in the future. He would have to give some valuable pledge of sincerity, he realized. So Careta excused himself for a few moments, and then returned silently to his seat on the dirt floor at Balboa's side.

Presently the tribal musicians entered, settled themselves in a dim-lit corner of the smoky room, and began an overture of weird pipes, reedy flutes, and tom-toms. Careta wanted his conqueror-guest to see, he announced, some of the traditional dances of the Coiba tribe.

The chieftain clapped his hands, and a curtain of deerskins at the far end of the room swung aside. There, crumpled in a graceful heap on the hard-packed floor, was Anayansi, Careta's daughter, of whose beauty Balboa had heard. She was bedecked in bracelets, earrings, bangles, head cord, all of flashing gold.

This, Careta explained, would be the Dance of the Sun.

As the music swelled, the Indian maid rose gradually to a sitting position, and slowly extended her gold-spangled arms overhead. Steadily she continued to rise, until she was on tiptoes, arms reaching high.

No mistaking that, Balboa thought; it was the dawn.

Then she stalked around the room, fingers spread wide like piercing rays, arms moving from one stylized position to another, stamping, whirling, in a violent dance, a dance of power; the relentless tropic sun was coursing the sky. When the copper-skinned princess had circled the room she halted over the spot whence she had risen, and slowly folded herself downward in a brilliant sunset. The curtain swung back across the scene.

Careta poured another shellful of chicha for his guest. Now, he said, Balboa would see the Dance of the Moon. The music softened, and the curtain opened again.

Anayansi was discovered in the same position, but this time her ornaments were all of silver. She rose, more lightly now, with none of the ponderous strength of the Sun Dance, and glided gently about the room in a dance of flowing repose, to sink slowly to the floor again. The curtain closed.

And lastly, Careta resumed, the honored guest would see the Dance of Love. Incidentally, he inquired, as he extended the tobacco pipe, would Balboa consider accepting the princess Anayansi, the Coiba chieftain's most treasured possession, as a hostage to enforce her father's future good faith?

Before Balboa could assimilate this arresting suggestion, the music softened again and the rhythm became slower and more pronounced. The curtain opened, and there stood the full-blown maiden, proudly wearing no ornaments at all. Now for the first time she allowed her eyes to meet the gaze of Balboa. She glided sinuously toward him, then away, weaving around the seated man, now near, now far, her arms undulating a warm invitation, her dark eyes flashing with savage fire, her full, vibrant hips circling voluptuously. Then slowly she retreated, to strike a final tableau which was modest despite her alluring nakedness. Her eyes remained riveted with those of the great white chieftain until the deerskins again swung between them. Wiping his brow, Balboa told Careta that he thought Anayansi, as a hostage, would do very well.

The American princess remained at the side of the white cacique until the tragic end. Many times in the ensuing years did Anayansi's diplomacy preserve the peace between brown men and white in the Chagres country. She was the first of three Indian princesses whose beauty and brains affected the course of New World history. After her came Marina, winning for Cortez bloodless victories over half the tribes of Mexico. The third, a century later, was Pocahontas.

To accommodate his new son-in-jungle-law, Careta assigned all the surplus of his abundant slave labor to work the gold sources of the Chagres valley. Production soared. The patriarch could not understand what the Spaniards could want with so much gold; he had long since traded them enough to make more ornaments than they could ever wear, and anyway they seemed to wear very little of what they already had. But what the hell? He might as well humor his queer allies.

So pestilential was Nombre de Dios, so quickly did the Chagres fevers thin the ranks of the men he sent there, that Balboa ordered the site abandoned. Then, since he was voluntarily adhering to the terms of concession of his late predecessor Nicuesa, which called for the maintenance of two garrisons, Balboa built a new city several leagues west of Antigua and named it Acla.

He divided his time between the two towns, enforcing his self-constituted government's regulations and making the Golden Castle into the best-run colony in all the New World. The success of his benevolent methods gave a forever unanswerable answer to the defenders of Spain's official colonial policy up to that time, which was based on the assumption that the American aborigine was incorrigible, vicious, treacherous, and unappreciative of just treatment.

In time Balboa's thoughts turned again to Enciso, who by now surely would be bearing black witness against him at the Spanish court. But it was gold that counted with Ferdinand. So Balboa loaded a caravel with treasure and dispatched it to the Spanish king, under an invoice drawn up as though he were acting by a proper appointment. Accompanying it he sent a letter, dated 20 January 1513, hoping that his Majesty would read between the lines:

> "Most Powerful Sire: There is one great favor that I pray your Royal Highness to do me, since it is of great importance to your service. It is for your Royal Highness to issue an order that no Bachelor of Laws (or of anything else except of Medicine) shall come to these parts of Tierra Firme, under a heavy penalty that your Highness shall fix; because no Bachelor ever comes here who is not a devil, and they all live like devils, and not only are they themselves bad, but they make others bad, having always contrivances to bring about litigations and villainies. This is very important to your Highness' service in this a new country."

Enciso had appeared at court well before the letter arrived. The king had also received Diego Colon's letter, but had decided, understandably, to favor the account of an eyewitness. Enciso had charged Balboa with so many crimes that it took every ounce of gold which the loyal rebel had sent to re-establish his innocence.

The king had already appointed Pedro Arias de Ávila, a Segovian noble, to take the helm of his golden province. The new viceroy was then already in Seville, organizing his vast retinue. He was sorry, the king wrote in reply to Balboa, but the appointment could not at this late date be rescinded. Ávila—known in history as Pedrarias—had expended huge sums on the recruitment and equipage of his party. However, in view of Balboa's loyalty in sending along to the king his customary share of the gravy, he appointed him to the post of interim administrator with the rank of captain general.

The king also issued the requested antilawyer order. Soon the recruiting bulletins posted by Pedrarias promised to the dashing adventurers of old Castile not only free grants of land and mining rights but also freedom from lawyers for a period of four years, in Spain's fabulous new Castile of the Gold.

Along with his letter the king sent a shipload of soldiers to replenish the short-lived garrisons of Balboa's two cities. From the new arrivals Balboa learned that Pedrarias could hardly be ready to sail for several months. The capitán figured that another shipload of gold might yet win his case. So he arranged with Careta to provide guides for a visit to the capital of the great inland chieftain Camogre, in whose domain gold was rumored to be even more abundant than along the shore.

Paddles dipped into the Chagres waters, and the tropic sun glinted on Spanish armor, as the gold-seeking party pressed farther than any white men had ever ventured into the interior of the American continent.

The house of Camogre fronted on a spacious plaza, surrounded by palm trees which had been planted in exact alignment. Balboa was amazed by the advanced landscaping and by the house itself, which was the largest native structure he had ever seen. It was a thatch-covered building of hardwood logs with a foundation of stone, eighty paces wide and twice as long.

Camogre received the Spaniards cordially, and showed them over his palace. Each of his several wives had a spacious apartment, set off by low partitions of matted grass. There were many pantries full of bread, meat, fruit, and earthen jugs of chicha in various stages of fermentation. But Camogre's particular pride was a long, narrow hall, against each side of which hung the bodies of his ancestors, the former caciques of the valley. They had been dried carefully and shrunk by fire, then salted, and bound in cotton cloth trimmed with pearls and gold.

Camogre presented Balboa to each one as though it were a living person, and Balboa responded every time with a courtly bow. His men, standing at a respectful distance from the royal personages, crossed themselves. Then Camogre presented to Balboa the heir apparent, his eldest son Ponquiaca, a bright lad who took great interest in the arms and equipment of the Spaniards.

Finally Balboa steered the conversation around to the purpose of his visit: he would like to trade some tinkling bells, colored beads, shiny brass whistles, and other fine merchandise for gold. Camogre spoke briefly to an attendant, and soon several slaves entered, bearing baskets and trays filled with golden figurines, pearls, and precious stones. He could not trade with a guest in his house; Balboa would please keep his trinkets; these were offered as a gift.

In the interest of international amity Balboa accepted. Then, thinking to entertain his host, he rigged up a set of balances and prepared to divide the treasure among his men then and there. Using coins from his pouch as counterweights, he determined that the gold alone amounted to twenty thousand pesos; faithfully Balboa set aside the king's quinto. It amazed his host to see him distribute the gold on the basis of weight, rather than by the quality of the art work that had been done upon it.

As usual, the men began to quarrel among themselves over fancied errors in the division. Ponquiaca, disgusted with such avaricious conduct by guests in his father's house, struck the balances from Balboa's hand with his fist.

"Why do you quarrel about a little gold?" he chided. "If that stuff is so important to you, I will guide you to a land where it is as common as iron is with you." And he rapped a soldier's breastplate with his knuckles.

Columbus had told of hearing about such a country, said Balboa. Ciguare, he had called it.

"That is the place," said Ponquiaca, waving his hand toward the mountains to the south.

Balboa questioned the lad closely. About six suns of marching to the south, the native prince said, was a great sea "like to that on which you yourselves came." Beyond it was the country of Ciguare. The sea had been crossed directly to southward, by adventurous natives in balsa rafts with sails, in as short a time as ten suns. But the usual route, which was safer if longer, was along the coast line to the left.

Balboa was in favor of setting out immediately, but

the old chieftain advised against it. There were hostile tribes in and beyond those mountains. Even with their weapons of thunder and lightning the Spaniards would need many more men than this. But Camogre was enthusiastic about the idea.

"King Tubanama, our ancient enemy, who has much gold, lives on that sea," said he. "Could we for once bring low this hated Tubanama, no sacrifice would be too great. Prepare your army. I myself will accompany you with all the warriors of our nation. If my words prove false, hang me on the nearest tree."

So they agreed that Balboa would return soon with more men, and that Camogre and Ponquiaca would lead the way to Ciguare.

Before leaving, Balboa had his chaplain baptize Ponquiaca, giving him the Christian name of Charles in honor of the crown prince of Spain.

Upon his return to Antigua, Balboa dispatched a caravel to Santo Domingo with a gift of gold for the viceroy and an appeal for reinforcements from that province. Another ship he sent direct to Spain, with a generously measured quinto for his king.

A shipload of frontier veterans and campaign supplies arrived promptly from Diego Colon at Santo Domingo, and among the special items of equipment was a pack of vicious hunting dogs which had been trained to attack naked Indians on sight.

The presence of these war dogs proved to be more effective than the Spanish clergy in persuading the Indians of the Golden Castle to adopt the ways of Christian civilization—at least in the matter of indecent attire. Because the dogs attacked only naked Indians (clothed ones being considered docile), many of the hostiles adopted the protective measure of killing Spaniards in order to get their clothes. Some of the braves began to take the warpath wearing cassocks which they had taken from the bodies of murdered priests who had urged them to cover their sinful nakedness.

The most ferocious of Balboa's dogs was a huge black-faced mastiff named Leoncico—Little Lion, the leader of the pack. He served for many years as Balboa's bodyguard. (Some historians record that Leoncico drew the pay of a captain, but neglect to explain how it could have been paid to him. This preposterous report probably grew out of a remark by Balboa that Leoncico was worth as much to him as an officer.) The remarkable dog was a special gift from Don Diego, in consideration of the hefty pouches of remembrance that Balboa had sent to him.

While Antigua and Acla bustled with preparation for the drive to the south, Camogre's braves labored to make extra arrows and darts as his priests disemboweled many slaves upon their altars to make big medicine for victory over King Tubanama.

VIII: THE GREAT SOUTH SEA

On the morning of 1 September 1513, Balboa assembled his expedition at Acla and set out on his fateful march to the south. He had with him 190 picked men several hundred Indian slaves to serve as scouts, porters and trailbreakers, and his pack of war dogs.

For six days they trekked toward Camogre's village. Every day more of the white men came down with the calentura, so that by the time they arrived at the rendezvous the natives were carrying 135 of the Spaniards on their shields. But the fever epidemic which had swept the party must have been of a mild type, for none of the victims died.

At the village they discovered that the old chieftain had died and joined his shriveled ancestors on the wall; Ponquiaca had dropped the diminutive syllable from his name, and was now Ponca, the new cacique. But to Balboa and his men, Camogre's son had been Charley—Carlocito—ever since his baptism.

The young chief ordered several apartments in his house cleared, and the porters bore the ailing Spaniards into the first, and probably the only, hospital ward ever operated by the Indians for the white invaders. The others took quarters in the huts of the village, while any of the regular occupants who could not find room slept outside by order of their chief. For a week the party remained in the village, cleaning weapons, packing food, and watching the bloody sacrifices to victory on the native altars.

Then one daybreak the column plunged into the jungle. Far in advance and on each flank the scouts of Ponca's army probed the underbrush for signs of ambush. Next came a phalanx of knife-wielding slaves, who hacked away at the heavy growth on either side of the trail to widen it for the most formidable force that had ever moved across Tierra Firme. Balboa and Ponca marched together at the head of the main body, which included sixty-six Spaniards, a thousand braves in war paint, the pack of dogs, and the hundreds of bearers. Well behind them ranged more scouts, guarding against a surprise attack from the rear.

A little before dark they halted, and the machetemen cleared a space beside the trail large enough for the entire party to gather for the night, inside a watchful circle of sentinel men and dogs.

Thus they traveled for several days, often meeting hostile parties which Ponca's men captured and brought before the two leaders. With characteristic tact, Balboa negotiated treaties of peace between Ponca and his neighbors, and exacted tribute of treasure from each chieftain. Before the column crested the Cordillera he had accumulated ten thousand pesos of gold.

Then, one midmorning, Charley signaled for a halt. A little way ahead was the continent-dividing ridge toward which they had been climbing, and beside the trail rose a steep green mountain, higher than its fellows, with a branch trail winding up to its bald pate. Showing a fine sense of the dramatic, Ponca invited Balboa to climb the mountain alone.

Balboa climbed, and when he reached the top he saw,

beyond the miles of forest-covered hills and plains that yet remained, the endless expanse of the blue Pacific. There he remained, transfixed, for several minutes. Then he signaled for his men to come up. No word was spoken as each one gained the view and stood.

After all had seen, Balboa motioned them to gather around him. Then he fell on his knees, and the others—Charley Ponca included—followed silently.

Balboa removed his peaked helmet, turned his eyes upward, and said:

"Blessed Virgin, give me good success to subdue these lands to the glory of His name and the increase of the true religion."

It was a devout heart that made that prayer, but it was a landsman's heart. Balboa had seen what no European had ever seen before him, the world's greatest ocean, the hemispherical sea. Yet he thought only of the many lands that must lie beyond it. Six decades later, when Francis Drake stole across the Chagres and became the first Englishman to set eyes on the Pacific, he prayed out of his seaman's heart for "life and leave to sail once, in an English ship, on that sea."

It was still a long journey ahead, and as Balboa hiked along the trail he pondered the question of the formalities that he should follow when he reached the shore. No one had ever discovered an ocean before, or at least no one had laid formal claim to one. He knew of no precedent. Fortunately he had witnessed Bastidas' ceremonies after his landing on the coast of Paria, and his recollections of the occasion furnished some ideas. But this case merited more elaborate treatment. Balboa cudgeled his imagination for words and actions which would be equal to the unique circumstances.

Four days later, after climbing and descending the several lesser ridges that stepped down from the divide to the plain, Balboa strode forward from the party and waded, clad in full armor, into the water up to his waist. Turning to face his men as they lined the water's edge, he waved overhead a banner, on one side of which was a painting of the Virgin and Child and on the other the arms of the royal house of Spain. Then he drew his sword, raised it aloft, and cried:

"Long live the high and powerful monarchs Don Fernando and Doña Juana, sovereigns of Castile and León and Aragon, in whose name and for the royal crown of Castile I take and seize real and corporeal possession of these seas and lands, and coasts and ports and islands to the south, with all thereto annexed, and kingdoms and provinces which belong to them, now and in all time while the earth revolves, and until the universal judgment of mankind."

Then he scooped up a handful of water from the South Sea and drank it.

A notary recorded the procedure in detail and affixed the names of all the Spaniards who had witnessed it. It was 29 September, the day of Michaelmas, in the year 1513, at a point whose exact location has been lost, somewhere between San Miguel Bay (which Balboa so named in honor of the day) and the future Pacific entrance to the Panama Canal.

Chief Charley Ponca, whose loyal service had made the great discovery possible, now received satisfaction of the bargain Balboa had made with his father. Their combined forces fell upon the village of proud King Tubanama, who hastened to surrender after seeing a few of his braves torn to pieces by snarling monsters which the strange white warriors called back to their leashes with a whistle. He swore his entire tribe to perpetual allegiance to Ponca, and through him to Balboa and the Spanish crown, and in earnest surrendered to Balboa a great hoard of treasure. Then, at Ponca's insistence, the dogs were turned loose upon him.

The plan had been to commandeer seagoing cayucos and rafts from the coast natives and push on to Ciguare. But Balboa had not reckoned on such a staggering discovery; he had expected the sea of which the Indians had spoken to turn out to be nothing more than a vast inland lake. Instead, here was another ocean: salt water, which rose and fell in mighty tides. Even with his limited knowledge of such matters, Balboa realized that it would rival in size, or even excel, the great Ocean Sea on which he had sailed for months to reach the New World. Had he ever apprehended its true extent, he would have smiled at the recall of his heroic declaration; he had claimed for his sovereigns virtually the whole world.

Ciguare would have to wait. Mere gold could not delay the loyal rebel in getting this news to his king. It would rocket Balboa from an obscure upstart, a bankrupt frontier farmer who had been raised by circumstances to a moderate and rather precarious notoriety, to the world's man of the century, who would live forever in history with a prominence equal to that of Cristobal Colon himself.

Anyway, here at hand was more treasure than they had yet seen anywhere in the New World. Ciguare, it would seem, could be richer only by being larger. Not only did they find gold in abundance, but also pearls of rare beauty and breath-taking size, in such quantity that the natives attached little value to them. Every canoe on the South Sea beaches had a string of huge pearls as a decoration; the children played with them as with glass beads or marbles.

These gems came mostly from several ridges of land which rose out of the South Sea in the distance—the first and only land of his own ocean on which Balboa was destined to set foot. He and his men paddled out to them for a bloodless conquest, and Balboa christened them, obtusely enough, the Pearl Islands. When he was far from shore he rose to his feet in the shaky canoe and, in a new surge of exultation, swung his sword about his head in all directions over the South Sea, repeating over and over his formal speech of annexation.

The glistening pellets were not exactly a nuisance to the island people, who subsisted largely on the produce of their oyster beds, but certainly they were an insignificant by-product of the industry. The children's habit of decorating the trees about their villages by embedding huge pearls in the bark led some later white visitors to the islands to suppose that they had found jewel-bearing plants. Some of the pearl-studded trees they laboriously uprooted and nurtured carefully all the way to Spain, in the hope of propagating them.

Balboa talked with the seacoast chieftains, and they all verified that there was a land beyond that sea where even the drainage sewers were made of gold. They drew for him pictures of the queer, long-necked, cud-chewing beast of burden in that land. The huanaco, they called it. Could they somehow be looking toward an arm of Africa or Cathay? Balboa wondered, for surely these pictures were of camels. Balboa did not live to see a llama.

Always during these interviews regarding Ciguare—

or Peru, as these people called it—there stood nearby in rapt attention a lieutenant whose name was Francisco Pizarro. . . .

When the party had enough treasure to make the expedition also a smashing commercial success, it struck camp and wound its way across the mountains, to rejoin its convalescing members in Ponca's village. On the way Balboa fell victim at last to the calentura, and the bearers carried him in a hammock along the trail, with Charley walking ever at his side.

For many weeks Balboa lay in the native palace, running the gamut of the Chagres country's many varieties of fever. While the native priests danced about him in grotesque costumes to drive the evil spirit from his brain, and brought huge wooden statues of grinning devils to stand guard over his bed, the chaplain said masses in an improvised chapel. Charley took no chances; he prayed for his friend at both altars.

When he had regained enough strength to continue his journey, Balboa took leave of Chief Charley Ponca, assuring him that he would return before many moons had passed to complete their interrupted plans. But he had not reckoned with the new governor, whose stately ships were then being assembled for loading in the harbor at San Lucar.

Balboa arrived at Antigua 19 January 1514, without having lost a single man. "The feat which he had accomplished," wrote Ira Bennett, "from whatever point of view it is regarded—whether from the smallness of the force, the difficulties surmounted, the shortness of the time, or the results achieved—must be classed as one of the greatest performances of man."

Again Balboa displayed his scrupulous sense of fairness by distributing the expedition's share of the treasure, which amounted to forty thousand pesos, not only to the men who had made the march but also to those who had remained behind in Antigua and Acla.

Shortly after his return Balboa dispatched a ship to Spain. It carried the greatest treasure that had yet crossed the Atlantic, including a special gift of two hundred magnificent pearls for the queen, and the world-shaking news. All this, Balboa felt certain, would lead the king willy-nilly to withhold Pedrarias' expedition or send it to another province.

But it was too late. Balboa's treasure ship passed the eighteen pennant-gay galleons of Pedrarias' fleet in mid-ocean.

IX: FURY OF THE LORD

NEVER before had the New World seen such a display. Into the harbor at Antigua sailed the greatest fleet that had yet crossed the Atlantic, and from it landed a colonization party fifteen hundred strong, replete with the finest equipment that money could buy.

The sun-browned pioneers of Balboa's garrison stood in their rusty armor and gaped as the American mainland's first bishop, Juan de Quevedo, marched around the plaza in full robes, with a retinue of Franciscan friars chanting a Te Deum. Behind them Don Pedrarias, clad in solid gold brocade, minced along on a fiery Oranian thoroughbred, flanked by the members of his staff. After them rode hundreds of caballeros in silk and satin uniforms of gold over scarlet, wearing Toledo blades with jewel-crusted hilts, their prancing mounts shiny in silver-studded trappings, their pennon-flying lances and foundry-new armor agleam under the tropic sun. Among them were Hernando de Soto, who was destined to discover the Mississippi, and Hernando Ponce de León, who later explored Florida in search of the Fountain of Youth.

Next came the infantry, hardly less ornate, with muskets of the latest type, crossbows, halberds, and packs of war dogs. At the rear ambled a long baggage train of Pyrenean burros. Also in the party, but refraining of course from the ostentation of the parade, were several ladies of the Spanish court. Doña Isabel de la Bobadilla, wife of Pedrarias, was the first white woman to set foot on the American continent.

Within a month, because the Chagres country always took lives in exchange for its treasure, half of this glittering entourage were dead. A hundred more fled to Española, leaving the European population of Golden Castile, old and new, at about eleven hundred. But the fevers which slaughtered the young adventurers could not down the viceroy, although he was seventy years old. While his followers died all about him he clung to life through days of babbling torment, and rose from his sickbed to begin a systematic exploitation and carnage. For years Balboa had labored to unify the natives and gain their loyalty; now Pedrarias ground it all under the heel of his polished Córdoban boot.

The new governor was, as Mack expressed it, "that rare phenomenon, a scoundrel to whom not a single historian, contemporary or modern, has ever thrown a kind word."

He dissembled his rage upon learning that the rumored South Sea, which his expedition had come to seek, already had been discovered, and assigned Balboa to the writing of a detailed report of all that he had learned about the province. For two days Balboa labored, and tendered an exhaustive summary of his experiences. When Pedrarias had the valuable document in his hand, he dropped his false air of cordiality and ordered Balboa's arrest.

Pedrarias carried orders to punish Balboa for mutiny and a part in the assassination of Nicuesa, but the old man knew that the news of Balboa's feat must by now have reached the king. This would make Balboa a royal favorite rather than a rapscallion, and Pedrarias knew better than to deal too harshly with him. Pointing out that his sentence normally would be death, Pedrarias levied a stiff fine and threw Balboa into prison.

The other officials prevailed upon Pedrarias, in the interest of his own standing with the king, to remit the jail sentence. Then Bishop Quevedo, who desired harmony in his diocese, negotiated a betrothal of Balboa to Pedrarias' schoolgirl daughter María, who was then in a Spanish convent. But when bishop and governor urged Balboa to put aside his native mistress Anayansi because of the engagement, Balboa declined; he knew that it might be years before María arrived. His refusal further enraged Pedrarias, and doubtless gave the final scratch to Balboa's death warrant.

When the treasure ship returned from Spain it brought orders which showed the reaction at home to Balboa's discovery. Ferdinand had commissioned him admiral of the South Sea for life and governor of the Pacific side of Castilla del Oro; but because Balboa had been involved in mutiny and assassination, and probably also because his social station was below that of Pedrarias, he had been placed under the orders of the viceroy. These papers Pedrarias conveniently mislaid, intending to put off delivery of them as long as he safely could.

Another order, framed by the Council of the Indies in the light of Balboa's signal success through fair treatment of the Indians, revised the official policy. Henceforth all bargains and promises would be scrupulously kept; the natives would be treated kindly; their conversion to the Roman faith would be by suasion rather than force. Pedrarias reacted queerly: he placed the papers on his head, apparently as a gesture of subservience, and said, "I honor, but I do not execute." It was a masterpiece of understatement.

Pedrarias organized his men into small parties and sent them out to scour the isthmus for treasure. At first they were cordially received in the native villages. The people ran to bring out the gold they had mined since Balboa's last visit, and assembled to get down to the business of trading for it. The newcomers seized the gold out of hand and carried it away, with no pretense at compensation.

When they came again, naturally there was no gold. So the Spaniards seized the chieftains and tortured them until they gave orders for their gold to be brought out of hiding. Most of them refused to show weakness before their people; rather than face a lifetime of disgrace they allowed themselves to be tortured to death, all because Pedrarias disdained to hand out a few trinkets.

One of the raiders, Gaspar de Espinosa, distinguished himself by being the first man to cross the American continent on an ass. The interior Indians of the isthmus had never seen an equine animal before, and were terrified by its braying. Espinosa told them that here was a dragon, a gold-eating dragon, who bellowed thus when he felt hungry. If he did not promptly receive a good meal he began to breathe fire, and destroyed everything about him. This was no more preposterous to the Indians than sticks which spit thunder and lightning and caused men to fall dead at great distances, or howling monsters which tore Indians to pieces and returned when the Spaniards whistled to lick their hands. They surrendered every ounce of their gold, and continued to do so on subsequent visits until they realized that they had been duped.

The tribes whose leaders had been roasted alive or thrown to the dogs retaliated by ambushing the raiding parties along the trails and massacring them. The Spaniards slaughtered whole villages in reprisal. Soon Spaniards and Indians attacked each other on sight.

Spaniards who fell into the hands of the Indians were in equally bad case. The braves poured molten gold down their throats, crying:

"White man love gold. Give him all he wants."

They also enlisted the natural forces of the country to do their vengeance for them. They stripped the Spaniards and spread-eagled them under the equatorial sun to suffer hours of torture before they succumbed. Others they trussed up and laid on great anthills, which meant that their bones would be clean and dry within a few days. During the rainy season they staked the white men out over sprouting beds of bejuco, whose sharp shoots grow as much as six inches overnight.

Gold production came to a standstill. So Pedrarias sent out his raiders to capture whole villages and herd the people in chains to the mines. There they were overworked without mercy, and died by the thousand. Several tribes were thus wiped out, their cultures and anthropographies forever lost.

When the Spaniards learned that some of the tribes had for centuries been burying their dead with full-sized skeletons of gold and quantities of golden ornaments, they began to dig into the guacales and carry off rich hauls. This brought extinction to many villages, for Indians of both sexes and all ages attacked the violators in suicidal frenzy and impaled themselves on the Spanish spears.

Inland by several days' march through densest jungle

stood the richest of the Darién mines, known as the Tsingal. It became a graveyard of Indians, and finally was the scene of a revolt in which the natives massacred the white overseers to a man. They stacked all the equipment inside and piled debris over the openings, then retreated down the narrow trail sowing bamboo sprouts. Days later they reached the plain, and there they stood guard for weeks, until no trace of the trail remained.

Since then numerous expeditions, one as late as 1927, have scoured the Chagres country trying to rediscover the Tsingal, without success. Isthmian legend has it that the Chuquenaqui tribe, which still roams the Darién in complete independence, has reopened the Tsingal. It is true that members of the tribe sometimes bring quantities of raw gold to Colon or Panama, and refuse to reveal its source.

Under date of 16 October 1515, Balboa wrote to aging King Ferdinand and described the situation. "Whereas the chieftains and natives used to behave like gentle ewes, they have now turned into savage lions," he said. "If this state of things continues only a year longer, the country will be so completely devastated that it will never be possible to restore it."

Pedrarias, Balboa wrote, "is excessively impulsive; he was not greatly distressed by the loss of half of his people at the very beginning; he has never punished his men for causing damage and death . . . nor . . . for stealing gold and pearls . . . He is highly pleased to see discord . . . and if there is no discord, he will stir it up by speaking ill of one group to the other." He described the viceroy as "consumed by all the envy and cupidity in the world," and added that "he wholly lacks the ability or talent to govern."

Truly at last, as the Cuna-Cuna prophets had predicted for centuries, the white Tuyra had come on the water from the direction of the sunrise, to blight the world of these simple people forever.

Not content with slaughtering the Indians for their gold and working them to death, Pedrarias enlivened the weekly bullfights by driving numbers of slaves into the ring after the picadors had goaded the bull to frenzy, to be gored to death before the entry of the matador. His colonists tried to appeal to his practical side by pointing out that this needless slaughter destroyed valuable manpower.

"They will breed again," Pedrarias replied.

It is estimated that the population of the isthmus decreased from two and a half millions to less than half a million during the eleven years that he held sway. Toward the end even his closest henchmen wrote to King Ferdinand to urge his replacement.

Frenesi de Dios—Fury of God, the helpless clergy called him.

When Balboa could stomach it no longer, he registered at Antigua for passage to Spain by the next ship. Only then, almost a year after the orders had been received, did Pedrarias deliver to him his royal commissions. And as the viceroy hoped, Balboa decided to go instead to the other side of the isthmus and try to restore some of the devastation.

Shortly afterward word came that Ferdinand's successor, Emperor Charles V, was sending Lope de Sosa to replace Pedrarias. The news reached Balboa as he was supervising the construction of ships on the shore of San

Miguel Bay, for he had decided to set out in search of the land of Peru.

"Pedrarias' days are numbered," commented Balboa. "I must press forward with my plans in all haste, before I have to fight the new governor as well as the old one."

Nearby stood Andres Garabito, one of Balboa's lieutenants, who had long been enamored of Anayansi and had been rebuked by Balboa for attempting to seduce her. It was singular bad luck that Balboa sent him to Antigua that day for a supply of pitch for his vessels.

Garabito reported the remark to Pedrarias, and the old man saw his chance to finish off his rival before he had to yield to his successor's authority. He wrote a friendly letter to Balboa, begging him to come immediately to Acla for a conference on a problem of state. Balboa set out with the messengers of the viceroy. As they hiked along the trail, the messengers told him that they suspected a ruse, but Balboa took no stock in their fears.

Outside Acla they were met by a detail of soldiers led by one of Balboa's old lieutenants. They seized Balboa and put him in chains.

"What is this, Francisco Pizarro?" demanded Balboa. "You were not wont to come out in this fashion to receive me." Pizarro looked away and made no reply.

Before a jury which had been hand picked by Pedrarias, Garabito embellished Balboa's innocent remark with tales of a plot to cast off the yoke of Spain and set up an independent kingdom on the great South Sea. (The testimony may have planted in Pizarro's mind the germ that later flowered into his Peruvian revolt against the king.) When Pedrarias received his dictated verdict of guilt, he sentenced Balboa to be beheaded in the public square one week from that day.

While Balboa sat in his dungeon, Pedrarias heard his own officials plead on behalf of the loyal rebel. Would not the excellent viceroy report the trial to the king and ask his approval of the execution? Or would he not at least wait for his expected successor to arrive, and let him confirm the sentence?

Pedrarias had for each one the same answer: "Since he has sinned, let him suffer for it."

Accordingly on 17 January 1517, in the forty-fourth year of his life, Vasco Núñez de Balboa, discoverer and admiral of the South Sea, conqueror of Tierra Firme, friend of the Indians, first European governor in fact of the Chagres country, prince consort of the Coiba nation, greatest of the Conquistadors, marched with a firm step to the center of the plaza at Acla. Before him walked the town crier, shouting:

"This is the justice which our lord the king and Pedro Arias de Ávila, his lieutenant, in his name, command to be done upon this man as a traitor and usurper of the lands subject to the royal crown."

Balboa mounted the specially erected platform and spoke:

"It is a lie that is charged against me. Never did I entertain such a thought. It was always my intention to serve the king as a faithful and loyal vassal, and my desire to enlarge his domains with all my power."

A priest received his confession and administered the sacrament; then Balboa laid his head on the block. One blow of the executioner's hacha severed it cleanly. Nearby stood Pedrarias, observing through a lattice of reeds which had been set up to protect him from Balboa's gaze. On the opposite side of the plaza stood the princess

Anayansi, erect and proud, her features frozen so that Pedrarias would not see her grief.

By order of the viceroy, Balboa's head remained on display atop a halberd in the plaza until it withered away. The nearby Chagres flowed on.

Balboa had struck the first blow in the conquest of the isthmus. Four centuries and a New World later, a Yankee soldier led the final drive of the campaign. At the southern end of the Panama Canal he built a model city, overlooking Balboa's great South Sea, to serve as the Yankee capital. And on the four hundredth anniversary of the loyal rebel's landing on the unknown land of Tierra Firme, George Washington Goethals christened that city Balboa.

Shortly after the execution Pedrarias' successor, for whose timely appearance every Indian and Spaniard had prayed, arrived from Spain. But the Castle of the Gold was not yet destined to be free of its Scourge of the Lord. Lope de Sosa died in his cabin aboard the ship that had brought him, without ever setting foot on American soil. King Charles took this for divine intervention, and so Pedrarias remained in power in the Chagres country for eight more bloody years.

X: KING'S HIGHWAY

FERDINAND had ordered Pedrarias to establish a line of forts across the isthmus, in preparation for exploring and exploiting the South Sea. Accordingly, the viceroy had given to his treasure raiders the incidental mission of locating the best route for the project.

It was in November 1515 that Antonio Tello de Guzmán, leading a large party westward along the Pacific littoral from San Miguel Bay, came upon a fishing village which the inhabitants called Panama—a Cueva word meaning Place of Abundant Fish. ("Your Highnesses should know," Pedrarias wrote, "that Panama is a fishing village on the coast of the South Sea, for the Indians call fishermen Panama.") Northward from the village ran a well-used trail, of unknown antiquity; the natives told Guzmán that it continued to Porto Bello, and was the best and shortest route for travel from sea to sea.

And it was in truth the best. Without benefit of surveying instruments, the Indians by their uncanny instinct had settled upon a line which, for its purposes, was as efficient as the future laboriously determined axis of the canal. Their transisthmian route could have been shortened slightly if they had entered the uninhabitable Black Swamp and come out at Navy Bay, but to them the muck was an insurmountable barrier. Instead the trail ran a few miles to the east, avoiding the lowland and circling the headwaters of two large tributaries of the Chagres, thereby eliminating all watercourses of consequence except the unavoidable crossing of the Chagres itself.

Across our river the aborigines had long since swung a bridge of withes, at a dizzy height above the water, because they knew the destructive force of its sudden floods. A large cable of twisted lianas provided a foothold, and two smaller ones, waist high above it, served as handrails. An open network of vines, which gave the structure the shape of a trough, furnished added protection against a slip of the foot. This crossing the Indians called Barba Coas—Bridge Big, in the Kunah tongue. It is a tribute to their engineering that the railroad builders, at least four centuries after the barba coas was built, selected the same site for their spanning of the Chagres with a great bridge of iron. And it is appropriate that the crossing retained its Indian name.

If the Indians had assigned a present-day engineer, with complete equipment, to the job of determining the most practical walking route across the isthmus, for use in all seasons with an irreducible minimum of grading, bridges, and other works, he could not have deviated materially from the old Porto Bello-Panama trail.

Guzmán sent Diego de Alvitez with eighty men to reconnoiter this trail, and thus Alvitez became the first white man to cross the River of Crocodiles on foot.

Three weeks later the party returned, with ten thousand pesos of gold which it had extorted from the villages along the way. This trail, Alvitez reported, was much better than the one between Antigua and San Miguel Bay. While it was slightly longer—he estimated it at eighteen leagues—the mountains were much lower than

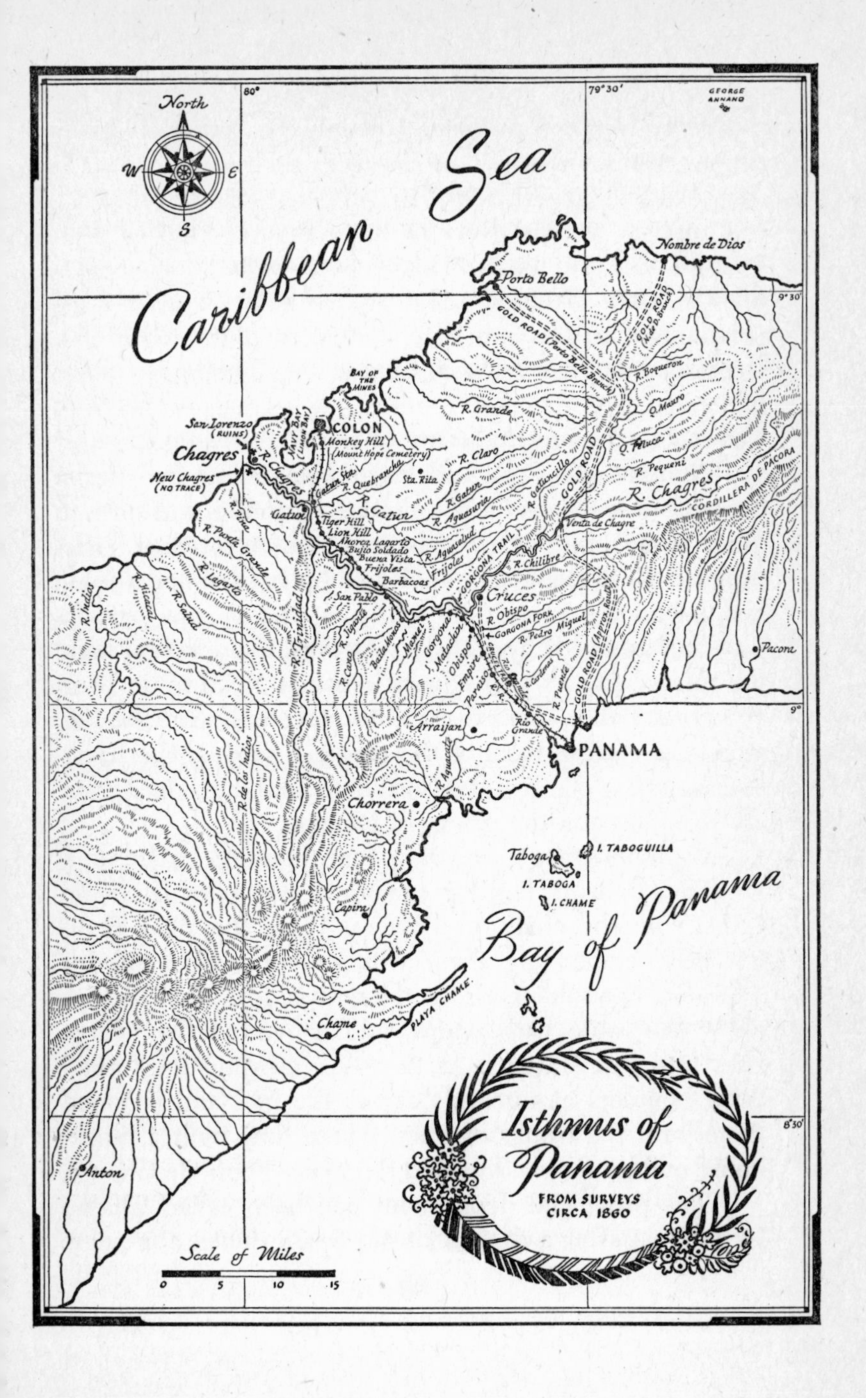

Caribbean Sea
Bay of Panama
Isthmus of Panama
FROM SURVEYS
CIRCA 1860
GEORGE ANNAND
North
W
E
S
80°
79°30'
9°30'
9°
8°30'
Nombre de Dios
Porto Bello
GOLD ROAD (Porto Bello Branch)
GOLD ROAD (N. de D. Branch)
BAY OF THE MINES
NAVY BAY (LIMON BAY)
COLON
Monkey Hill
(Mount Hope Cemetery)
San Lorenzo
(RUINS)
Chagres
New Chagres
(NO TRACE)
R. Chagres
Gatun Sta.
R. Quebrancha
Sta. Rita
R. Gatun
Gatun
Tiger Hill
Lion Hill
Ahorca Lagarto
Bujio Soldado
Buena Vista
Frijoles
Barbacoas
San Pablo
Cruces
R. Obispo
GORGONA FORK
R. Pedro Miguel
R. Cardenas
R. Puente
GOLD ROAD (Approx. Route)
GOLD ROAD
GORGONA TRAIL
R. Chilibre
Venta de Chagre
CORDILLERA DE PACORA
R. Pequeni
R. Boqueron
Q. Mauro
Q. Fluca
R. Grande
R. Claro
R. Gatuncillo
R. Aguasuria
R. Aguasalud
Frijoles
Gorgona
Matachin
Obispo
Empire
Paraiso
Memei
Baila Monos
R. Caño
R. Jigante
R. Trinidad
R. Pina
R. Punta Grande
R. Lagarto
R. Salud
R. Hicaco
R. Indios
R. de los Indios
Pacora
Arraijan
R. Aguacate
Rio Grande
PANAMA
Chorrera
Taboga
I. TABOGUILLA
I. TABOGA
I. CHAME
Capira
PLAYA CHAME
Chame
Anton
Scale of Miles
0
5
10
15

those of the Darien route. It could be traversed in a shorter time, and with less hardship.

When the party arrived in Antigua, Guzmán reported to Pedrarias the discovery of the village of Panama and its trail to Porto Bello. The viceroy waited for several months, until his raiders had probed as far westward as Guatemala, to be sure that no better route would be encountered. Then he sent Gaspar de Espinosa, he who had been first to cross America on an ass, to build a Camino Real along the route of the Alvitez trail.

Nombre de Dios had been abandoned five years before, but it still had a blockhouse, a cabildo, and several other stone buildings which could be restored at little expense. Here Espinosa established his base of operations, and began the project by widening the narrow branch trail that extended from there westward to a junction with the main route about midway between Nombre de Dios and Porto Bello. There the trail turned southward and ran along the eastern bank of the Pequeni, crossed the River of Crocodiles, climbed the Cordillera, and descended onto the plain to enter the village of Panama.

Espinosa's men rounded up four thousand Indians and set them to work hauling smooth-worn stones from the beds of nearby creeks and rivers. These they laid along the trail, embedding them with only the clay soil for a binder. The soldiers drove the natives from their bohíos along the route with whips, and converted the village sites into rest stations. At the river crossing they piled huge boulders at intervals across the bed and spanned them with the trunks of trees. There they built a blockhouse and an inn, and named the place Venta de Chagre.

The provincial department had been called Chagre by Balboa, after a district of old Spain; hence the name of the principal inn on the road. Soon its great River of Crocodiles came to be known by it. For three centuries it remained the Río de Chagre, or the Río Chagre, and then for some reason the name acquired an *s*. How this came about—through colloquial accretion or as the result of an error by a writer or cartographer—is not clear. But the present name of our river can thus be traced, albeit deviously, to Balboa himself. Its earlier name was given by Columbus, the other of the two greatest discoverers of all time.

In August 1519, Pedrarias and his staff made their official inspection of Espinosa's work, riding from Nombre de Dios along a cobbled road which averaged three feet in width all the way to Panama, where they arrived on the 15th.

"Here," said Pedrarias, "I shall build my capital."

Bishop Peraza, who had succeeded Quevedo when the latter returned to Spain in protest against the inhumanity of Pedrarias, blessed the undertaking and marked the site of his future cathedral by drawing a cross on the ground.

To reward Espinosa for his services, Pedrarias appointed him alcalde of the city of Panama, and returned to Antigua, leaving the ass-borne pioneer to begin the construction of his domain.

A royal decree dated 15 September 1521 created the city of Panama, assigned it a coat of arms, and transferred to it the capital of Castilla del Oro. Within five years Antigua and Acla were ghost towns. The Indians eschewed their former village sites, doubtless because of their melancholy associations, and in time the jungle reclaimed them. Today their locations are unknown.

The revived Nombre de Dios, at the northern

terminus of the first paved highway to cross the American continent, continued for almost a century to hold the distinction of being the oldest living European city on the mainland of the New World. When it was abandoned in 1597, by order of Philip II, the honor passed to Panama, at the southern terminus. There it will remain as long as ships sail the sea. . . .

Another milestone had been passed in the conquest of the isthmus. The King's Highway had taken thousands of lives in the building; in time it would take many thousands more.

At Nombre de Dios arrived galleons from Spain, bringing ironwork, sailcloth, rope, pitch, and other shipbuilder's items which the new land could not furnish. These supplies crossed the isthmus on the backs of burros and slaves, and at Panama the Spaniards built hundreds of ships. In them they sailed toward the setting sun, and returned with the spices, the oils, the perfumes, the silks, the precious stones of the Orient. The cargoes in turn shuttled back across the hump to Nombre de Dios, to be picked up by the galleons of Spain's Atlantic fleet.

The cities at the two ends of the King's Highway to the South Sea prospered, but only on the profits of their trade. No industry grew up in the Chagres country other than the building and maintenance of ships. Money flowed freely, but food was scarce; the Council of the Indies sent out very little of it, for the shipping space was needed for trade goods, and the grandees in Seville saw no reason why this land could not produce enough victuals to take care of its people's needs.

Disease was rife. Yellow fever, malaria, cholera, leprosy, dysentery took a steady toll, and occasionally flared up in frightful epidemics, for the white man had not yet learned how to live safely in the tropics. A quarter of the white people of Panama died each year, and at Nombre de Dios the rate was even higher. The military garrisons received twice the normal pay and seniority for the time they served in the Chagres country.

Every ship from Spain brought new colonists to replace the victims of the pestilences. These were a hand-picked lot, by order of the Casa de Contratacion in Seville: no Jews, no Moors, no migrants from the other countries of Europe, no one who had not been born in the Roman Catholic faith—thus excluding Jewish and Moorish merchants who professed conversion in an effort to acquire eligibility.

The life was hard, but the reward for those who survived the plagues and the privations was proportionately great. Here was the one gateway to the East, the greatest monopoly in all history. (Only Magellan had succeeded in rounding the Horn.) Through this monopoly Spain became the richest country in the world, and many of her people who went to the isthmus penniless returned to the old country in a few years with their fortunes made.

Across the Chagres valley, a paved highway had spanned the American continent a full century before the Pilgrims landed on Plymouth Rock.

While Europe's explorers continued to probe the western shore of the Ocean Sea in search of an opening, Spain began to consider the idea of a canal. One of Los Ríos' first acts as governor was to order the military engineer Captain Hernando de La Serna to explore the Chagres for the possibility of connecting it to the Pacific by means of a ditch.

La Serna reported that a canal would be feasible, so Charles ordered that a detailed survey of the route be made for estimating the cost. Pascual de Andagoya was placed in charge of the project, and, on 22 October 1534, he wrote to the king from Nombre de Dios that "No prince in the world, however powerful, could accomplish the union of the two seas." He opined, however, that he could keep the Chagres channel clean and maintain the connecting highway to Panama if his Majesty would send him "another shipload of Negroes from Cape Verde."

Tomás de Berlanga arrived in February 1535 to succeed Peraza as bishop of America. In a letter to Charles reporting his arrival, he called the isthmus "in truth the top of the world," for to the north was one of its seas and to the south the other. "But the summit is so difficult to mount that it costs much wealth and many lives of men."

The good bishop evidently had been preyed on by the tradesmen at Nombre de Dios, for he described the town as "a den of thieves and a graveyard for travelers."

He recommended that the northern terminal city "be moved to the mouth of the Río de Chagre, where ships of two hundred tons could anchor, unload half of their cargo on barges, and proceed upriver to within five leagues of Panama to unload the rest." As an engineer, the bishop was no slouch. It took Spain a century of losses to the buccaneers to see the wisdom of his words and comply.

"If this pass, in the manner aforesaid," Berlanga concluded, "there is no more necessity to seek another strait, because your Majesty will be lord of so great a World as in this Sea of the South is discovered, and waits to be discovered, and hold it all as under key, and go in and out of it for a countinghouse; since doing what I have said, there remains but one day's journey by land."

On the question of a canal, the clergy was divided. In 1555 Francisco López de Gómara, chaplain to Cortez, wrote to Philip II:

"If there are mountains there are also hands. Let but the resolve be made, and there will be no want of means . . . To a King of Spain, with the wealth of the Indies at his command, what is possible is easy."

But the Jesuit father José de Acosta, after crossing by the Chagres route, wrote to Philip that "No human power will suffice to demolish the most strong and impenetrable mountains and solid rocks which God has placed between the two seas, and which sustain the fury of both oceans. And when it will be to men possible, it would in my opinion be very proper to fear the chastisement of Heaven for wishing to correct the works which the Creator, with the greatest deliberation and foresight, ordained in the fabrication of this universe."

For two centuries the fear of God's displeasure was a factor in Spain's hesitancy about attempting a canal.

XI: GOLD ROAD

FRANCISCO PIZARRO in time received his reward from Pedrarias for turning on Balboa: a repartimiento of land and slaves in the new city of Panama. There for five years Pizarro lived the indolent life of an encomendero—pensioner of the viceroy. He had risen far since his illegitimate birth in old Trujillo and his boyhood as a swineherd.

But he could not dismiss from his mind the tales of the unknown land to the south; even though he was in his fifties, he heard the call of adventure and gold. So he found a partner, one Diego Almagro, a common soldier who had come out with Pedrarias and who was illiterate as well as illegitimate. These two sought the aid of Hernando de Luque, a schoolmaster-priest in the new cathedral.

Father Luque persuaded a rich merchant of Panama to finance an expedition, and wangled a permit for the voyage from Pedrarias by promising him a fourth of the profits. Then the priest drew up a formal agreement, placing Pizarro in command of the expedition, himself in charge of the base of operations in Panama, and Almagro as supply and contact officer between the expedition and the base. The three partners swore to the terms on the altar of the cathedral, and Bishop Peraza gave the enterprise the episcopal blessing.

It did not take long to recruit a party from the streets

of Panama. In a few weeks the first expedition sailed: one caravel with a hundred men, among whom was Hernando de Soto. Ten months later it returned, with stories of awful weather, impenetrable jungle, and savage seacoast tribes. Half the men had perished.

Reluctantly the wealthy squire handed out more money; replacements were recruited, and a second attempt was launched. Its emaciated survivors were back in three months, reporting no better luck. But the partners had had their faith renewed by talks with island natives; they paid Pedrarias two thousand castellanos for his interest.

The first financier had had enough, so Father Luque scoured the town for others. Recruiting was dampened by the fate of the previous expeditions; only fifty volunteers could be found. They set out in two large pinnaces.

Four months later one of the pinnaces sailed into the harbor at Panama with Almagro in command. This time they had the evidence; he produced a box of golden ornaments and fine cloth, of a texture unknown to the Spaniards, which the party had taken from some native traders on a balsa raft. Pizarro, he reported, was waiting with the other boat and most of the men on a desolate island off the coast of Peru while Almagro returned for recruits and supplies.

But now Pedrarias was gone, and the new viceroy was indifferent even when he saw the treasure. Governor Los Ríos ordered the project abandoned, forbade Almagro to leave the city, and sent a government caravel southward to pick up the rest of the party and bring them home.

Two months later the boat returned, with most of Pizarro's men and this report for Los Ríos: the party had crowded around the caravel, expecting to welcome

Almagro; the order had been conveyed; unhesitatingly Pizarro had drawn his sword, traced a line in the sand from east to west, stepped across it from north to south, and said:

"Friends and comrades, there lies Peru with its riches; here Panama with its poverty. Choose, each man, what becomes a brave Castilian. For my part, I go to the south."

Thirteen of his men had followed him across the line, and the rest had boarded the boat to return to Panama. The rescuers had then given the insurgents what food could be spared, and had sailed for home after assuring Pizarro that his determination and his appeal for help would be conveyed to the governor.

Los Ríos could not help admiring such tenacity, especially when he learned that the men had lived on the island for four months on coconuts alone. He grudgingly sent Almagro out with his latest recruits, under orders to have the caravel back within six months.

In six months to the day the party returned. They had visited several coast cities of Peru, and produced huge chests filled with gold and silver to prove it. Pizarro had wanted to stay, but Almagro had prevailed upon him to comply with the time limit. Every man in the party affirmed that gold was as plentiful in Peru as iron in Europe.

But Los Ríos, probably because he did not have any stock in the venture, forbade further voyages. The proceeds, he pointed out, covered all advances from Luque's various backers and left a neat profit.

"Be satisfied with what you have," the governor advised them.

So Pizarro sailed for Spain, to present the case to the king himself. . . .

Two years later he was back in Panama, with King Charles's commission as viceroy of Peru, ample funds, and a draft on Los Ríos for ships and supplies. Father Luque had been appointed Peru's first bishop. Almagro was incensed to learn that he had been relegated to the obscure job of operating the base of the expedition in Panama.

Then, in January 1531, Pizarro and Luque set sail from Panama with a picked force of two hundred men and twenty horses, on the voyage that enslaved the golden empire of the Incas. ("Use the point!" Bishop Luque shouted to the men as they slaughtered the Peruvians; they were damaging their fine Toledo blades by using flat strokes.)

Within a year the undreamed-of volume of treasure flowing to the isthmus from Peru, augmented by the looting of the Aztecs of western Mexico, made it necessary to construct huge vaults at Panama and Nombre de Dios. Across the Atlantic came shiploads of horses and burros from Spain, and Negro slaves from Africa, to move the treasure across the Chagres valley. Entire blocks in the terminal cities were given over to buildings for stabling the carriers. Soldiers ranged the countryside, rounding up Indians and driving them into the cities like cattle, to turn them over to the slave drivers whose job it was to keep the treasure moving.

The King's Highway became the Camino del Oro. But the Highway of Gold could have been called as aptly the Highway of Blood, for while the treasure flowed ceaselessly to Spain the blood of the people who carried it washed every mile of the cobblestone paving. Chained together and harnessed to trundle carts, they strained

HIGHWAY OF GOLD

—AND OF BLOOD

forward with their loads while merciless masters lashed their backs. What if they lived only a few weeks? There were plenty of them in the jungle.

Even today the Indians of Panama will not go near the Gold Road after dark. At night, they say, it is haunted with the clack of hoofs, the tinkle of mule bells, the creak of wheels, the shuffle of feet, the whir of whips, the groans and shrieks of the hapless people whose shades still flicker along the rock-paved trail. It is la Via Maldita, the Way Accursed; they cross themselves at the mention of it.

The road was improved and widened, so that carts could pass in double file. More inns and rest stations were built, until every five-mile stretch had at least one. From dawn to dusk the traffic moved in both directions along the banks of the Chagres, and when the king's galleons were waiting at Nombre de Dios the carriers worked in shifts, so that the treasure moved on through the jungle darkness by torchlight.

The river was cleared of logs and boulders up to the head of navigation, thirty river miles below Venta de Chagre. A branch trail was cut from the Inn of the Little Bed to the new river station, and there was built Venta Cruz—Inn of the Cross (the engineers had marked the terminal point on their maps with a cross). Then in the rainy season they loaded the treasure on boats and rafts, and floated it down to the mouth of the Chagres. Thence the lighters skirted the coast line to the harbor at Nombre de Dios.

A town grew up around the new inn on the River of Gold, and for three centuries Las Cruces continued to be the most important inland city of the isthmus. Its vaults and warehouses did such a volume of business that the king sold the concession to operate them for ten thousand pesos a year.

There is no means today for calculating the sum of the billions in treasure that flowed across the Chagres valley throughout the rape of Peru. But the world purchasing power of gold shrank by more than half between 1530 and 1550, which seems to indicate that the total supply of gold in all the world's commercial channels was at least doubled during the time.

As viceroy of Peru, Francisco Pizarro was the richest man in the history of the world—richer, in fact, than all the kings of Europe combined. It is not surprising that he beheaded his sworn partner Almagro, nor that Diego the Lad, Almagro's son by his Panama Indian mistress, then murdered Francisco Pizarro, nor that he in turn was garroted by Gonzalo Pizarro, Francisco's younger brother, who thereby gained a tenuous control over the empire of the Incas.

Thus it was another Pizarro, who held no royal commission, that Vasco Núñez de Vela came out from Spain to depose and replace as viceroy of Peru. For several years King Charles, at the instance of the kindly priest Bartolomé de Las Casas, had been decreeing more laws to protect the Indians from enslavement, and the Peruvian dictators had disregarded these laws. (If they were also giving the king short measure on his quinto, there is no official mention of it.) Vela, a member of the high council of the Spanish Inquisition, arrived at Nombre de Dios with an imposing retinue in January 1544, and there he confiscated a large shipment of Peruvian gold as the product of slave labor. Marching along the banks of the Chagres, he stopped each train as he met it. By the time he reached Panama he had collected half a million pesos of illicit treasure and freed three hundred Peruvian

Indians who had been sold into slavery in the Panama marts.

"I have come not to tamper with the laws," he commented, "nor to discuss their merits, but to execute them, and execute them I will, to the letter, whatever may be the consequence."

He thus continued to execute the laws all the way to Lima, and the consequence was that Gonzalo Pizarro executed him.

Now Peru was in open revolt against Spain. But the highway across the Chagres valley was the only door to the Andean empire, and King Charles could break the rebels simply by bolting the door and letting them dry up on the stalk. Pizarro realized that he must control the Gold Road or die.

So he sent Hernando Bachicao with seven hundred soldiers in thirty vessels to secure his life line. Having been warned of the scheme by an enemy of Pizarro, the citizens of Panama took up arms and sent out a warning to the rebel captain not to come ashore. Bachicao replied that he had come only to drop some passengers and to buy provisions for his fleet. The merchants saw no reason to forego this sizable item of business, and they insisted that the force be allowed to land. Once inside the city the Peruvians seized the food and arms depots, and almost without a fight the southern terminal of the Gold Road was in the hands of Pizarro.

Bachicao seized the ships in the harbor, giving the crews a choice of hanging from the yardarm or joining his force. After a few had been hanged the others signed up. This taste of authority sent Bachicao off on a spree; he began to loot the city, beheading the citizens wholesale on the slightest provocation. The reign of terror continued for a month, until Pizarro learned of it and recalled his power-drunken emissary.

Pizarro outfitted a second force under Pedro de Hinojosa. Ahead of it he sent a messenger, with a letter which disclaimed the acts of Bachicao and announced that Hinojosa was coming to pay for the damage that had been done. Again the prospect of gold was too much for the merchants; they insisted over the objections of all others that the adjusters be allowed to enter the city. But Governor Francisco Robles was not taken in. He armed a force of seven hundred men.

The fleet hove to in the cove under Ancon Hill; Hinojosa landed his force, and marched along the shore toward Panama with the ships following, their guns trimmed for action. As the army came in sight of the city, the clerics filed out of the cathedral, clad in mourning, and marched back and forth between the opposing groups chanting:

"Is it necessary for Christians to imbue their hands in each other's blood?"

This intercession led to a 24-hour truce; hostages were exchanged, and Hinojosa left his army encamped outside the city to confer with the Panameños. Insisting that he had come to pay damages, and not to make war, Hinojosa persuaded Robles to extend the truce to forty-five days and allow a bodyguard of thirty men to join him. The armistice terms were sworn to before a notary.

Hinojosa put his case before an assembly of leading Isthmians: Pizarro ruled Peru, and intended to rule its gateway; he would use force if necessary, but first Panama could have an opportunity to submit peaceably and reap a golden harvest as part of the richest country in the world. In earnest he distributed gold freely to all, including the delegations from Nombre de Dios and Las Cruces. That did it. At the end of the truce he led his army in triumph into the city.

He sent a detachment under Hernando Mejía de Guzmán over the Gold Road to occupy Nombre de Dios, and, in October 1545, Panama became a part of the independent empire of Peru. Elaborate carnivals celebrated the change of nationality. It was the first but not the last time that the isthmian people tailored their patriotism to fit their pocketbooks.

Despite minor uprisings by loyalist factions, matters held thus for about a year. Spain was involved in a war at home, and so could not spare a force to put down the rebellion. But Spain sorely needed her quinto from Peru to help finance the war, and so she sent Pedro de la Gasca, as "President of the Royal Audience," to try to patch up the trouble through diplomacy.

Gasca arrived at Nombre de Dios in July 1546, with an unarmed but regally accoutered party. Guzmán was so much impressed by their finery that he saluted them with cannon and turned out his garrison in dress uniform to stage a welcoming review. Gasca told the lieutenant that he came with power to change the laws to suit the colonists, thereby remedying the cause for rebellion, and to grant amnesty. Guzmán ushered him in state across the Gold Road to confer with Hinojosa.

Hinojosa was cagey; he examined Gasca's credentials, and asked him point-blank whether he had authority to confirm Pizarro as viceroy of Peru. The ambassador gave an evasive answer, so Hinojosa interned him pending advice from Lima.

A delegation came to Panama bearing a petition from

the caballeros of Peru that Pizarro be confirmed as viceroy, and advising that Gasca not come south of Panama in the interest of preserving the peace. Gasca's eloquence won over the delegation, and then Hinojosa climbed on the bandwagon and turned over his fleet. Gasca levied a force from the towns and garrisons on the Gold Road and sailed south with more than a thousand men, arriving at Tumbez 13 June 1547.

"Had Gonzalo Pizarro been a great man," wrote Anderson, "he would have chopped off the head of Pedro de la Gasca, and have become king of Peru. As it was, Pedro de la Gasca chopped off the head of Gonzalo Pizarro, on the field of Xaquixaguana; and Peru remained, for two centuries and a half longer, a province of Spain." It was the cheapest war that Spain or any other nation had ever waged. One clever emissary had talked his way into the enemy stronghold, alienated a faction, and manipulated it to conquer the rebellious regime.

Gasca reorganized the Peruvian government and returned to Panama with eleven million castellanos of gold and silver. Commandeering all the slaves and pack animals in the town, he rushed the treasure to Las Cruces. Thence he shuttled it by lighter down the river and coastwise to Nombre de Dios, seized all nineteen of the merchantmen which happened to be in the harbor, and packed the cargo off to hard-pressed Spain.

While this heavy shipment was crossing the isthmus, trouble came from another quarter. Revolutionists from Nicaragua, where Pedrarias had gone after Los Ríos deposed him, landed unexpectedly at Panama and seized the city on the night of 20 April 1550, shouting "Death to the traitor!" Whom they were accusing of treason is not clear.

The party was led by Hernando Rodrigo de Contreras, grandson of Pedrarias through his daughter María, of the ill-fated transatlantic betrothal to Balboa. He was planning to seize control of the expanded empire of Peru on plea of inheriting Pedrarias' rights in the proceeds of the voyage of discovery—a ludicrous excuse for brigandage which marked him as his grandfather's grandson.

When Contreras learned that the bulk of Gasca's treasure had already gone forward to Venta Cruz he set out with his entire force on the Gold Road, and thereby he allowed the Panameños full opportunity to organize their resistance. He arrived on the bank of the Chagres in time to see the last of the lighters rounding the bend, so he sent part of his force on to Nombre de Dios by road in the hope of intercepting it. The rest of the party he led back to Panama.

Alcalde Rodrigo de Villalba's soldiers, lying in wait outside the city, fell upon them. After extensive slaughter Contreras surrendered, and he and the ninety other survivors were herded to the dungeons in the Sea Wall. There the alcalde put them all to death that same night with his own dagger, refusing even the last rites of the church. Upon hearing of this, the detachment that had gone on to Nombre de Dios lost heart and disbanded without molesting Gasca's gold.

Contreras' head was cut off and displayed in an iron cage in the plaza; at last the isthmus was free of the curse of Pedrarias. But the interocean gateway across the Chagres valley had had only a foretaste of another curse that would not be laid until the twentieth century: bandits.

XII: BLACK MAGIC

AMONG the thousands of slaves whose lives were a never-ending trudge along the Camino del Oro appeared increasing numbers of black savages from Africa, their naked bodies scored with the welts and tattoos of the Congo country, their brilliant white teeth filed to shark-like points as the unfailing badge of cannibalism.

These lithe and powerful people, the Spanish soon found, were admirably well suited to the cargador service. Even the females among them were taller, broader, and stronger than the pick of the males among the natives of the Chagres country. And the hulking males could carry almost as much as could the donkeys. They did not sicken and die under the whips of the soldados as readily as the Indians did. And they shared the natives' virtual immunity to the fevers.

There could be no better gauge of their value than the prices paid for them at the Portuguese slave marts in the Spanish cities of the isthmus: an average of three hundred pieces of eight for a healthy young male, and almost as much for a female of similar quality. The aborigines of the country seldom brought more than a fourth of this amount.

The mere fact that they were brought there at all, in view of the expense of buying them from their black-Judas captors in Africa and shipping them across the ocean, was a supreme endorsement. For the Chagres country itself offered a seemingly inexhaustible supply of brown-skinned people who were already there at hand for the comparatively easy taking.

Week in, week out, month in, month out, they shuffled over the uneven cobblestones under staggering burdens, iron collars around their necks and heavy chains swinging between them. Beside each single-file group on the ground dragged two large chains, fastened by smaller chains to each ankle on that side. This arrangement forced them to swing their legs outward on every fourth step, in order to haul the gang chains forward and leave play for the next three steps. This meant that they must walk in rhythm and kick the chains ahead in unison.

The fine Spanish ladies, watching the treasure trains as they moved in and out of the terminal cities, observed this rhythmic walk and imitated it at their fandangos. In time it became one of the most popular dances of the Spanish Indies, with a name brought straight from Africa and Hispanicized into La Conga. From Cuba it spread over the world; but those who trace its origin to the Cuban chain gangs should look further back into Time—to the Gold Road of the sixteenth century.

Beside each gang traveled a soldier, sometimes walking, sometimes riding, always wielding a lash. When one of the carriers faltered and broke the rhythm of the group, the whip laid open and red the black flesh of his naked back. He screamed, but he caught step, somehow he caught step, for if he did not the lash would come again and again . . .

Often their voices rose in the weird minor-scale fugues, already aeons old in the Congo country, telling now of their former freedom, their treacherous enslavement, and their blazing hatred for their masters. Some of the guards, feeling uneasily the strange power of their harmonies, forbade them to sing.

When the column halted, they swung their burdens down and stretched their weary bodies on the humid ground of the Chagres country, the muscles under their shiny skins relaxing just as long before they had relaxed against the humid ground of the African jungles.

Overhead and to either side of them stretched the same inscrutable mesh that they had known as home before the white man came with his gifts of shackles and whips and endless, unrewarded labor. True, they had traveled for many moons to westward across the rolling water, chained in the holds of slave ships which stank with their waste and their vomit and their rotting dead. But this new Chagres country was still home, for here were the bright-colored birds, the lush green plants, the slithering serpents, the dark paths, the sparkling waters to remind them of the Congo. Here was the brilliant sun, the drenching rain, the abundant life of their own land.

It was inevitable that these creatures should hear and heed the call of the wildness all about them.

In the still midnight, as the mail-clad guards nodded beside the fire at a rest station, whole squads of the black cargadores rose quietly to their feet. Silently, slowly, holding their chains taut, they stole across the clearing and vanished into the welcoming darkness. To counter this their swarthy masters tried chaining themselves to their gangs. After several guards disappeared with their charges, the idea was abandoned.

Once they had been swallowed up by the jungle, the chains were a simple matter. They pounded them between stones until the links broke. From the broken links they fashioned rods for spreading the staples on their collars. Soon they were free, free of the white man and his fetters, free to return to the wild life that boiled in their blood as it had boiled in the blood of their mothers and fathers before them from the dawn of the race.

Now they fashioned each an assagai, using the straight, stout bejuco of the Chagres swamps to make the shafts and the very iron that bound them to pound out the heads. With these they killed the animals whose cousins they had known in their native land. And the bones of these animals they split, tooled, and polished, as their ancestors had done before them, and thrust the sharpened slivers through the gristle of their noses and the lobes of their ears.

With the latent lore of the Congo country again astir in their breasts, they wove palm fronds into thick mats and covered them with animal skins for shields; they cut straight shafts of hardwood for bows, and twisted monkey gut to make strings; across the ends of long, slender gourds they stretched animal skins, and upon these tympani produced unscorable rhythms, more audible at great distances than close at hand, by gentle pounding with open palms and agile fingers; with the juices from berries, blossoms, and roots they painted their bodies after the styles and colors of their former untrammeled life.

From myriad concealments they watched the treasure trains which were the symbol of their erstwhile slavery, and when the moon was down they crept among the sleeping guards, killing silently as they had learned in the jungles of Guinea to do, and releasing their manacled brothers and sisters. Soon the Chagres country had a new people, taller, stronger than the denizens found there by Columbus, and every jot as savage, crafty, and wild. The

Spaniards had added to the already vicious jungle a new hazard of their own making.

From many different African tribes they had come: Mondongo, Jago, Angola, Ansiko. Now they were united as los Cimarrones—the Untamed.

Among them were certain ones who had ruled supreme in their old haunts: the bocos, the priesthood of the voodoo—a harmless little green snake possessing all knowledge and all power in all things. These leaders resumed their old authority, entrenched as it was by the ageless mores of the race, and began to scour the jungle for the ingredients of their potent medicines and charms.

Then, on moonlit nights, the Spaniards could hear in the distance the eerie pounding of voodoo drums as the Cimarrones gathered at their council fires beside their new Chagres and performed the same bloody rites which for ages their ancestors had followed beside their old Congo:

From the jumpy shadows around the fire leaps the high priest, the father boco, his naked body agleam with many colors of paints and dyes, his head enclosed in a horrific horned mask whose grotesque features depict his idea of the countenance of the devil himself.

He stands motionless for a moment before a cage of woven twigs, in which a tiny green snake rears its head after the style of the deadly cobra, darting out its forked tongue and hissing. Then he begins his wangah, an incantation which he hopes will please the little serpent: a single note of varied syllabics, held for eight beats of the drums, then another note, a half tone higher, for another eight beats, then the original note again . . .

Now the drums begin to inject figurations between

the relentless major throbs, and the other worshipers, seated on the ground facing the fire in even rows, begin to sway forward and back, chanting with the drumbeats: ahya-a-*uh*, ahya-a-*uh*, ahya-a-*uh*. The priest sways from side to side. The little snake, hypnotized by the drums, the chanting, and the priest's motion, sways in time.

Then the priest begins to dance. He shuffles forward and back, his feet padding the relentless rhythm. In short, jerky movements he brings his fists up beside his head, then aloft, then down, then forward, then upward . . .

From the darkness steps the naked priestess—mother boco. She raises one arm and then the other overhead, and sways sinuously. She bends her knees and pounds her heels, swinging her hips from side to side. As she moves toward the priest, the voices of the women rise to shrill screams; as she shuffles away, the chanting of the men sinks into pulsing groans.

Now the others leap to their feet and begin to dance, with a shuffle forward and a shuffle back, closing in around the two principals, who have danced to a spot directly in front of the one person in the group who seems to take no interest. It is the zombi, perhaps a man, perhaps a woman, possibly a child, who has been marked for sacrifice under the rites of the bamboola—the feast of the goat without horns. (Throughout the world, cannibals use some euphemism. With most Africans it is "the goat without horns." With most Polynesians it is "the long pig.") It is indifferent because it is under the spell of the rong-dah, the most powerful of the voodoo charms; it sits beside the little snake and stares into the fire with open but unseeing eyes, apparently not knowing and not caring what fate awaits it.

The zombi may be a wrongdoer of the tribe, condemned by the high priest. It may be an outsider who has been caught spying on its rituals. In either of these cases the sacrifice to the little snake serves as a penalty for offense. But guilt is not necessary. The zombi may be an innocent captive from a neighboring tribe, or even a half-grown child of one of the participating couples.

The priest drops the loop of a thong about the feet of the zombi and tosses the other end across an overhanging limb, and the men haul away until the victim is hanging head downward. The priest steps close, without interrupting his shuffle, and places his hands at various spots on the zombi's body. His movements are furtive and rapid, and in the uncertain light it is impossible to see exactly what he does, but presently the zombi regains consciousness—for the voodoo demands a knowing victim.

Perhaps the awakened zombi, realizing its predicament, struggles and screams; perhaps it quakes in speechless terror. In either case its time is not long; the priest seizes a knife, dances briefly with it, and slashes the zombi's throat. Then, as women shriek and men groan in ecstasy, the priest buries his face in the gash and takes a draught of the blood that spurts forth. The priestess follows, then each of the dancers in turn, until blood no longer flows. During all this time the drumming, the chanting, and the dancing have not slackened; the celebrants maintain their shuffle even as they bend over to partake of their grisly communion.

Now the priest wields the knife again. He lays open the torso of the zombi and tears out its vital organs. These he cuts up into pieces small enough to ensure that no one present will be left out, and distributes them to be eaten raw. The heart he keeps separate, and ceremoniously serves it piece by piece to the little snake.

Next he severs the head and hands it to the priestess, who places it in a simmering caldron over the fire. The body is then hauled down and placed on a spit. While the dancers slowly circle round, father boco tends the roasting and mother boco prepares the stew . . .

The harmless little snake, possessing all knowledge and all power, would have preferred a nest of young birds as his share of the feast. But he shows that he is reasonably well pleased by this sacrifice in his honor by curling up and going to sleep. The cultists thereupon feel assured that their god the serpent will bring good fortune to them all for a little while.

The Cimarrones ranged the Chagres country, attacking the mule trains, killing adult Spaniards of both sexes on sight and carrying off their children.

In 1549 the viceroy of Panama sent a regiment which had been specially trained in jungle tactics to clean them out. The regimental insigne, which each man wore on his helmet and breastplate, was a lizard; this gave rise to a battle cry of the black ones: "Ahorca lagarto!"—Hang the lizard!

For months the soldiers beat the jungle in pursuit, with nothing more than an occasional lame prisoner to reward their pains. One of the officers lamented in a letter to the governor that "there is no way to catch them on account of the incredible impenetrability and ruggedness of the country, access to which is greatly impeded in thick undergrowth and thorny bushes, through which the Negroes pass unharmed, because they smear their bodies with a kind of pitch which protects them from the thorns."

When one of the soldiers became separated from his fellows he was likely to turn up next morning hanging by his neck before the Spaniards' camp, or to become a pile of charred bones following a bamboola.

One night the regiment camped on the lower Chagres, on a sábana adjoining a tiny Indian village several miles above Gatun. The Cimarrones surrounded the camp and attacked, shouting "Ahorca lagarto!" They cut up the Spaniards so badly that the expedition was abandoned, and the handful of survivors who had hacked their way through the ring of black devils was sent back to Spain. Three hundred years later the village was still known as Ahorca Lagarto; as such it became a station on the Panama Railroad.

Each gang had its boco, and all were organized under the leadership of a strapping saw-toothed nightmare named Ballano, who stood six feet six inches tall. His skull was so thick that in one encounter with the Spaniards it broke a soldier's sword and in another it deflected a pistol ball without noticeable effect.

A second expedition in 1552 succeeded in capturing Ballano, but upon the strength of the boco's promise to discontinue his attacks along the Gold Road the governor naïvely released him and formally recognized the sovereignty of the three largest Cimarron villages: Palenque, near Nombre de Dios, San Juan, near Las Cruces, and Diablo, near Panama. (Today near the former site of Diablo rises one of the model towns of the Panama Canal Zone—Diablo Heights.) Once free, Ballano resumed his depredations, and another expedition was sent out. For two years he eluded his pursuers, all the while taking toll of their stragglers and the treasure trains. When he was finally recaptured he was sent to Spain in a cage for exhibition before the royal court.

The Cimarrones carried on under new leaders. Soon

the blacks outnumbered the combined white and brown races of the Chagres country. (This numerical superiority has ever since increased; today four-fifths of the population of the isthmus is Negroid.) By 1570 they had grown strong and bold enough to attack Nombre de Dios; they fought their way into the city, but the chance arrival of a regiment of soldiers from Panama interrupted the massacre.

A year later Francis Drake arrived on the scene, to usher in a century of piracy. The Cimarrones joined his forays, and thereafter were the allies and friends of all the buccaneers.

In some of the Caribbean lands, particularly Haiti, the voodoo priesthood still exerts a strong influence over the people and their leaders, because of its knowledge of strange, jungle-brewed poisons and its notorious willingness to apply it ruthlessly against any opposition to its activities.

Across the Chagres country the cult flourished for three centuries. As late as 1868 the devil-priests were powerful enough to bring about the death by poisoning of Governor Vicente Olarte, who was conducting a campaign to stamp them out. Even today there are occasional rumors of mysterious disappearances of children from native villages.

The Indians fall silent when asked about it: "Yo no se nada de eso."

For one of the rules of the cult is that no one may discuss its activities. The penalty, if the offender can be reached, is the rong-dah, the most potent of the voodoo charms. It is a poison, investigators agree, of a formula that is unknown except to the priesthood; its ingredients apparently are available in the flora or fauna of all tropical lands, for its use has been observed in the jungles of both the Old World and the New. The method of poisoning also is unknown: perhaps in food or drink, possibly through the skin from deposits dusted into clothes or bedding.

The followers of the cult know nothing of its use by the priests to give effect to their charms. They are allowed to see only the ritual in which a small wooden figure is called by the name of the marked one, and then pierced through with a sharp object, to the accompaniment of incantations. The sorcerer himself then attends in secret to the planting of the poison. Later, when the marked one begins to waste away, the believers attribute it directly to the mumbo-jumbo.

Rong-dah appears to be a cumulative poison. A mild dose merely sickens the victim, who becomes gaunt, hollow eyed, and listless. If at this stage he makes whatever restitution is required, the sorcerer withdraws the hex, and the victim recovers health. Otherwise the administration of the drug continues until it induces a state of catalepsy which gives every appearance (to the primitive family at least) of death. The body is buried without benefit of embalming, and that night the minions of the boco exhume it for delivery to the voodoo sanctum, where a stimulant is given to restore life long enough for it to be sacrificed at a bamboola.

In rare instances the rites have been interrupted and the zombi rescued before the sacrifice. But complete recovery, after enough of the poison has been absorbed to induce a coma, apparently is impossible. Thus there have been voodoo victims who lived for years with certain brain centers impaired—noticing little, speaking only an occasional halting word, and moving grotesquely, with much difficulty.

Little wonder that reopened graves, empty coffins, and the sight of such hapless people give rise to stories of wraithlike figures, stalking through the jungle night along the banks of the Chagres, heeding only their voodoo master and doing his will, even to murder. Little wonder that the initiates of the cult believe that throughout life they must do the bidding of the voodoo, on pain of resurrection after death to the zombi's timeless, soulless limbo of death-in-life.

While all tropical lands are rich in the grist of superstition, the Chagres country is opulent. It is the home of the only true vampire bats (genus *Desdemonus, Diphylla,* etc.) of the world. The voodoo priesthood teaches that it can change its zombis into these bats at will, and send them forth to create more zombis.

By night the vampire flits silently into an open hut, and settles lightly on the foot of a sleeper. Gently it slivers its needle-sharp teeth between the nail and the flesh of the great toe, all the while fanning the wound with its wings. It sucks blood until its stomach is bloated, then it withdraws its fangs just as gently and flits soundlessly out.

The bampiro is no larger than an ordinary bat, and it takes only a few ounces of blood at a visit. But in the uncertain moonlight, aided by rioting imaginations and the Draculine tales brought from old Spain, it grows into a winged beast of human shape, who in a single visit drains every drop of a person's blood and leads his victim out into the night, a soulless zombi.

No specific disease is usually transmitted by the vampire bat, but its repeated visitations will cause even an adult victim to waste away—somewhat as does the voodoo poison. The witch doctors diagnose the trouble readily, through slight discolorations underneath the toenails. Their treatment includes a jingo chant, and a charm pouch to be worn about the neck, but its effective ingredient—which must seem just as queer as the rest of it to the ignorant patient—is an order to sleep with the feet wound in heavy cloth.

The voodooism that survives today in the cities of the isthmus is milder than the primitive variety as imported four centuries ago direct from the Ivory Coast. In the slums of Panama and Colon are meeting places where monkeys captured in the nearby jungle are drained of life and eaten by the cultists. Afterward the grinning participants stamp their bare feet to the sensual rhythm of the Black Rumba and drink raw cerveza.

The bocos, having seen horror movies from Hollywood in the modern theaters of Balboa and Cristobal, preside over these sessions wearing black capes which have been ribbed so that the extended arms resemble bat wings.

Adjoining the voodoo sanctum's dance floor are rooms with cots which rent at 25 cents for 15 minutes. The bocos also offer a variety of charms and potions: Man (or Woman) Come Close, Man (or Woman) Stay Away, Husband (or Wife) Stay Home, Other Man (or Woman) Grow Ugly, at prices ranging according to the potency from 50 cents to $5. They perform operations to encourage or to terminate pregnancy, and sell nostrums for venereal diseases.

Do they still brew the charm which makes people into zombis?

"Yo no se nada de eso," answer the devil-priests.

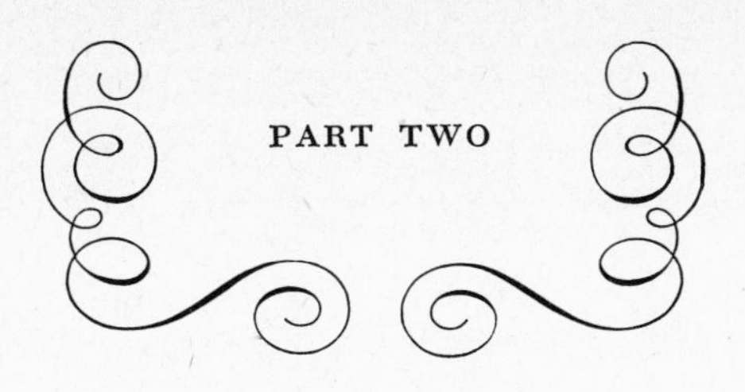

PART TWO

Ye Spanish Mayne

XIII: THE KING'S BEARD

IT ALL grew out of an obscure incident at Río de la Hacha, in which Francis Drake, merchant mariner, from South Tavistock, Devon, felt that he had been cheated by the Spanish port officials. Because of it he dedicated his life to "singeing the beard of the King of Spain." Before Drake was done, he had not only singed that monarch's beard. He had wrested control of the high seas forever from Spain and left it to England as her heritage. . . .

Philip's beard, Drake readily perceived, was most luxuriant where it lay across the Chagres valley. There were concentrated the gold of Veragua, Peru, Darién, and Mexico, the pearls of Isla Rica, the gems of the Orient—wealth, fabulous wealth, flowing to the king of Spain.

With it, Spain was furiously building ships to invade England.

Across the Caribbean in 1571 came Drake in the *Swan*, a 25-ton midget among the mighty ships of Spain. He nosed about, making charts of the isthmian coast line and probing into its remoter inlets and bays. Occasionally he took a prize from among the galleons plying between Nombre de Dios and Cádiz, but only to replenish his supplies and amass enough funds to pay his little crew and finance the next phase of his campaign.

He sneaked ashore, disguised as a Spanish trader, to mingle with the crowds in the market places of Nombre de Dios, noting the lie of the fortifications and the roads, observing the habits of the treasure trains, and raising the eyebrows of the Spaniards in the cantinas with his thickly accented "sí, señor."

Finally he found what he had come primarily to seek: a small, well-concealed inlet a few leagues to the east of Nombre de Dios. There he took his men ashore and cached several chests of arms and other supplies. Then he marked the spot on his charts, christening it Port Pheasant after the gaily plumed birds that seemed to be the principal inhabitants, and set sail for England.

In a year he was back at his "Swan's Nest," with the *Swan* and another, the *Pasha*, of 70 tons, and crews totaling seventy-three. All the men had been recruited in Devon. The only man among them who had reached the ripe age of thirty years was the sailmaker.

They dropped anchor 12 July 1572, and found that the caches had been rifled. On a tree was a leaden plate with this inscription:

> "Captain Drake. If you fortune to come into this port make haste away; for the Spaniards which you had with

you here last year have bewrayed this place, and taken away all that you left here. I departed from hence this present 7th July, 1572. Your very loving friend, John Garret."

The Spaniards referred to were prisoners from Spanish merchantmen. It was Drake's habit to keep them as long as their labor could be used, and then release them unharmed. He never killed unnecessarily, and never used torture.

Drake weighed this intelligence. The caches were badly grown over, yet loving friend Garret had been there only a week before. How could he know who had done it? Natives, more likely. And even if it was as Garret said, the Spaniards were merchant sailors; doubtless they had kept the loot and said nothing to the military authorities, who, in turn, probably ignored them if they did. It had been a long time anyway. And best of all, they could not suspect the purpose; only he and his queen knew that, and Elizabeth was not on speaking terms with her brother Philip on the Spanish throne. Another base as good as this one would be hard to find. . . . He decided to stay.

The lads set to work felling trees, and soon had raised a 30-foot palisade enclosing almost an acre of land, and opening only at the water's edge. Inside they built themselves native-style nipa shacks.

From this base Drake preyed upon the ships of King Philip, collecting his alleged debt a thousand times over. The small band lived on the fare of the grandees, and the treasure of the grandees they cached in the jungle. At odd times they practiced archery, sipped rare wines from old Spain, and played at tenpins on an excellent bowling green, sing hey. The leader became El Draque to the Spaniards.

His operations had an objective deeper than occasional piddling amounts of treasure. Drake had his eye on the treasure's artery, the Gold Road across the Chagres valley, and its reservoir, the king's treasury at Nombre de Dios, where the wealth was stored pending arrival of the gold fleet once each year. No buccaneer could take one of Philip's treasure ships without braving Spain's navy—the mightiest afloat. Drake's activities at sea were partly to keep the Spaniards from realizing that they were vulnerable on land.

One day Drake's patrol sighted an English ship which had just taken a Spanish dispatch shallop carrying a pouch of Chagres nuggets as a gift from the governor of Nombre de Dios to the viceroy of Cartagena. The master, James Ranse, had liked his first taste of Spanish bacon, so Drake signed him on for a major venture.

He picked the twenty stoutest lads from Ranse's crew and added them to his own; then, leaving Ranse and his older men in charge of the base, they sailed westward along the coast in the captured shallop and three "dainty pinnaces" which Drake had brought along from England.

They stopped at a small island, and found it inhabited only by a work gang of Negroes whom the Spaniards had put there to cut timber for Nombre de Dios. There was no guard over them; they could not swim away from the island because of the sharks, the black men explained. Every so often the Spaniards came out with a lighter to load the timber they had cut. If they had not cut enough to suit their masters since the last visit, each slave got a flogging.

'Marrones, they called themselves. (Then and there the word "maroon" was born into the English language.)

Drake took them aboard and set them over on the mainland, little surmising how well they would one day repay the favor. He recruited Diego, the brightest one of the lot, to remain with him as a guide; then he shoved off for Nombre de Dios.

At dusk they slipped behind an eastern promontory of the bay. Around a campfire Drake spent an hour rehearsing the plan of attack, which was to begin at daybreak; then he told his lads to turn in and get some sleep. But they were too excited to sleep. Time dragged on, and Drake worried lest they start the attack a tired lot. When, shortly after midnight, a brilliant full moon rose, he decided that it would serve. Silently the four boats shoved off, rounded the promontory, and glided into the harbor, with the extra raiders packed between the oarsmen.

A lone sentinel was catnapping on the wharf when they swarmed ashore. He scrambled into the lookout tower and jangled the alarum for dear life, while Drake and his lads tumbled all the harbor-defense cannon into the water. Then the raiders formed up in two columns.

The smaller, under Drake's younger brother John, silently skirted the town just inside the wall. Drake himself led the other down the main avenida, with trumpet and drum adding to the clang of the alarum and the shouts of the wakening garrison. His archers sent broadsides of fire-tipped arrows into the thatched roofs all about, and soon the town was ablaze.

The Spaniards formed in the plaza and, as Drake himself reported it, "presented us with a jolly hot volley of shot." The English, having discharged their firearms, "feathered them with our arrowes," and, as John's men showed up on their flank, "came to the push of pike." Soon they "took such order among these Gallants" that "they, casting down their weapons, fled all out of the Towne."

The raiders made for the governor's palace and broke into the vault, where they found a neat pile of Peruvian silver, cast in 40-pound pigs. It measured 26 paces long, 4 paces wide, and 12 feet high—say five million dollars. But it was gold they wanted, so they trooped across the plaza and set to work mining the massive door of the king's treasury. Then Drake fainted.

Demmed nuisance, he mumbled, after they had dashed water in his face and poured a spot of brandy down him. He had got a musket ball in his leg during the first brush, but had neglected to mention it. Carry on!

But the lads would not. They forgot loot and carried him tenderly back to the quay. As one of the pinnaces shoved off with him, the men of the others noted that one of the newly arrived ships in the harbor had brought a cargo of choice wines from old Spain, so they paused long enough to load a few kegs. Then the tiny fleet made for an unoccupied island just outside the bay.

Next morning out skimmed a Spanish pinnace flying a white flag, and an officer of the garrison jumped ashore. Drake's archers had wounded several of his soldiers; he wanted to know if they were poisoned. Over a bottle of old Amontillado, Drake said no, he never used poisoned arrows. He complimented the Spaniard on the quality of his wine, but said frankly, as he shook a pouch of nuggets, that he was more interested in the "special commodity" of the isthmus.

"So tell the jolly old governor," he concluded the interview, "to hold open his eye."

Captain Ranse, who had just arrived in one of the pinnaces, figured that this was asking for trouble, so he begged to be excused. Drake agreed, and the chance ally took his share of the excellent wine and sailed away.

While he nursed his wound, Drake sent brother John with one of the pinnaces to see whether there were any new fortifications at the mouth of the Chagres. Then, feeling better than he had counted, he took the other two pinnaces down to Cartagena, stole into the harbor at night, and stole out again in a handsome new frigate with the pinnaces in tow. As he neared Nombre de Dios he met another trim frigate leaving for Spain, so he took it along.

With these fine ships, far better than the tubs he had been looting and scuttling, he had no more need of the *Swan*, so he sank her in her own nest.

Knowing that the garrisons on shore would be alert for a while, Drake turned again to the sea. He preyed on shipping out of Chagres and Nombre de Dios, stowing treasure in his frigates until they were like to sink. In time it again became necessary to begin burying their loot in the jungle, where much of it undoubtedly remains to this day.

Once the governor sent out a frigate loaded with soldiers. It drifted about on the horizon, apparently abandoned or in difficulty, so of course Drake hove to. Just in time he saw the glint of armor behind the rail; as he pulled away, the soldiers peppered the water around his pinnaces with ineffectual musketry. From the quarterdeck the Spanish captain screamed at him in frustration, while Drake and his lads thumbed their noses between contemptuously unhurried strokes.

So it went until January, when the fevers of the Chagres country swept Port Pheasant and laid more than half of the lads low. The surgeon, casting desperately about for a remedy, made a concoction of voodoo medicine as instructed by Diego. Like a good doctor, he tried it first on himself, and it killed him. Diego was nonplused. He made up another batch, from a less violent formula, but the lads declined with thanks. Before it was over, twenty-eight had died, including Drake's second brother Joseph. Then brother John and another of the men were killed while boarding a Spanish ship. The situation was grave.

Diego sent out word by the jungle telegraph that the blond warriors who were so successfully hacking the hated Spaniards needed replacements, and the next morning Drake found a mob of black volunteers chafing outside the palisade. He selected thirty of the best among the savages to fill his ranks, and told Diego to send the others back to keep watch on the treasure trains.

After he had given the recruits a week of intensive training in English commands and weapons, word came through Diego that the king's plate fleet had arrived at Nombre de Dios. Now the treasure trains would start across the isthmus in earnest.

Drake left the convalescents to guard the base, and took eighteen of his Devonshire lads and the thirty Cimarrones into the jungle. Diego led them unerringly over almost-invisible trails to the upper Chagres, and they followed the river down toward Las Cruces. At the nightly halts on this march, another queer sight was added to our river's extensive collection: Francis Drake, pirate, teaching thirty savage, black, snake-worshiping anthropophagists to recite the Lord's prayer in English.

When the party arrived in the vicinity of Las Cruces the Cimarrones learned from their fellows that no trains had yet gone through, so Drake decided to move cautiously along the road toward Panama in the hope of meeting one.

There was a little trouble when a lone rider came down the road and the Cimarrones rushed out of the tall grass, dragged him from his horse, and knifed him. That sort of thing, Drake told them gruffly, would have to stop. No one exposes himself without orders. The Cimarrones, who habitually killed Spaniards on sight, could not understand this queer edict, but they shrugged and complied.

When they crested the divide Diego showed Drake a tree from which he could see the Pacific. The Spaniards had built a platform in the branches with a ladder leading to it, so Drake climbed up and became the first Englishman to set eyes on Spain's private ocean.

"Almighty God," prayed Drake, as he gazed out over the azure expanse, "of Thy goodness give me life and leave to sail once in an English ship on that sea." His prayer was answered in a blaze of glory five years afterward, but that, unfortunately, is not a part of the Chagres story.

Two days later they had crossed the Cordillera and gained the plain before Panama; in another two days they were hiding just outside the gates. Diego removed his jungle trappings, thereby disguising himself as a loyal slave, and walked boldly into the city. He was back shortly, with news that two trains were to move out at dusk, carrying a little gold and silver for the fleet and rations for the garrison at Nombre. In the convoy, happy day, would be the treasurer of Lima and his daughter, with eight mules carrying gold and another carrying jewels looted from the Incas.

The party withdrew to the foothills and planned an

ambush. The Englishmen put their shirts on over their armor, so that the Cimarrones could distinguish them from the Spaniards in the expected fray. The signal for attack would be a blast of his whistle; absolute quiet, Drake ordered, until then. At supper he authorized the issue of a dram of spirits to each man; then they deployed on either side of the road and took cover.

Shortly before night fell there came a clop-clop of hoofs on the cobblestones, from the direction of Cruces. It was a lone horseman, and going the wrong way, but one of the lads, Robert Pike by name, who had taken more than his quota of brandy, started up from the grass and lunged toward the road. The Cimarron next him dragged him back and sat on him, but the fat was in the fire. The rider spurred his horse to a gallop. Drake, at the other end of the ambush, had not seen, and so thought nothing of the rider's change of pace.

When the rider met the convoy he told its captain about seeing an hombre in a shirt tussling with a Negro in the grass. They didn't know what to make of it, but to be on the safe side the commander detached the treasure-bearing mules and sent them back to Panama.

The ambush came off as planned, and Drake found himself in possession of a convoy of beans, nothing but beans. (For years afterward, they say, he would not allow beans to be served at his table.) When the sensible Cimarron and one of the muleteers pieced the story together for him, Drake gave Pike a sermon, in well-chosen words, on temperance.

Anyway they had plenty of mules, so they each one took a mount and the party clattered down the high road to Cruces. As they approached the town a sentry called a challenge.

"English party," bawled Drake. "Stand aside in the name of her Majesty, Queen Elizabeth!"

Undoubtedly the sentry knew no English, but he did know that this was not the countersign. He fired his piece, and the other soldiers of the outpost came up on the run. They were met by a squad of Cimarrones who, with El Draque's permission, took care of them in their own way while the column rode into town.

Cruces, being higher and cooler than Panama or Nombre de Dios, was popular as a resort for the fine Spanish ladies of both cities who were anticipating confinement. Hearing the uproar, all the pregnant women ran into the monastery, on the heels of the soldiers of the garrison. As they barred the door, Drake shouted through it that they need have no fear. Then he barricaded it on the outside to keep the soldiers in—a precaution hardly necessary, he commented—and proceeded to sack the town.

Before daybreak the party had vanished into the jungle, following their old route back along the Chagres toward their base.

The Spaniards left off sending treasure across the isthmus for a time. The gold fleet languished in the harbor, and Drake turned again to the sea.

The French vessel had been without water for almost a week, during which time the crew had been subsisting on wine taken from the cargo. It had been great fun for the first day or so, said Captain Tetu, with everybody feeling very brotherly and the lookouts sighting a sea serpent on every wave. But now they were all weak and bleary eyed, stomachs badly upset, heads and hearts pounding, minds foggy. Drake led them to his anchorage and gave them the run of the grounds to recuperate.

Some days later, after the guests had regained their health and sobriety, a spy brought word that the treasure trains were moving again. So Drake organized a party of his own lads, the pick of the French crew, and the Cimarrones, and shoved off in the pinnaces, leaving Tetu in command at the base. This time they carried no brandy.

They rowed in a wide, leisurely arc around the harbor at Nombre, and hove to a few miles to the east of Chagres. There they hid the pinnaces in some overhanging foliage and posted guards near them.

By sundown the party had worked back along the shore line to a point just outside the western gate of the city. Here, Drake figured, within sight of journey's end, the treasure guard would be more relaxed than at any time before. But the garrison in Nombre probably would hear the scuffle and come to the rescue, so he posted a group of his best archers in a clump of trees which commanded the gate, with orders to hold them back.

It was the height of the dry season, and Nombre was so hot that its people slept by day and worked at night. The Devon lads outside the gate heard the city waken as darkness closed in, saw the guards light the torches around the plaza, heard the hammering of carpenters, watched the tradesmen unload their Oriental finery from donkeys and arrange their dazzling displays on the ground.

Word from the spies was that a train of some two hundred mules, all carrying gold and silver, would arrive shortly after dark. This time the ambush did not miscarry. The usual guard of one soldier for each ten mules had been tripled, and they put up a stiff fight, but soon all of them were done in or routed, with only one of the raiders, a Cimarron, killed.

Sure enough, a party of soldiers from the city started out to investigate the hubbub, and the archers nailed the entire front rank as it passed through the gate. The others ran back inside and reported that the city was surrounded, so preparations were made to withstand an assault. The gates were closed—serving Drake's purposes admirably—and fires were set under the caldrons of pitch on the walls.

About twenty tons of gold there was, and fifteen of silver. All the silver and most of the gold they cached in the jungle, using the mules to carry as far as the trails would allow and then feverishly lugging it by hand to several widely spaced places of concealment. Finally each man shouldered as much gold as he could carry, and they staggered back to the place where they had left the pinnaces.

The pinnaces were gone.

What to do? They could not carry these backbreaking loads much farther, and there was no place to go anyway. Drake had to have a vessel, any sort of vessel, to go out and hunt for his pinnaces.

Diego ventured that he knew of a Spanish logging camp on the banks of the Chagres, a long way up from the mouth but only a few miles through the jungle from where they were at that moment.

Drake left a small guard over the gold and took everyone else under forced march to the logpile by the river. Through the night they labored, lashing unstripped logs together to make a huge raft. A tall, thin sapling they stood up amidships, with an old biscuit sack for a sail. They split a big log and laid a flat section of it in a notch in the stern for a rudder; they split some small logs and hacked on them with their knives to make paddles.

Then, as dawn spread over the mouth of the river,

the sentinels of the village garrison saw this strange craft come wallowing down the Chagres, with a black and white crew, deck awash, and Francis Drake at the tiller, shouting his commands in bad Spanish, in the hope that this would persuade the sentries that here was a local yachting party. The guards were too entranced to move until the raft was past them and on the open sea; then they sent a cannon ball skimming after it, so wide of its mark that they were ashamed to try another.

Around the promontory Drake spied his pinnaces; they had left the rendezvous the night before when a land patrol, beating the jungle for the gringos who had made off with their gold, had got too near for comfort. The boats drew alongside to pick up the crew of the raft. How had things gone? they asked.

"Well," said Drake.

Back at the rendezvous they met the rest of the party and learned that intemperance again had reduced the winnings of the voyage: one of the Frenchmen, finding a bottle on one of the late Spaniards, had got himself drunk and had wandered into the hands of the pursuers—who had finally come out after realizing that the city was not being assaulted after all. Under torture he had revealed where much of the loot was hidden; even then the Spaniards were busy recovering it.

But they still had gold aplenty, all that they could ship and more. They spent the rest of the day caching the surplus in the jungle, and at first dark they shoved off.

Back at Port Pheasant, Drake and Tetu calculated the division of the spoils, and as a favor the Frenchman accepted equivalent value in silver from Drake's previous raids, since his vessels already were low in the water and he needed to concentrate his cargo however possible.

As the French ship sailed away, Drake gave orders to strike camp. With barely enough men to sail the two captured frigates, he had to scuttle the *Pasha*—regretfully, for it could have brought home another fortune in loot which he was forced to leave behind, hidden in the jungle.

To the Cimarrones he gave the pinnaces and all the arms and ammunition that he did not need for the voyage home. Diego, when he learned that he was not to sail away with his friends, ranted so that the other Cimarrones had to hold him. Drake knew that Diego had long had his eye on a jewel-hilted Turkish scimitar which had been found on one of the prize ships; he offered it to him as a parting remembrance, knowing that it would see full service at singeing Philip's beard in the Chagres valley for long after he had gone.

In return, Diego insisted on giving Drake a heavy pouch of gold coins which he had collected at various times from his victims along the Gold Road. It was a personal gift, but Drake lumped it with the other winnings, and thereby set a precedent which grew into an inviolate law of the buccaneers: that no man will withhold any acquisition, however insignificant, from the "common stock of the voyage."

With the two erstwhile Spanish frigates freighted so that their decks were almost awash, the Devonshire lads sailed for England. What the French wits of that day called "Spanish bacon" these genuine boucaniers were bringing home.

Francis Drake had singed King Philip's beard to the tune of some twenty millions of dollars' worth of treasure, plus a sizable fleet of scuttled and stolen ships.

XIV: MUFFLED DRUMS

TWENTY-TWO years after he had abandoned his secret base at Port Pheasant, Francis Drake sailed in a mighty fleet of the English navy as it crossed the Caribbean and stood off Nombre de Dios.

He was no longer Captain Francis Drake, privateer, conducting a personal war against those blackguards of the Spanish Main who had cheated him. He was no longer an adventurer, challenging the world-wide maritime supremacy of Spain with a handful of stout English lads in rowboats.

He was Admiral Sir Francis Drake, destroyer of Spain's "invincible" armada, savior of England and of Protestantism, circumnavigator of the globe, discoverer of California, favorite of good Queen Bess, idol of his country, the greatest mariner of all time. Since sailing off the stage of the Chagres Theater two decades before, he had singed King Philip's beard on every sea.

This time England and Spain were formally at war; he was after booty rather than loot. This time he had brought along a crack regiment of war-seasoned English marines. Already Spain's empire was beginning to disintegrate; her navy had been hacked to pieces by staggering blows from the swelling sea power of England under Admiral Drake's command. Already King Philip was on the ropes, but still holding doggedly to his golden life line across the Isthmus of Panama. This time Drake's mission was to cut Philip's jugular vein, rather than singe his beard.

Drake's intention was to sweep across the Chagres valley and push the Spanish off into the Pacific, to annex Panama as a colony of the English crown, to clinch forever England's mastery of all the seas. For Sir Walter Raleigh had said to Elizabeth: "Seize the isthmus of Darien and you will wrest the keys of the world from Spain."

But he was not the same Drake. As a young man with a slender rapier, he had pinked the enemy at will; now as an old man with a ponderous broadsword, he could only lunge straight forward and dull his weapon against the enemy's armor where it was thickest.

Very foolishly, he had sacked and burned several Spanish ports in the Caribbean en route, thus destroying his chances of staging a surprise attack. Warning of his presence in those waters had got to Panama weeks ahead of him, and preparations for his reception had been thorough; for the isthmus still bore visible scars of the ravages of El Draque and his little band, and the Spaniards had not forgotten.

The news that he was coming back, and with a hundred times his former strength, had sent a quaver of fear through every Spanish heart. But that had been followed by the cool determination of desperation. Every able-bodied Spaniard on the isthmus had been called up hurriedly to be armed and drilled; concealed forts had been built along the roads; all treasure had been lugged into the jungle for concealment; Nombre de Dios and the new harbor city of Porto Bello had been abandoned except for lookouts, who had orders to speed inland with the news as soon as Drake's fleet appeared.

So, into a lifeless, treasureless city walked Drake, with Colonel Sir Thomas Baskerville, commander of his fleet marine force, who had earned distinction in the recent campaigns in Ireland. Drake pointed out to him the road to Panama, and then settled down in the governor's palace to wait for news. The Drake of old would have led the way. And the way would have been some daring feint, some wholly unexpected stratagem, instead of a blunt, unimaginative frontal assault.

Baskerville moved out with eight hundred men—about half of his available force. The mission given him by Drake was to take and hold the city of Panama. The plan was then to work from these two bases, with Baskerville in command at Panama and Drake leading the remainder of the marine force out of Nombre, to subdue the rest of the isthmus. Too late did Baskerville realize that Drake had sent him straight into the elaborate network of defenses which the Spanish had labored desperately to prepare.

On the march toward Cruces, well-placed snipers harassed every mile, inflicting heavy casualties and driving the invaders from one exhausting deployment into another without any visible enemy to attack.

As they crossed the Chagres at Cruces, the first of the concealed forts mowed down a platoon before Baskerville's vanguard could even locate it. Then the handful of entrenched defenders threw back two attacks by the English advance element with alarming losses. It required a full-scale assault by the entire force to reduce the strongpoint, and the price paid was dear.

The scouts then brought back the intelligence that

there were at least two more such forts before Panama, each with more defenders than this one had had, and snipers in every tree along the way. Baskerville could hear in the distance the felling of trees across the Gold Road.

With a third of his original force already lost, he saw that he could never reach Panama, and that if by some miracle he should, it would be with only a handful of men who would never be able to take the city. So he sent a runner back to Drake with word that he was in full but orderly retreat.

Drake got the news in Nombre, early on the morning of New Year's Day, 1596, and had the empty satisfaction of burning an empty city while waiting for the return of his broken army. Later that day Baskerville brought in the remnants of the force, which had been further reduced by snipers during his retreat. The scores of wounded men who had been unable to walk unaided he had abandoned to the ministrations of the Spaniards.

The disheartened fleet put to sea and sailed westward, with Drake speaking bravely of gold and glory to be had in Nicaragua. But contrary winds held them back, and in two weeks they had made less than a hundred leagues.

So they put in at the pestilential island of Escudo de Veragua to clean and water, and there dysentery swept the fleet. Drake took it, and with his grief-stricken, befuddled mind now also feverish, he ordered the fleet to sail eastward again to Porto Bello.

During the night of 27 January, Drake rose from his sickbed against the protests of the fleet surgeons and had himself dressed in full armor. He drew his sword and swung it about, mouthing incoherently and lunging unsteadily at an imaginary opponent, while his attendants shook their heads. Then he fell back onto his bed, still mumbling. Shortly before daybreak, as the fleet was passing the bay which one day would become the Atlantic entrance to the Panama Canal, he died as a great fighter should—with his boots on.

The fleet continued to deserted Porto Bello. As it sailed into the harbor, the lookouts ran into the interior, alerting the snipers and the men in the concealed forts that had been built along that route. The isthmus trembled again. El Draque was coming back, and though they had driven him off once, the Spaniards knew him well enough to expect that he would strike again, and this time with something new and unpredictable. The Spaniards did not know that this was not a combat operation, that the sorrowing fleet had come to Porto Bello only to carry out its beloved admiral's last command.

Next morning the fleet put to sea again, and hove to a league from the shore, not far from the spot where Drake had died.

On the deck of his flagship, the *Defiance,* lay Drake in a leaden coffin, draped over with a flag bearing the cross of St. George. The trumpets of the fleet sounded. Then the fleet's muffled drums began a roll, which swelled and swelled as the casket slid over the rail, and stopped short as it struck the water. The guns of the fleet roared again and again in a thunderous salute to their greatest admiral.

The Reverend Mr. Bride, fleet chaplain, made a sermon in rhyme:

Where Drake first found, there last he lost his name,
  And for a tomb left nothing but his fame.
His body's buried under some great wave,

The sea that was his glory is his grave.
On whom an epitaph none can truly make,
For who can say, "*Here* lies Sir Francis Drake?"

Then the ships weighed anchor, and moved one by one slowly over the spot, with their crews, in full dress, lining the rails at rigid attention. When all had passed, onto the spot moved two good English ships which had been piled high with timbers. The crews anchored them, poured gunpowder over the decks, ignited it, and escaped overside into dainty pinnaces such as Drake had loved.

The Spanish lookouts, who had returned cautiously to the coast when no enemy appeared, watched the ritual, half wondering whether this might be some sort of ruse. Then, as the admiral's funeral pyre on his own high seas blazed, and the mighty fleet turned away to the northeast, they realized that Francis Drake would never harass them again.

The Cimarrones of the Chagres valley wept. And as the ships of the fleet dropped one by one over the horizon, some old Devonshire lads on board recognized the distant mournful throb of voodoo drums.

Seen today across the perspective of the years, Drake's failure to take Panama for his queen shows the pervading wisdom of Providence. Instead of becoming a part of a rising empire, which later tried with all its might to crush a budding democracy in the New World, the isthmus remained a part of an empire whose inexorable decay in time left it free. Then, when science at last had conquered the pestilences of the Chagres valley, the high mission of dividing the land fell to Americans.

XV: PIRATES!

FRANCIS DRAKE had shown how it should be done, so in his wake followed the notorious buccaneers of the Spanish Main—as lurid in fact as in song and story.

The original buccaneers were cattle rustlers (boucaniers) on the island of Haiti. When Spanish trade in the Caribbean reached such a volume that outlawry on sea offered greater opportunities than on land, they took to the ships in which they had previously smuggled away their buccanned (barbecued) beef and began to waylay the rich galleons from Seville on the high seas. It drove the Spanish to build the greatest navy that the world had ever seen, and led to the invention of the convoy system for the protection of ocean commerce.

English geographers of the day charted a "Spanish Mayne Sea" (which Magellan in 1520 had misnamed Pacific in his vast relief at getting through the strait that bears his name) and a "Spanish Mayne Land" (the Caribbean arc of the new continent, which curved west and north from Cartagena to Santa Cruz). It was not the Spanish Mayne Sea that the English and French raiders roved; piracy was virtually nonexistent in Pacific waters. Ships could reach that ocean only by braving the blizzards of Tierra del Fuego at the southern tip of the pan-American continent, where even the master mariner Drake lost two of his three vessels. Drake's success at raiding Spain's South Sea ports and ships with his one remaining frigate made other pirate mouths water, but few of those desperate men were desperate enough to try the voyage around the stormy Horn. Those who did were never heard from.

It was on the Caribbean that the buccaneers "sailed the Spanish Mayne"—the mayne in this case being the mainland. They called the northern shore of the isthmus, with the Chagres River and its Camino del Oro as its artery of riches, the Gold Coast. From this inexhaustible till the English pirates drained so much specie that Spanish coins became more common than pounds, shillings, and pence in the English colonies of North America.

(The Spanish silver peso was divided into eight reals, which the English called bits. The term "pesos of eight reals" they corrupted into "pieces of eight bits," which they soon shortened to pieces of eight. The Spanish silver peso served as the model, as to weight and fineness, for the first U.S. dollar, and the piece-of-eight symbol —a figure 8 with a vertical line through it—evolved into the dollar sign. Despite the introduction of Thomas Jefferson's decimal system of fragmentation for United States money, the old division into eight parts survives today in the expressions two, four, and six bits.)

The first buccaneer to harass the Spaniards in the Chagres country after El Draque departed Port Pheasant was John Oxenham of Plymouth ("John Oxnam of Plimmouth")—one of the Devonshire lads who had been with Drake when he first sighted the South Sea. Oxenham returned to the isthmus in 1575 with seventy men, including a number of veterans from the Drakian expedition, in a ship of 120 tons.

News of his presence at the same old base spread quickly through the jungle; black Diego and a troop of his Cimarron campaigners came joyously to greet him. The Spaniards, Diego informed him, now were sending formidable detachments of soldiers with every treasure train that crossed the Chagres valley. But if the English leader cared to resume the old operations in the face of this extra hazard, Diego would gladly place at his disposal any desired number of his Cimarrones for reinforcements.

Oxenham decided instead to undertake another bold plan. With the help of the savages, the party beached the vessel and camouflaged it with jungle foliage. They buried its ordnance, and then set out across the isthmus by secret trails which paralleled the Gold Road, under the care and guidance of the Cimarrones. When they arrived on the Pacific coast the Negroes pilfered a Spanish lumbering camp for a supply of carpentry tools. With these the Englishmen built a 45-foot pinnace, as dainty as those which Drake himself had used. Soon the first pirate crew ever to sail the South Sea began boarding vessels of the Peruvian plate fleet as they neared the harbor of Panama.

Within a few weeks their raids had netted for them nearly a million pesos of treasure, and the governor of Panama was beside himself. He sent out all available ships and men to scour the bay and the littoral. One of the patrols, consisting of a hundred soldiers in four barques under the command of Juan de Ortega, encountered the Englishmen and chased them into San Miguel Bay. There the raiders dragged their pinnace ashore and hid it in the jungle, stationed a guard of six men over it, and fled inland with the treasure. Ortega's men came upon the guard and routed it, killing one of them; then they destroyed the pinnace.

While beating the jungle roundabout, the pursuers

came upon a fresh-dug mound of earth which turned out to be Oxenham's cache. Ortega's men opened it and recovered the loot, then abandoned the chase and started back toward Panama. The infallible Cimarrones brought the news to Oxenham's hideout, and the pirates attempted to ambush the Spaniards along the homeward trail. But the Englishmen were routed, with eleven killed and seven captured.

Under torture the captive Englishmen talked; then, while the beaten pirate band retreated along the back trails of the Chagres valley under forced march, a mounted messenger from the governor sped northward over the Gold Road. Soldiers from Nombre found the hitherto secret inlet of Port Pheasant, and when the mud-caked Englishmen arrived at the base their hidden ship was gone. Again the Cimarrones filched tools from them, and they set to work building another pinnace. But then the Chagres fever came again to Port Pheasant, and all but fifteen of the Englishmen died. While the survivors were convalescing under the tender care of the savages, the Spanish patrol that had taken their ship returned and captured them.

When the fever-weakened prisoners arrived in Panama, the governor asked Oxenham whether he held a privateer's commission from his government.

"No," said he, perhaps realizing that his fate would be the same no matter how he answered, "I and I alone am responsible for this voyage."

So the ten surviving adults of the party were beheaded in the plaza, and the five cabin boys became servants in the governor's household. The first execution of English pirates in the New World climaxed the first crossing of the isthmus by Europeans other than Spaniards.

Thereafter adventurers from all the ports of Northern Europe gravitated to the Caribbean, to lie in wait for the shiploads of treasure that fanned out from Nombre and Porto Bello. While there was war with Spain they sailed under their national colors, carrying commissions from their sovereigns. Such operations were cheaper than formal warfare, and the booty was the legitimate spoils of war, which the privateers kept as payment for their services.

But while there was peace, Spanish gold still flowed across the Chagres valley and on to Seville, and stout fellows could still prosper by tapping the channel. So they hauled down their national colors and ran up the black flag with white skull and crossed bones, which the English lads christened the Jolly Roger, or Rover. Their governments loudly disclaimed their activities while secretly providing them with men, money, and ships.

Even in wartime, when captured privateers were legally entitled to the same consideration as any other prisoners, the isthmian governors openly hanged them in the plazas and pinned their commissions on their chests with daggers. During peace they were not granted such merciful execution; they went instead into the torture chambers under the fortresses of Nombre, Porto Bello, San Lorenzo, and Panama. Knowing what they faced in the event of capture, the pirates asked and gave no quarter.

A ponderous galleon was no match in maneuver for the lighter craft used by the raiders. The assaulting longboats ran under the stern of the floating castle; the men jammed the rudder, swarmed up the rigging, and poured over the bulwarks, with cutlasses in their teeth. Once on deck they drew pistols and laid about them with lead and steel, shooting, yelling, lunging, seeming to be everywhere at once, until the deck ran with blood.

Sometimes the Spanish sailors went overside into their own longboats as soon as the pirates appeared on the horizon, but usually they fought to the last man. Those who surrendered were held for ransom or sold into slavery at Jamaica; anyone who proved untractable was forced to walk the plank, with eyes and arms bound and weights in his boots.

Spanish ladies never embarked on Caribbean travel without a locket containing a capsule of poison, but when the dreaded moment came many of them lacked the courage to swallow it. Those who threw themselves on the mercy of the corsairs usually regretted the decision, although some grew reconciled and lived for years aboard pirate ships, wearing the silks of the Orient and the jewels of Inca queens.

François L'Ollonois of Calais was the cruelest man of this heartless profession. He once beheaded seventy Spaniards with his own sword, and sent the heads in a Cuna Indian's cayuco to the governor of Nombre de Dios. Women he tortured and butchered after ravishment no longer entertained. Once he laid open a señorita with a stroke of his cutlass, tore out her still-living heart, and ate it, washing it down with a cup of her blood. (What copy he would have furnished had there been tabloids in those days!)

In contrast with the usual cordiality between the buccaneers and the native tribes of the isthmus, L'Ollonois was as cruel with them as with Spaniards. He often went ashore along the Gold Coast seeking food, and instead of offering trinkets in exchange for it as the other pirates did, he seized the Indians and tortured them until they met his demands. Then he shot a few, so that next time they would be more agreeable.

One day he fell upon a galleon as it was leaving Porto Bello, not knowing that it had a large detachment of homing soldiers on board. In the battle that followed the pirates were almost wiped out; L'Ollonois himself was wounded, and barely escaped overside into a pinnace with a handful of his men. The master of the galleon assigned enough of his crew to sail the pirate ship into the harbor, and continued on his way.

L'Ollonois and his followers landed on the Darién coast without weapons, nursing their wounds. The Frenchmen, thinking that they had the natives cowed, demanded food, shelter, and care until they could return to the sea. But the Indians, realizing that they had the upper hand, put the entire party to death. L'Ollonois they tore limb from limb, and threw the pieces into the fire.

Edvart Mansveldt of Rotterdam conceived a plan for putting piracy on a more respectable footing. He enlisted several independent outfits, and by 1664 was the admiral of a buccaneer navy: fifteen ships and five hundred men. He led them in a successful assault on a Spanish island, known variously as Santa Catalina, St. Catherine's, and Old Providence, fifty leagues off Panama. Here he built a permanent base and began a systematic pillage of the Gold Coast and the galleons leaving there.

Then Mansveldt sailed to Jamaica, where he called on Governor Thomas Modyford and placed before him a plan to make of the island a permanent pirate independency, even to the extent of sending diplomatic representatives to the courts of Northern Europe. From this commanding position athwart the Chagres coast it would be simple to tap Spain's pipe line of gold, and it could be done without the complication of declaring war. He asked Modyford for money and supplies, in return for which England would participate in the profits of the venture.

England and Spain were then at war, so this would have been a legitimate as well as lucrative investment, but the governor declined—undoubtedly because it was already planned to seize the island and annex it to the British empire. Soon after this Mansveldt died, leaving his vice-admiral, Henry Morgan, in command of the greatest pirate organization in the world.

The greatest exploit of Morgan, the greatest pirate, was the murder of Panama la Vieja. (See The Rape of Panama.)

After Morgan the Chagres spotlight shifted to Bartholomew Sharp of Liverpool. In 1680 he led a company of three hundred English across the isthmus by the wild Darién route, far to the east of the Gold Road. For three months they battled treacherous jungle, rugged mountains, swift rivers, and tribes which used poisoned darts in their blowguns and were permanently hostile even toward their neighbors, until they reached San Miguel Bay. There the party seized native canoes and crept eastward along the coast toward the new city of Panama.

They were in luck. A fleet of ten galleons was lying in the lee of Perico Island, unloading chests of Peruvian gold onto a string of rafts which was shuttling the cargo across the shallow water to Panama. Ships and men were lightly armed, so Sharp's band had a weighty advantage despite its small numbers.

Sharp assembled his force in an inlet from which the fleet could be seen, and assigned to each galleon, according to its size, a group of two, three, or four canoes. Then the pirates paddled out in a wide circle and approached the fleet from the sea. They were almost upon their objectives before the Spanish realized that they were being attacked. It was short work.

Most of the treasure had been taken ashore, but this was not too bad. They had gained the necessary tools of their trade. They selected the flagship of the fleet, *La Santissima Trinidad,* of 400 tons, for their own. The rest of the fleet they stripped to make their *Most Blessed Trinity* the best armed and provisioned ship in the Pacific, and scuttled the other ships at night in the harbor.

Within arm's reach of the pirates was the new Panama, by far America's largest and richest city, with all the treasure that had been taken ashore from the fleet and more. The Spaniards at that moment were busy unlimbering their defenses, clearing the vaults, lugging the gold to various hiding places, expecting Sharp to storm the city in imitation of Morgan.

The Englishmen clamored for Panama, but Sharp was as discriminating as he was daring. Panama had the strongest defenses on the South Sea; in fact it was the only Pacific city with any more fortifications than were necessary to keep out hostile savages. There were other prizes to be had at smaller cost.

So Sharp's rovers sailed to southward and out of the Chagres Theater, leaving a trail of burned cities, murdered colonists, plundered churches, and ravished women all the way to Cape Horn.

Before they were through, the pirates had murdered the three greatest cities of the Chagres country.

XVI: GOLD COAST

"I DARE boldly say and avouch," wrote the English traveler Thomas Gage in 1640, "that in the world there is no greater fair than that of Porto Bello."

Nombre de Dios was abandoned after Drake burned it in 1596. The Spaniards transferred its charter as the sole Atlantic port of Peruvian treasure to Porto Bello. The stone in its walls and most of its buildings was trundled over the old eastern and the new western fork of the Camino Real, and above the native town of Porto Bello, on a long arm of land which embraced a far better harbor than that at Nombre, rose the strongest bastion of the Spanish Main. It was six leagues closer than the old port to the mouth of the Chagres, where the Spanish built yet another fortress and named it San Lorenzo. The two strong points were in a position to reinforce each other in case of emergency.

The new treasure port was planned to be impregnable at any cost. Porto Bello's fortress of San Felipe was really a system of separate ramparts, joined by a continuing wall of stone nine feet thick, which was lined with cannon of the largest caliber ever cast up to that time. With tremendous labor the engineers cleared a field of fire almost a mile wide before the walls by cutting back the jungle. To keep this zone free of underbrush in the fertile tropics required the year-round attention of a hundred slaves.

No ship could enter the harbor without passing under the guns of San Felipe; no land force could reach the walls without moving across an open strip in full view of the defenders atop them. Picked troops of the Spanish army, veterans with records of bravery under fire in campaigns all over Europe and Africa, were sent to garrison Porto Bello and San Lorenzo. Underground passages within the walls contained stores of food, ammunition, and medical supplies enough for a year of siege. Every soldier, from the captain general down, drew a bonus for every shipload of treasure that was loaded and cleared from the harbor without loss at the hands of the buccaneers.

Yet William Parker, of Tortuga and London, with about two hundred men, invested Porto Bello in 1602, less than a year after the fortifications were completed. His ship entered the harbor at night; at the rail stood Parker, holding a pistol at the head of a captured Spaniard. When the lookouts shouted a challenge, the prisoner called out in Spanish that it was a Seville merchantman from Cartagena. Back came instructions as to where to cast anchor.

Quietly, in small groups, the Englishmen came ashore, and soon were holding the key officers of the town and its garrison at sword's point. Without firing a shot they made off with half a million pesos of treasure, and because the Spaniards did not resist the Englishmen refrained from damaging the port. It was one of the least bloody and most profitable raids in all the annals of piracy.

For a century and a half Porto Bello was the world's greatest trading center. "However detestable its climate," wrote Antonio de Alcedo, "this city was the emporium of the riches of two worlds, and the most considerable commercial depot ever known." The Casa de Contratacion at Seville, which was quite as monopolistic in policy as its later British counterpart, the London Board of Trade, required all the Spanish colonies of South America to buy goods only from old Spain. They could not trade even with each other. Their only chance to acquire merchandise was at the great annual trade fairs at Porto Bello. By this means the Seville merchants controlled the quantities of goods so that supply never approached demand. Scarcity kept prices high and profits large. It also encouraged smuggling and aided the eventual breakup of the empire.

Once a year the Spanish commercial fleet sailed out, and because Porto Bello was so pestilential it put in at Cartagena to wait for word that the Pacific plate fleet had arrived at Panama from Peru. When the Peruvian galleons appeared in the harbor at Panama, a horseman set out like Paul Revere across the Gold Road. At Porto Bello a waiting shallop shoved off when he clattered up, and the crew tacked and paddled furiously along the coast to Cartagena. By the time the treasure had begun to move by mule train across the Chagres valley the Seville fleet was on its way to Porto Bello.

When the fleet anchored, the president of the fair came ashore and assembled the merchants of Panama, Mexico, Peru, the Argentine, the Antilles, and the Philippines. At conferences in the customhouse they fixed the prices that would be paid for the goods which were already being unloaded in the harbor and which were piling up at the mule-train terminal. Then followed two months of wholesale trading, in which gold, silver, pearls, cotton, cacao, vicuña wool, bezoar, quina bark, dyes, wax, leather, and other raw materials were exchanged for the manufactured products of the industry of old Spain, and for shiploads of Negroes from Guinea. Even the hides from the Pampas reached the bootmakers of Córdova by the circuitous route of Porto Bello; the months of winding through the Andes by llamaback to Lima, the ocean voyage to Panama, and the costly land transport from there to the fair made them cost five times what they had first sold for. The trade goods exchanged for them were worth ten times their normal price by the time they reached Buenos Aires.

Around the plaza nearest the wharves, opposite the custom house, the seamen built booths of jungle logs and made tents of sailcloth to hold the vast stacks of merchandise. The silver bars from Potosí were piled in the plaza like firewood; only gold and gems were dignified by storage under lock. A special guard of five thousand soldiers patrolled the city and its approaches.

Thousands of merchants from all the cities of new and old Spain rented the rickety trading booths at a hundred pesos a day, and paid as much for each night's verminous lodging. The land-office activity continued through the night, when the soldiers set out lanterns and torches in such numbers that it was possible to write contracts and receipts anywhere in the trading district.

The fevers of the isthmus took an appalling toll during the fairs. Soldiers and tradesmen who had never been exposed to tropical pestilences died by the hundred. Porto Bello had a hospital large enough to accommodate more than its entire permanent population, and it overflowed throughout the weeks of trading.

Jaguars, pumas, and ocelots from the surrounding jungle prowled by night through the great corrals where the two thousand mules of the transisthmian freight service were stabled, and despite the vigilance of the guards made occasional kills. The muleteers left the carcasses aboveground as long as any meat remained on the bones, in the hope that the big cats would not need to kill more mules. When the wind was from the east it brought this stench over the town, and when it reversed it wafted in the noxious odors of the Black Swamp. Also, along the shore at low tide was "a black, filthy Mud" which, wrote Wafer, "stinks very much."

Jefferys was appalled by the toad population. "The streets and squares in the morning are paved with these reptiles, so that you cannot step without treading on them." They were a giant species, averaging six inches in length, and he "could not imagine anything more dismal than their croakings."

Gage suggested that the place be called not Porto Bello, but Porto Malo. "What most I wondered at was to see the requas of mules which came thither from Panama, laden with wedges of silver; in one day I told two hundred mules laden with nothing else, which were unladed in the public market place so that there the heaps of silver wedges lay like heaps of stone in the street, without any fear or suspicion of being lost." He also marveled at "the multitude of people in those streets which the week before had been empty," and the merchants who "sold their commodities not by the ell or yard, but by piece and weight, not paying in coined pieces of money, but in wedges which were weighed and taken for commodities."

The spectacle of Porto Bello's dazzling wealth brought on many attacks by the English.

Governor Modyford of Jamaica in 1669 commissioned

Henry Morgan to raid the port with the great pirate fleet he had inherited from Mansveldt, and assigned to him for a guide an English tar who had just escaped from prison at Porto Bello. The seaman had worked under Spanish whips on maintenance of the Gold Road and the fortifications, and he knew the surrounding trails.

Morgan sailed his fleet into a concealed bay several leagues to the east, and as night came on a string of thirty pinnaces stretched out westward along the coast line, feeling for the mouth of the Chagres.

The first hazard of the expedition was the passing of the fortress of San Lorenzo, which overlooked the river's mouth. It was occupied in strength only at the height of the rainy season, when the land routes from Cruces were impassable. At other times the Spanish kept there only a maintenance crew of soldiers and slaves. There were no lookouts at night, since there was nothing to guard.

Morgan felt no concern at the strength of the garrison; one of his pinnaces could have paused and taken the fortress, probably without losing a man. But this might result in a warning to Porto Bello by runner. So he gave an order: no talking above a whisper, and no splashing of the oars. Silently the line of small boats glided into the mouth of the Chagres and filed past the sleeping castle in bright moonlight. San Lorenzo slept on.

About six miles up the river they unloaded, and Morgan ordered the boats to return to their ships in the same manner. Then, with the sailor leading the way, the force marched northeast on a little-used jungle trail.

Shortly after daybreak they came upon the Gold Road. Cautiously the party moved over the cobblestones, and by midafternoon the tips of the lantern-shaped sentinel towers of San Felipe were in sight. Now they took to the tall grass and marched blindly forward in single file, as the sailor led them to a place on the edge of the cleared strip from which they could study the lie of the fortifications.

Then the weary men slept until dark, while Morgan planned the attack.

At dusk he saw the sentinel outside the gate of the southernmost fortress relieved by a fresh man, who immediately began patrolling a beat some three hundred yards out from the walls and back. As the soldier faced about in his third round, three pirates rose silently from the ground behind him, dropped a cloak over his head, and forced a gag into his mouth. They carried him writhing and kicking back to Morgan.

Morgan drew his dagger and laid the blade against the soldier's throat, then nodded for the gag to be removed; the prisoner made no outcry, and told freely the details of the defenses. While a small group of Englishmen stole across the strip to the gates of the fort and flattened themselves against the wall on each side, the kidnapers escorted the soldier back to the place where they had seized him.

"Sarjento de la guardia!" the soldier shouted obediently. "Help! I have been hurt."

In a moment the massive gate swung out and the pirates just outside poured through, cutting the sergeant down as he appeared in the opening. The first two men fell upon the soldier at the windlass that operated the gate, and the third thrust the staff of his halberd through the links of the pulley chain and bent it double, which ensured that the gate could not be closed for a while.

After them came the rest of the party, shooting and yelling. They made short work of the garrison as the men piled out of their barracks. Then Morgan climbed upon a parapet and called out to the sentinel of the next fortress in the chain that it must surrender immediately or he would destroy every man inside its walls.

For answer a musket ball whizzed past his head, so Morgan turned his pack loose. Some ran along the connecting wall and dropped inside the enclosure; others seized ladders from a tool shed and placed them against the walls so that the moat was spanned, and swarmed up. Many of them fell dead or wounded from the ladders into the moat, but others got over. While the defenders fought stubbornly, the tide of attackers rose again and again, until only a handful of soldiers was left. Seeing no need for them all to be slaughtered, the officer in command surrendered.

But Morgan had stated his terms, and they had been rejected. He herded the survivors with their wounded into the powder magazine, and exploded it.

By now the city was in panic. The townspeople ran screaming through the streets, throwing their valuables into wells, crowding into the church in the hope of sanctuary, making for the jungle. Through the mad throng moved the governor, calling on the citizens to keep their heads and assemble in the key fortress. Few complied.

The pirates descended on the town, slashing and shooting until the streets were littered with dead and dying. But the governor had gathered his remaining forces in the main fort, and there they prepared for an indefinite siege.

Morgan assembled his men and tried an assault, but the pirates were thrown back with heavy losses. From every firing bay bristled a cannon or a musket. Over the parapets came sizzling bombs, with fuses cut so that they exploded as they struck the ground. Caldrons of blazing pitch tipped and spilled on the pirates whenever they approached the walls.

Morgan called off the assault, and the pirates picketed the fortress at a respectful distance while he led a group back into the town and down to the monastery. The monks and nuns they dragged from behind the altars where they were crouching in terror, and marched them to the scene of battle. Morgan called out to the governor that these innocent people would be forced to lead the next assault if he did not surrender immediately.

"Surrender?" shouted the gray-bearded Don. "Not while I am alive."

As the sun appeared on the horizon, the governor watched helpless from the parapet while Morgan divided the clerics into groups and assigned them to the ladders, with orders to place them against the wall and climb up. At first they refused, but he flogged them until they agreed. When the front rank of nuns neared the walls with the ladders, followed by pirates using them as shields, the governor gave the order to fire. Many went down. The others cried out piteously, begging him to yield, but he "consulted only his official duty."

Not all the soldiers, however, could bring themselves to fire accurately at such targets, and soon a few of the pirates gained the top, where they occupied the defenders while their fellows poured over in greater numbers. Once inside, they began such a merciless slaughter that some of the soldiers dropped their arms and escaped down the attackers' ladders. But most of them fought desperately on. As the Spaniards lost their weapons or suffered disabling wounds, they fell on their knees and begged for quarter. The pirates laughingly kicked off their helmets and split their heads.

Soon only the governor remained, his back to the wall, bleeding from several wounds, but still blazing defiance. Morgan called off his men and offered him quarter.

"I'd rather die like a soldier than be hanged like a coward," hissed the fiery Don, and he waved the pirates to come on.

To give him a sporting chance Morgan sent his men in one at a time. But the governor, who was famed as the best swordsman in all New Granada, was too much for them. Soon he had a pile of dead before him, and Morgan had to try other tactics. He had a group of men rush the stubborn Spaniard and try to seize him, but as they closed in the governor laid about him and drove them back. So Morgan shrugged, drew his pistol, and shot him.

Immediately he sent a lieutenant in a Spanish pinnace to notify the ships. At noon his fleet sailed triumphantly into the harbor, under the now harmless guns of the "impregnable" fortress.

There ensued two weeks of the wildest debauchery.

The pirates herded the surviving old men and boys into cells and locked them up. The higher-class women Morgan set aside and held for ransom, and the rest he distributed among his men for their entertainment. The wine cellars of the Dons were well stocked; soon every man, except Morgan himself and a handful of his lieutenants, was beastly drunk.

Men and women were tortured pitilessly to make them disclose where their valuables were hidden. Those who could not or would not produce treasure were broken on the wheel, torn on the rack, drawn and quartered, hacked to pieces, boiled in pitch, flayed alive, roasted on spits.

Then the maddened pirates fell to fighting among themselves, over the choicer women, the choicer wine, or unimportant things. While they killed each other, women killed themselves rather than submit further to their unending violations. Every day dozens of corpses, Spanish and English, were flung from the sea wall of San Felipe. Wrote Exquemelin, an eyewitness: "If there had been found fifty courageous men they might easily have taken the city and killed all the Pyrates."

Morgan had no objection; Porto Bello had been taken, and the fewer men there remained to claim the spoils the larger would be each one's share. When news of this voyage had spread over the Caribbean, he would have more volunteers than he would need to replace the losses.

Then an Indian brought him word that a force was on its way from Panama to rescue the city. Morgan sent his lieutenants scurrying about the disheveled town to muster the besotted mob. The men responded to discipline, and fell to work putting the city's defenses in order, while a lieutenant led a detachment of the soberer ones southward on the Gold Road. At the foothills of the Cerrania the party laid an ambush along the trail, the musketeers climbing trees and the pistoleers lying in the tall grass.

The rescuers walked squarely into the trap, and the pirate marksmen mowed them down. Then they pursued the survivors, yelling and shooting until the soldiers took to headlong flight.

Their commander hurried back to the governor of Panama, telling a story of strange new weapons, with greater range and accuracy than any firearms before known to him. Promptly the governor sent back a messenger under a white flag, begging that Morgan send him "some small token of the arms wherewith you have taken with such violence so great a city."

Morgan gave the courier an ordinary pistol and a handful of bullets, with a note reading:

"I desire the viceroy to accept this slender pattern of the arms wherewith I have taken Porto Bello, and beg that he keep them for a twelvemonth. After that time I promise to come to Panama and fetch them away."

Hastily the governor sent Morgan's pistol and bullets back to him, together with a gift of a handsome emerald ring and a note advising that he not trouble himself to travel so far on so trivial an errand, for he "would not speed so well at Panama as at Porto Bello."

Now with the wine exhausted, the vaults of the king's treasury scraped clean, and the people squeezed of as much ransom as he figured could be extracted, Morgan gave the order to prepare to withdraw. But first he demanded a hundred thousand pieces of eight as the ransom of the city itself. The people demurred, so he made ready to set fire to their houses. At this they scraped up the last of their hidden money and paid.

Morgan and some two hundred survivors sailed away to Jamaica with a quarter of a million of gold and silver, and a like amount in precious stones and Oriental finery.

Within a matter of weeks the goods had been converted to cash, and the cash had been converted to wine and finery for the harlots of Jamaica and Tortuga, and the Brethren, as lean and impecunious as ever, were chafing for more.

XVII: THE RAPE OF PANAMA

BACK to Tortuga sailed Morgan's fleet, and his fame spread to every pirate lair in the Caribbean. From all directions they came to join him, while the sands ran out the twelvemonth of grace that the Welshman had promised to the governor of Panama. That city was by far the greatest in America; there lived ten thousand Spaniards and thrice as many slaves, in a splendor patterned after the Oriental capitals whose goods funneled through it toward old Spain.

In due time Morgan circulated a letter, addressed "To All the Ancient and Expert Pyrates inhabiting Tortuga," summoning them to a voyage for "Gold and Gems beyond your wildest Dreams." It gave no hint of the objective, but his reputation was guarantee enough. Dozens of independent rovers sailed into the harbor to enlist, ship and crew. Respectable English and French merchants, unabashed by the technicality that the war had ended, came from Jamaica and Haiti to offer capital for the venture.

At the organization meeting, 24 October 1670, Morgan found himself at the head of thirty-seven ships, the largest mounting twenty-eight guns and the smallest four, and some two thousand fighting men in addition to the crews. A conference of captains drew up detailed articles of agreement.

Bonuses would be paid as follows: loss of both eyes or both hands, 1,800 pieces of eight; both legs, 1,500; right hand, 600; left hand or either leg, 500; thumb, forefinger, or either eye, 100; special acts of bravery, 50 to 100.

Slaves, regardless of age, sex, or color, would be valued at 100 pieces of eight (somewhat below the average market price, to allow for the trouble and expense of selling). They could be taken in lieu of an equal amount of cash.

The captain general would receive a hundredth part of the loot, and other commanders smaller proportions based on the value of the vessels they were risking. Remaining loot would be divided equally among the rank and file. The contract ended with the standard clause: "No prey, no pay."

"Fair enough!" shouted the Englishmen; "Eh bien!" cried the Frenchmen.

Then they repeated in unison the oath of the Brotherhood, to obey their leaders, to turn in all loot to the "common stock" and conceal nothing for themselves, not to desert or show any cowardice.

Next morning the greatest pirate fleet that ever sailed the Spanish Main weighed anchors and stood out to sea, on a southerly course.

Santa Catalina had been retaken by the Spanish, and made into a penal colony; the fleet sailed openly into the harbor, expecting the island to submit listlessly to another routine pillaging. But lo! a shore battery opened up and sent a cannon ball ripping through the sails of Morgan's fine flagship. Hastily he broke out a flag of truce and went ashore.

The governor had been inspired by reports of the bravery of his colleague at Porto Bello, and was ready to fight to the last of his men. Morgan described for him the latest refinements in torture which his hearties had developed. Anyway, he pointed out, the war had ended.

The governor thought it over.

"Well," asked Morgan finally, "is it peace or war?"

The governor licked his lips. "It's peace," he answered.

"Peace it is, then," said Morgan. "You have the satisfaction that I am taking only loot, not booty."

But the governor could not let the pirates come ashore without a show of resistance; his Most Catholic Majesty might hang him. So they agreed to save the governor fore and aft by staging a mock assault. For three hours fortress and fleet fired cannon without ball; then the governor surrendered.

While Morgan made himself at home in the governor's palace, his men stripped the island. Stores of beef, pork, and flour shuttled out to the ships, while the surrendered garrison and the townspeople looked on. All weapons they appropriated; guns too large to mount on their ships they spiked. Fifteen tons of gunpowder went aboard. In the dungeons Morgan found three Spanish felons from Panama, who agreed to join the party as guides for the crossing of the isthmus.

Then Morgan assembled his captains to plan the next phase.

It was the dry season, so the way to Panama overland from Porto Bello was at its best, and the way by the Chagres River was at its worst. Thus truthfully did the Spanish outlaws advise Morgan. But he suspected treachery, and chose to go by the river and the Cruces trail. This meant that the fortress of San Lorenzo had to be reduced;

and to take the entire fleet over for this purpose would expose their intentions too soon. So he assigned Captain Joseph Brodely, of Tortuga and Bristol, to the mission of conquering San Lorenzo with four ships and four hundred fighting men.

While Morgan and his other lieutenants enjoyed choice wines from the governor's cellar, Brodely set sail with his little fleet.

They landed several miles west of the castle on the Chagres and worked their way back along the coast on foot, to find the fortress circled by two newly built log palisades, filled between with earth. Every foot of the ring was exposed to fire from the parapets. No bally chance of snaring a sentry here, so Brodely decided to wait for dark and fire the palisades.

But it is hard to start a blaze unobserved even at night; the alarum sounded, and the defenders began to pour a hail of lead through the darkness. Despite this annoyance several fires were set, and presently the earth ring lost its supports and crumbled into a sloping breastwork which the pirates later used to advantage.

For the rest of the night they rushed the walls of the fort, placing ladders and swarming up through a rain of blazing pitch, only to have their ladders pushed away just as they reached the top. They left dead and wounded lying in the moat after each assault.

At daybreak Brodely ordered his musketeers to crawl up to the ruptured earthwork, burrow foxholes in the soft spoil, and open a duel with the gunners and archers on the parapets. With volleys of fire they forced the soldiers to keep their heads down whenever the assaulting force started for the wall with ladders. This should have served to get a few of the pirates over. But the defenders, many of whom were veterans of the sack of Porto Bello, knew what it meant to fall into the hands of the rovers. They shoved the ladders away with the strength of desperation while the pirate marksmen sniped at them. Thus the stubborn battle continued until midafternoon.

"Come on, English dogs!" shouted the defenders. "You will not go to Panama this bout."

Then luck turned the tide for the attackers: one of the pirate musketeers got an arrow through his shoulder; he pulled it out and ripped up his shirt to bandage the wound; then, on impulse, he wrapped the remaining strips of cloth around the arrow, rammed it into his musket, and fired it back at the parapet. The exploding powder ignited the cloth, and the flaming missile sailed over the wall and struck the thatched roof of a magazine inside the compound, unnoticed. The magazine blew up, killing scores, breaching the wall, and jarring several cannon from their mountings. The men on the parapets turned to see what was up in their rear, just as a wave of ladders started for the walls.

This time the pirates got over. Soon the whole force was inside; with expert infighting they drove the survivors into a corner of the enclosure. When the comandante got a pistol ball in the head, the rest surrendered.

Brodely learned from them that the garrison at the start had numbered 320; now he counted thirty left, most of whom were gravely wounded; not an officer was alive. Of his own force more than a hundred had been killed, and about as many wounded. He also learned that a warning was on the way to Panama; runners had slipped through the pirates' cordon the night before.

While one of the ships sailed back to base with word of victory, Brodely set his men to work repairing the defenses and tossing the dead from the north parapet into the sea.

Morgan decided to make a clean sweep of Catalina. With the island picked bare, he herded its people into the holds of his ships, fired the town, and blew up the fortress as he set sail for the Chagres coast. A storm came on as the fleet entered the mouth of the river, and four of the largest vessels, including the flagship, broke on Sentinel Rock. While the water gushed through the breached hulls, the pirates labored to save the loot of Catalina from the holds. For the prisoners there was no time; they were chained to the beams, and the keys were not at hand. But the cargo was for the most part salvaged, and not a pirate life was lost.

Morgan ran up the English color over San Lorenzo —illegally, for his commission as a privateer had expired with the signing of the peace. The prisoners from the holds of his remaining ships he chained in gangs and set to work rebuilding the palisades and remounting the cannon; he had no wish for a fleet of Spanish men-o'-war to happen along and bottle him up in the Chagres.

As soon as he was satisfied with the state of the fortifications, Morgan set out upriver with about twelve hundred men in five large boats and a string of canoes. Brodely's force had seen its share of action; it stayed behind to garrison the fortress and guard the fleet as it lay in the river. Some two hundred more, who were weak with dysentery or fever, stayed behind with them.

Morgan knew that the governor of Panama had had three weeks of warning, so he ordered lookouts for signs of an ambuscade. At each village he sent scouts ashore, and his fears increased as they found no sign of life. On the second day he realized that the governor's strategy was deadlier than ambush: grainfields were charred and smoking, orchards were picked clean of fruit. Foraging parties returned empty-handed.

Expecting to live off the country, the men had packed no rations. Food was an impractical item anyway, for each man was already laden with necessaries: armor, musket, pistols, cutlass, daggers, knives, crossbow and arrows, powder, lead, and wadding, and his share of the organization's special items, such as cannon, bombs, trumpets, and drums.

At the village of Cruz de Juan Gallego, where they arrived late on the second day, they had to abandon the pinnaces because the river had become too shallow. This forced almost a thousand men to take the trail, their bellies empty and their backs straining under grievous loads. The field pieces they transferred to the canoes, which could still follow along.

On the third day, which was the second without any food, the column moved along arduously, to break into a stampede whenever the men spied a village ahead. Every hut they tore apart, hoping to find a forgotten morsel. Curses filled the air at each new disappointment, and the men discussed how they would barbecue any Indian or Spaniard who fell into their hands.

On the fourth day they ate their leather pouches. Says Exquemelin: "Some persons who were never out of their mothers' Kitchens may ask how these Pyrates could eat, swallow, and digest these pieces of Leather so hard and dry. To whom I only answer: That could they once experiment with Hunger, or rather Famine, is that they would certainly find the manner, by their own necessity as the Pyrates did. For these first took the Leather and sliced it in pieces. Then they did beat it between two Stones and rub it, often dipping it in the water of the River to render it by these means supple and tender. Lastly they scraped off the Hair and roasted or broiled it upon the Fire. And being thus cooked they cut it into small morsels and et it, helping it down with frequent gulps of Water, which by good Fortune they had near at hand."

On the fifth day, as the men straggled through a narrow defile, a broadside of boulders lumbered down from the ridge, crushing several men and breaking the legs of others. Then came a shower of arrows. No one was strong enough to scramble up the bank to investigate. Being well covered with armor, the men received only a few insignificant scratches, but several of the slightly wounded sickened and died in agony. Morgan assumed that the attackers were Indians in the pay of the governor, using poisoned arrows: an inland tribe, he figured, which was unfamiliar with the universal comradeship between pirates and natives. The injured and ailing they piled into the canoes and labored on.

On the sixth day they found, in a cave beside the trail, two jars of wine, several baskets of plantains, and two sacks of meal. Morgan examined the food carefully, suspecting poison, but saw nothing amiss, so he allowed some of the sick to try samples. Nothing happened, so he distributed the supplies to the canoes. Some of the marchers broke into frothy babblings at the sight of food, and had to be held back by their fellows. But Morgan, whose belly was as empty as any other, had taken nothing, so they accepted his decision.

Whenever a sick man died, they tossed his body into the river to make canoe room for another heat-stricken marcher. The men talked of eating their dead, but Morgan gave orders against it.

Next day they reached Las Cruces, and found a binful of maize and a cellar of wine which somehow had escaped the governor's scorching. Morgan gave each sick man two ears and each marcher half an ear, and the wine he distributed in the same ratio. About the town were several old dogs and cats, which some of the men tore apart and ate raw; it made them violently ill.

Now the trail left the riverbank and turned toward the Cordillera, so the canoes had to be cached, along with the field pieces, which were too heavy for the famished men to carry. The men with broken legs Morgan allowed to take a canoe and try to drift back to San Lorenzo.

The marchers struggled up and over the divide, and then came upon a rancho where a herd of cattle was grazing. Cheering and cursing, their wizened mouths adrool, they fell upon the animals and hacked them to pieces. Says Exquemelin: "They more resembled Cannibals than Europeans at this Banquet, the Blood running down many times from their Beards to the middle of their Bodies."

Then they built fires and roasted the meat for their second course, and soon the entire party was sprawled about the field, recuperating from the shock. Hours later, as they prepared to move on, each man stuffed great hunks of raw meat inside his armor and other equipment; it was a bloody band that pitched camp that night in sight of the Cathedral of San Anastasio.

Morgan called in his lieutenants to plan an attack at dawn. While they talked a troop of cavalry trotted across the plain with sabers clanking, plumes flowing, armor and gay trappings agleam in the moonlight. Morgan interrupted the council long enough to survey the size of the force, instructed his sentries to fire on them if they came within range, and returned to the conference.

The horsemen skirted the camp and paused just beyond musket range to taunt the "hijos de perras." Finally tiring of this, they posted scouts to watch the camp and withdrew. In a little while the heavy artillery in the city opened up, sending several broadsides harmlessly over the camp. Then it grew quiet.

Daylight found the pirate camp astir. After a breakfast of buccanned meat, the men formed three battalions of three companies each. With trumpets and drums sounding, they marched toward the city on a wooded trail which the guides had assured Morgan was proof against cavalry ambush.

When the woods were past and they gazed down from their eminence on the plain before Panama, they saw the Spanish host, formed in battle array with pennons flying: two squadrons of cavalry, four regiments of infantry, a battalion of Negroes and Indians. Behind them in a great corral milled a herd of two thousand wild bulls —a year's quota for the municipal torearía; they had been bred in old Spain for the arena, and were particularly big and vicious. The governor planned to turn them loose if the pirates broke through his forces on the field.

The pirates were outnumbered four to one, not counting the bulls. They had only a few small cannon, while the Spaniards had cavalry and heavy artillery. The invaders, in their rusty, blood-caked armor, had been wearied by eleven days of hard marching, eight of them without food. (Exquemelin: "Yea few or none there were but wished themselves at Home, or at least free from the obligation of that Engagement, wherein they perceived their Lives must be narrowly concerned.")

But Morgan harangued them: "You are Englishmen!" to the English companies; "You are Frenchmen!" to the French. "They are only Spaniards; it would not differ if they had twice their numbers!"

The pirates cheered, trumpets blared, drums rolled, and they swung out to attack. At their forefront was a solid line of musketeers; they marched forward with muskets at the ready, well into range but holding their fire, as Morgan had ordered, until they heard the Spanish officers shout "¡Apuntán!" Closer they came; the governor saw that he must fire a volley soon or they would be upon his men, and the Spaniards had little taste for the infighting with cutlass and dagger which the pirates loved. He gave the command, and instantly the pirate musketeers fired, killing scores. The return volley was scattered and ineffective.

The pirate vanguard would have closed with them, but the cavalry, which had been waiting for the full flank of the advancing column to expose itself across the field, charged from the left. The ground to that side was soft and boggy; the cavalry mired up, and the pirates saw their chance. They turned and charged into the lances to fall upon the horsemen and drag them to the ground. Soon hardly a mounted man was left, and the Spanish musketeers stood helpless, holding their fire because their own men were as thick before them as the enemy.

The pirates soon disposed of the caballeros with their knives, and this taste of blood turned them into the howling monsters that every Spaniard had learned on his mother's knee to fear. Forgetting tactics and all else, the pirates turned and stalked toward the Spanish infantry, brandishing their bloody weapons. The ranks of smart armor broke. The pirates were too worn to give chase, but their musketeers sent volleys after the fleeing Spaniards while the others followed them across the field, finishing off the wounded.

It was time, the governor decided, to release the bulls. By now, roused by the shooting and the smell of blood, they were surging dangerously about their enclosure. The vaqueros kicked down the bars and fled; the bulls poured through the gates and charged across the field toward the pirates. The sea rovers had never encountered a foe quite like this, and not knowing what else to do they turned and ran. Close behind the front line was Morgan; quickly he told his trumpeters to turn their horns toward the bulls and blare the loudest and highest notes that they knew.

The trumpets shrilled a piercing blast, and the perplexed bulls wheeled and stampeded toward the fleeing Spaniards. They gored a few, trampled some of the wounded, and then dispersed into the jungle, leaving the pirates in undisputed possession of the field.

Morgan ordered that the murder of the wounded be restricted to those who could in no wise walk; the ambulants he assembled at the edge of the field. Among them was a captain with a knife wound in his shoulder. By gouging into the gash with the muzzle of his pistol, Morgan persuaded him to discuss the defense plan of the city. Meanwhile the surviving defenders were assembling behind the arched stone bridge at the main entrance to the city. Old Panama had no walls, for the Pacific had no rovers, and what army could conquer one of the Caribbean fortresses and then cross the isthmus?

Over the bridge came a group of priests, who walked onto the field and began to administer last rites to the dying.

"Bring 'em in," Morgan ordered; soon the priests were standing before him, crossing themselves and mumbling prayers. Being a devout Protestant, Morgan shot them, one by one.

As soon as his men had collected their wounded and rifled the bodies on the field, Morgan announced that they would go into the city over the arched bridge. He distributed the prisoners for use as shields in the approach.

The pirates moved across the plain, each with a captive walking before him, through a whirlwind of arrows, musket and cannon balls, grapeshot, and scrap iron from howitzers. Most of the prisoners were dead by the time the bridge was reached. For a while not many pirates got over; then, as the few who did laid about them with cutlass and pistol, the bridgehead widened. For hours the attack was contained just inside the city by a solid mass of defenders.

Finally the wall of Spaniards crumbled, and the pirates spread over the city. Crazed by blood and enraged at their heavy losses, they shot and stabbed and slashed until hardly a soldier was left on his feet.

Morgan knew that he must restore discipline before they found the wine cellars; he had to shoot several of his men to make the mob listen to him.

Only a third of the pirate force that had attacked that morning was still alive, he told them. Each late-lamented brother had "taken five or six Spaniards with him to Hell," but the situation was still precarious. Reinforcements from Porto Bello might at any moment march into the town. Therefore, no man must touch liquor until he gave the word. He had learned, he lied to strengthen his point, that poisoned wine had been planted all around the town.

Then he turned them loose to gather in the sheaves.

But now, mysteriously, fire broke out at several points over the city, and for a week pirates and Spaniards together fought the common enemy. When it was over, little was left of Panama la Vieja except the walls of its central buildings of stone and its more elaborate suburban homes of tile.

The pirates broke into the nunneries and dragged the richly gowned ladies before Morgan, but hardly one was wearing any jewelry of value. They surged into the churches, but the golden altars, the jeweled chandeliers, the silver candelabra were gone. They blasted into the king's treasury, but it was empty.

The governor, after hanging by his thumbs for a while, remembered that all the treasure of the city had been sent to sea. There were several ships in the harbor, so Morgan sent Captain Daniel Searles in a frigate to probe the inlets of the coast.

Searching parties beat the jungle, dragging in fugitives to be tortured until they died or told where some treasure could be found. One oaf of a servant, wearing taffeta breeches that obviously belonged to his master, denied that he knew the use of a small silver key which hung from them. Morgan racked him until he was disjointed, cut off his nose and then his ears, twisted a cord about his head until his eyes popped out, and held a flame to his face until it rose in a solid blister before he decided that the man was speaking truth. Then he had him run through with a lance.

"No use letting him suffer," he remarked.

Women and children of the aristocracy were herded

into a wing of the governor's palace and guarded from the lustful mob, pending ransom. Among them was the beautiful wife of an Andalusian merchant; Señora María Eleanora López y Ganero caught Morgan's eye. She had led the sheltered life of the women of her caste, and was amazed to find that the "heretics" had ordinary human form.

"Jesú, bless me!" she exclaimed. "They are like unto us Spaniards!"

Morgan was charmed. He kept her by him in his headquarters while he transacted ransom collections, and at odd moments he wooed her. In time she came to think better of him, for while she had been taught that his ilk "did neither invoke the Blessed Trinity nor believe in Jesus Christ," she had herself heard him "frequently swear by the Sacred Names." But his pleadings got him nowhere. Finally in a rage of frustration he had her cast naked into a mud-floored, pitch-dark dungeon which was infested with bats, mice, and fleas.

Her husband's frantic offers of all the ransom money that he could muster Morgan refused, but he did accommodate Señor López by taking the money "as a loan."

This was to evade the pirate law that money so tendered be accepted only if the hostage be released. It so infuriated his men that Morgan restored her to comfortable internment. When this did not satisfy them, he quibbled that the payment was not enough; for another hundred pieces of eight he would free her. López could not scrape up any more, but María had some money of her own hidden away. Not wishing to have her husband know of it, she told a priest. He got the money, but used it to ransom another priest. After several days of waiting, she told Morgan about it, so he sent for the priests. She confronted them, and they confessed. With typical caprice, Morgan returned to her the entire ransom, had the priests hanged before her eyes, gave her an escort home, and swept the ground with his plumed hat as she stumbled dazedly away.

Searles returned from his search at sea with a scheme. He had seen nothing of the missing gold, but he had taken with ease a galleon carrying a cargo of Oriental silks worth easily fifty thousand pounds. Ships in those waters, he reported enthusiastically, carried no armament; it was simply extending the open palm. If Morgan would release him and his men, they would forgo their share in the sack of Panama and give up their former ship to the common stock; they could get home by way of India, or find themselves a South Sea isle. . . .

"No," Morgan interrupted him. He needed them. For what, he did not say; he was simply in a contrary mood. He ordered the crew ashore, and burned all the shipping in the harbor to preclude any attempts at desertion.

After four weeks on the town Morgan decided that it had been bled white, so on 24 February a train of 175 mules and some six hundred prisoners filed out of the murdered city and wound across the plain into the jungle.

Castilian ladies, half naked, their shredded gowns splashed with mud, had to maintain the pirates' rolling gait despite their high heels. When they stumbled, they were jerked up by the hair; when they lagged, they were whipped. At the nightly halts, there were more than enough women to go around. The pirates, their unwashed bodies reeking with the blood and sweat of the month past, guffawed as women fell on their knees before Morgan, begging him to kill them. Some broke from the column and plunged into the Chagres to drown. Others fell in the line of march and let the mules trample them to death. For all their piteous wails Morgan had a standing reply:

"I came not hither to hear lamentations and cries, but rather to seek money."

At Gatún, the last bivouac before San Lorenzo, Morgan assembled his men and announced that each one would be searched for concealed loot, beginning with himself. The order was intended to confirm their confidence in him, for an idea was brewing in his brain; but it had the opposite effect. In all the history of the Brotherhood, no leader had ever subjected his men to this insinuating indignity, and a pirate's honor, queer as it was, shone bright.

The Englishmen were scandalized, but when the Frenchmen talked of mutiny it roused their suspicions. This forced everyone to insist on the search, which yielded nothing, but left resentment simmering in the hearts of the gentlemen rovers.

They found things in good order at San Lorenzo. The garrison had even picked up a nice cargo from a Spanish merchantman which unwittingly had run under their guns while fleeing from another pirate ship off Porto Bello.

"Every little bit helps," grunted Morgan.

After the garrison of the fortress had had its turn with the women, Morgan sent the prisoners in one of his ships to Porto Bello under a flag of truce, with a note to the governor demanding a club-rate ransom of 100,000 pieces of eight, and offering as a special inducement to allow this sum to cover also the ransom of the fortress of San Lorenzo. The governor of Porto Bello told his emissary to convey to the privateer admiral his compliments and tell him to go to hell; not a real would he pay, and Morgan could make of San Lorenzo what he pleased. As Morgan had instructed in case this should happen, the lieutenant gave the governor the prisoners ransom-free and sailed back.

The rebuff meant that San Lorenzo must be destroyed. Morgan put the Frenchmen to work mining the walls and setting charges; the English he assigned to loading the loot and provisions into the ships.

Somehow everything, including the cannon from the fortress, happened to be loaded into Morgan's own vessels; then he summoned the other English commanders "for a conference." A little later the men on shore noticed that the sails of Morgan's ships were being set. Probably moving the vessels up into fleet position, they figured. Into fleet position they moved, and, neglecting to wait for the rest of the fleet, sailed out of the Chagres onto the open sea, making straight for Jamaica.

Thus did Morgan add another unique ornament to pirate history: theft of the loot from followers who had toiled, starved, bled, and murdered for it, and maroonment of them in hostile territory without even their next meal. It was a delicate touch to leave their ships intact; they could not put to sea in pursuit without food, and the Spaniards were not likely to give them any.

At least the hapless ones were safe while they stayed within the walls of San Lorenzo, for the Spaniards did not know that they had no weapon heavier than a musket. They removed the demolition charges they had obediently placed (for who would blow up his only tenable abode?) and began to fish the Chagres and forage the countryside in their second siege of hunger; bats from the towers and rats from the dungeons of San Lorenzo became important items.

Morgan had sailed in chains from Jamaica for England (where he shared the wealth with Charles II and emerged from his arraignment with knighthood and the lieutenant-governorship of Jamaica) before another Spanish trader innocently sought shelter in the mouth of the Chagres. The Frenchmen seized the ship and sailed away, leaving its legitimate crew in their own former predicament.

Patiently the Spaniards set to work and built a new city, five miles west of the old site and only a stone's throw from the future Pacific entrance to the canal. Nearly all the stone of the old Panama went into the walls of the new, but the tower of the Cathedral of San Anastasio was left intact. Its remains stand today, a memorial tombstone for the greatest city of the old New World.

The fortifications of Panama la Nueva were the strongest in all America. The Council of the Indies, after auditing the construction account, inquired dryly whether the walls were of gold or silver. The king, standing at a western window of his palace in Granada, sighed and said:

"We are looking for the walls of Panama; they have cost so much that they should be visible from here."

The new city was never successfully assaulted.

XVIII: TIDE OF EMPIRE

But not all the alien ships that sailed the Gold Coast were men-o'-war. During the Porto Bello fairs, even in years when their countries were at war with Spain, English and French merchantmen anchored in the little coves between San Lorenzo and San Felipe and sent word to the buyers in the city that they would sell slaves and goods of excellent quality at reasonable prices—and without the bothersome taxes imposed by Seville.

Each year the Spanish officials categorically ordered the freetraders to leave, and just as categorically they received replies of "samples" of the strongest Negroes and the choicest merchandise in the foreigners' stocks, together with modest pouches of Spain's own golden coinage as tokens of esteem. Regularly each year after the fair the officials categorically assured the king that the reports of smugglers along the Gold Coast were mere rumors.

The illicit trade grew until it wagged the dog. In 1624 the king's treasury received revenues amounting to 1,446,346 pesos from the New World Fair. And, according to the estimate of Cristobal de Balba, special agent of the crown, the volume of smuggled goods handled in that year was five times that of the tax-paid commerce. Shortly before the opening of the next year's fair, by a funny coincidence, the Spanish Inquisition added smuggling and the accepting of smuggler's bribes to its list of mortal sins.

Thereafter for many years it chastened transgressors with its ingenious tortures.

But the sinning on the banks of the Chagres persisted, and finally provided a proximate cause of the War of the Spanish Succession. The Treaty of Utrecht, which terminated the war in 1713, awarded to England a monopoly on the slave trade to the Spanish colonies in America, and allowed the English to send each year one merchant ship of 500 tons burden to the Porto Bello fair.

English ingenuity made its Porto Bello trade ship a thing of wonder. The navio de permiso—"authorized ship"—approached the Gold Coast bulging with all the goods that she could safely carry on the high seas, followed by a string of tenders laden with more. Just outside the harbor the convoy hove to, and the trading ship divested herself of everything that could be removed in the way of equipment. All rigging except one tiny foresail (needed to pull the ship into the harbor), capstans, booms, bunks, provisions, even the navigation charts were transferred to the tenders, and the trade goods from the tenders were piled on the deck until she shipped water at the slightest roll. Then the anchor chain was cast off onto one of the tenders (for to weigh the anchor would have foundered the ship) and a skeleton crew sailed her into the harbor with the equivalent of five or six ordinary cargoes. Lacking an anchor, the crew made her fast to a pier with harbor chains. The Spaniards dropped their jaws at the skill of the English seamen.

When the fair was over she sailed out, this time carrying profits of millions in specie and a similar overload of Spanish raw materials. Outside the harbor she met her tenders, unloaded most of her burden on them, and took back her equipment and crew. It was all strictly according to treaty; only one English ship, of 500 registered tons, had visited the fair.

But appeasement never appeases. The lush slave-trade monopoly and the astronomical profits from the annual voyage of the navio de permiso only whetted England's appetite, and her encroachments in the Caribbean mounted. Openly in frequent wars and covertly in periods of armed truce she hammered at Spanish domination of the Chagres gateway to the Pacific. It came to a head in 1738 when a renegade shipmaster, who had lost an ear years earlier as a felon in the London pillory, appeared before Parliament and testified that his ear had been cut off by the Spanish port officials at Porto Bello.

A member rose and asked how he felt while the Spaniards were cutting off his ear?

"I recommended my soul to God, and my cause to my country," he replied. His words electrified England and set off the War of Jenkins's Ear.

At dawn 21 November 1739, a fleet of seven English men-o'-war appeared off Porto Bello. It had come to the isthmus after a tour of the English colonial ports of North America, where it had levied some two thousand men, mostly Virginians. In command was Admiral Edward Vernon, M.P. One of his aides was Lawrence Washington of Virginia, brother of the future first president of thirteen little United States.

Vernon had boasted in Parliament that he could take Porto Bello with six ships, so he entered the harbor with that number and sent the seventh out to sea. Throughout the day the fleet exchanged broadsides at point-blank range with the forts. While the turrets of San Felipe crumbled, scores of dead and wounded Virginia lads littered the decks of the ships; finally the Spanish comandante ran up a white flag.

The English admiral appropriated ten thousand ducats from the king's treasury and distributed the booty among his men; he loaded the best of Porto Bello's famed cannon on his ships, and spiked the rest; then he demolished the castles. "The Walls," he wrote, "were nine foot thick, and of a hard Stone, cemented with such fine Mortar that it was a long Work to make any impression in it to come to Mine at all, so that the blowing up took in all sixteen to eighteen Days."

For this exploit Vernon received wild acclaim in England and her American colonies. His next birthday was proclaimed a national holiday (with fireworks) by Parliament, and he was returned to that body *in absentia* by three different constituencies. The Washington family of Virginia christened its estate Mount Vernon, and the Hardy family, which had lost a son in the battle, named its plantation Porto Bello.

The fleet returned to Jamaica for repair and replacement, and the following March it sailed into the mouth of the Chagres. There for two days and nights the captured cannon of Porto Bello pounded the fortress of San Lorenzo, while the guns of San Lorenzo raked the decks of Vernon's ships with shrapnel. In this case the comandante refused to surrender, so when the English fleet finally sailed away with corpse-littered decks the fortress was a smoking heap of rubble.

Back again to Jamaica, where Vernon met Commodore George Anson with a fleet of six ships. Together they planned a co-ordinated campaign against the isthmus: Anson would sail around the Horn and attack Panama by sea, and Vernon would sweep across the Chagres valley and attack the city simultaneously by land.

While Anson sailed southward along the Atlantic coast of South America toward a hazard which had been surmounted only by Magellan and Drake before him, Vernon sent Lawrence Washington back to Virginia for more ships and men. In due course he sailed again into the harbor of Porto Bello (28 March 1742), this time with the greatest armament that the New World had ever seen: 120 ships and 25,000 men.

The city was still prostrate; since it could not resist, it sent out a delegation under a flag of truce. Vernon "sent their Deputies back," he chronicled, "and desired their Company on the next Morning to break Fast with me, where they came accordingly." He learned from his guests that Anson had lost five of his ships in the stormy Strait of Magellan, and had already plundered his way up the west coast in his remaining flagship *Centurion* without pausing at Panama. Obviously the commodore had felt that he had lost too much of his force to carry through the plan, and was making the most of his presence in the South Sea by taking some smaller prizes.

Vernon was for marching across the isthmus to attack Panama anyway, but his officers, Lawrence Washington included, counseled against it so vehemently that he abandoned the idea and yielded to their alternate plan for attacking Cartagena. The colonials could not have realized that they had forced a major turn in the history of the world, that they had struck a blow for their yet undreamed-of democracy, that they had saved the gateway between the oceans against a day when their own country, free at last from Old World domination, would take the Chagres valley in irrevocable trust toward the freedom of mankind. . . .

So the great fleet sailed to eastward and out of the Chagres Theater, and into disaster: the fevers and the defenders of Cartagena laid nine-tenths of its lads low before Vernon decided to call it off and carry the surviving English-Americans back to the colonies.

His popularity in the empire vanished as suddenly as it had soared, but his activities had one valuable and lasting result: the destruction of San Felipe broke the back of Spain's commercial isolationism. The Porto Bello fair was discontinued, and thereafter the merchant mariners of England were allowed perforce to trade in the ports of Spanish America upon the payment of reasonable license fees.

San Lorenzo was rebuilt, stronger than ever, to become the new clearing point for interocean traffic. Treasure and trade goods which had been lightered down the Chagres and along the Gold Coast to Porto Bello now went into the holds of the galleons from Seville as they stood in the river's mouth, under the guns of yet another bastion of Spanish might.

England continued to eye with envy the Chagres route between the world's seas.

The treasure of Peru had long since been drained off to Madrid when the Gold Coast returned to the limelight in April, 1819. Then one Gregor MacGregor, a British filibuster backed by private London capital, captured Porto Bello with a force of five hundred mercenaries. His plan was to march across the Chagres valley, take Panama, and then sell his conquest of the interocean link to the British government. It would mean profits for his backers, a fortune and probable knighthood for himself, bonuses and señoritas for his limeys, and an invaluable service to the empire.

But fever swept his tenderfoot army and delayed the departure of his transisthmian expedition. While most of his men were still flat on their backs in the famed Porto Bello hospital a rescuing force arrived from Panama and recaptured the city. "MacGregor's Raid" came a cropper as its leader fled ignominiously to the beach and escaped by swimming out to his ship.

England disclaimed responsibility for the attempt, but only because it had failed. Four years later, following this and other imperialistic efforts in New World territory, the fifth president of the United States proclaimed his Monroe Doctrine. It became a policy of the new republic, and gave to Simón Bolívar the moral support that he needed to break Spain's hold on the continent of America. Then it continued to preserve from European dominion the Chagres gateway to the Pacific.

Modern Porto Bello is as hard to reach as an island. The Chagres jungle has reclaimed the Gold Road except for a few isolated stretches, and the only land communication with the outside world is by unimproved trail. The once-imposing city had reverted to what it was when Columbus discovered it—a fishing village—when the Americans built a temporary town there during the construction of the canal. They quarried seven million cubic yards of Porto Bello's stone for the concrete mixers at Gatún, but left intact the ruins of the King's Customhouse and the remains of the massive fortress on the peninsula of San Jerónimo, which commands what was once the world's richest harbor.

Porto Bello has still another attraction which stems from its seventeenth century heyday. Boatloads of tourists and suppliants from every port of the Caribbean converge there each October to attend the weird Festival of the Black Christ.

According to legend, a Seville galleon which visited the fair in 1660 tried five times to leave the harbor, and each time was beaten back by a sudden storm. On board it had a life-sized statue of Christ carrying the cross, which had been carved of coco-bolo wood for shipment to Spain. The sailors blamed the statue for the queer weather; they threw it into the harbor, and on the next attempt the ship cleared without trouble.

The citizens of Porto Bello found the statue washed up on the shore—which was somewhat miraculous in itself, since coco-bolo does not float in water—and set it up in the Church of Jesus the Nazarene. It soon had a reputation as a healing shrine, which became world-wide in 1821 when a cholera epidemic swept the isthmus and left Porto Bello untouched.

For days preceding the climax of the festival on the 21st, thousands of visitors crowd the unpaved streets. Games of dice, cards, and roulette run continuously through the day and night. Down every alley is a crowd of shouting bettors around a cockfight. The cantinas sell more rum and beer now than throughout the rest of the year. It is a queer admixture of primitive gaiety and primitive faith.

In the church stands the Black Christ, so called not because the people of Porto Bello are almost entirely Negroes but because the statue's naturally dark wood has blackened with age. For the occasion it is clad in a robe of scarlet trimmed with gold, to which the suppliants pin sketches of their afflictions, pictures of wayward lovers, names of race horses running at Juan Franco, and tickets for the next drawing of the National Lottery.

At eight o'clock that night the ornate portals of the ancient church swing wide, and the statue moves out into the village, carried on a platform by scores of fanatics. Their bare feet sink deep in the mud as they stagger through the streets, which are lit only by thousands of votive candles in the hands of the pilgrims. The statue sways alarmingly overhead, and often seems about to topple over, but somehow they keep it erect.

It is the height of the rainy season, in one of the world's wettest spots; yet, it is claimed, the rain has always stopped during the procession. For four consecutive hours, during a time when an hour seldom passes without a shower, there is no rain. And the statue, say the people, refuses to return to the church until after midnight. Attempts have been made to carry it back earlier, but always an unseen force repels it from the threshold.

When it has been replaced, the revelry of the day is resumed, to continue through the night. By the following noon the excursion vessels have left, and Porto Bello settles back to fish and doze for another year.

Do you believe, old woman, that the Lord Jesus will cause you to win with that lottery ticket?

"Without doubt, señor. He has power over the Loteria Nacional as over everything else. We have an understanding, He and I. He lets me win much oftener than others do—almost every week, in fact, even if it is only a two-dollar proximation. And I give Him a third of my winnings."

The fortress of San Lorenzo still frowns down upon the native village of Chagres across the river's mouth. It was the last continental stronghold of Spain to be evacuated, two years after Bolívar's victory at Ayacucho in 1826.

No relic of America's era of the Dons is more perfectly preserved. One may see every line of the castle, which was built after its predecessor was destroyed by Vernon's colonials; it is probably the world's finest remaining specimen of military architecture from the period just preceding the introduction of rifled ordnance.

Inside a moss-covered outer ring of stone, which served as the first line of defense, rise the massive walls, their sheerness broken only by tiny air vents. They converge upon a tower whose drawbridge in other days clanged down to span a moat which now is filled with debris. The grooves and sockets worn into the stone by the bridge and its chains show clearly how the mechanism worked, although the iron parts have rusted entirely away.

In the courtyard is the rock-lined water reservoir, and above it in the wall is a deeply etched coat of arms. Around the patio are gaping cavities in the stone, once closed by solid hardwood doors studded with ironwork, in which tons of gunpowder were stored. Above them stretches an open gallery, covered by overhanging arches of stone, in which the garrison slept. From here terraces lead up into the cells where prisoners were held; still embedded in the masonry are the rusty manacles which held head, wrists, and ankles flat against the wall. ("About the only exercise one could take while in this position," commented Collins, "would be thinking.")

Below ground level are steep steps leading to the torture dungeons, in which are remains of various devices: a cage which holds its occupant on tiptoe by the chin, a wheel for breaking the bones of the arms and legs, a rack for pulling the limbs out of their sockets, an iron boot to be placed on the victim's foot and heated to redness. "A visit to San Lorenzo is strongly advised" by Collins, "because it will make one so much more contented with the time in which he lives."

There they stand, dotting the stage of the Chagres Theater: the King's Customhouse, the Cathedral of San Anastasio, the castle of San Lorenzo. They are pebbles which the ebbing tide of empire has left upon the beach of time.

BOOK THREE

CALIFORNIA OR BUST

By the River

XIX: THE FORTY-NINERS

THE TREASURE looted by the Conquistadors had made the Chagres far and away the dean of the world's gold rivers, but those sources had been depleted for a century. It was just a sleepy tropical river, carrying occasional boatloads of bananas downstream to be picked up by tramping fruiters, when a California pioneer named James Marshall discovered gold in Sutter's millrace 24 January 1848.

The burgeoning United States already had recognized the isthmus as the likeliest potential route to its newly acquired coast line on the Pacific, pending completion of a transcontinental railroad. Eleven months earlier Congress had offered ten-year subsidies which resulted in the organization, by New York capital, of:

(1) The United States Mail Steam Line. New York, Charleston, Savannah, Havana, New Orleans, Chagres, and return. Two sailings monthly.

(2) The Pacific Mail Steamship Company. Panama, San Francisco, Astoria, and return. One sailing monthly.

Contracts were let for the construction of steamships, but there was no great hurry; gold had not yet been discovered in the Golden West.

The shipyards failed to make timely delivery of the steamers which the U.S. Mail Steam Line had ordered, so the company chartered the small steamer *Falcon* in order to make the first New York-to-Chagres run within the time limit of its mail contract. The *Falcon* sailed from New York 1 December 1848 with 29 passengers, mostly federal employees and missionaries booked through to California.

The Pacific Mail's first steamer, the *California,* had left New York two months before to sail around the Horn to Panama. Most of her 250 passenger berths were empty; none of her handful of travelers was booked farther than Callao.

The *Falcon* was sailing down the Atlantic coast of North America and the *California* was sailing up the Pacific coast of South America, both bound for the isthmus, when the California gold fever broke over the world.

Covered wagons and stagecoaches went racing across the plains, the only means of overland conveyance, for completion of the Union Pacific Railroad was twenty years in the future. Many of them sank or floated downstream to destruction where rivers had to be forded, or racked apart on the rocks of the Bad Lands; wheels and axles gave way while crossing deserts, teams died or went lame on rugged mountain trails. Wild Indians massacred whole train-loads of travelers. The wagon route, while the most direct, offered the poorest odds for early arrival at the diggings.

Most of the Americans who could muster the extra money elected to try it by the isthmus, as did thousands more from Europe. Assorted vessels converged at Chagres from all ports on both sides of the Atlantic, dumped their frenzied passengers, and plowed back for more, while across the isthmus an equal variety of ships picked them up and shuttled them to the new Gold Coast. Despite delays and hardships, the chances of completing the journey by water within two months were fair. And the months thus saved over the best possible overland time might mean the difference between a rich claim and a fiasco.

Some of the passengers booked through to California. Others, hoping to gain a little time by shifting between packet and tramp, bought their tickets stage by stage. In either case, the traveler's crossing of the isthmus was his own problem. Construction of the Panama Railroad had begun, but its completion was to take six years. The only available means of transit were precisely those which had been open to the Conquistadors three centuries earlier.

When the *Falcon* docked at New Orleans, aboard her traipsed 178 southern backwoodsmen, carrying assorted pots, pans, axes, and picks. The *Falcon* had berths for only a hundred of them, but the rest refused to go ashore. As Captain Notestein talked of using force, the surplus candidates blandly twirled revolvers and spat tobacco juice on the deck. The captain compromised by rigging bunks in the dining saloon and the hold.

RESIGNEDLY THE

BUNGO BOYS CAST OFF

The *Falcon* sailed from New Orleans 19 December. Within a few days three New Orleans steamers, *Crescent City, Orus,* and *Isthmus,* and three Caribbean windjammers had been pressed into service, and were trailing her toward Chagres with overloads of passengers.

The *Falcon's* contingent descended upon the native village at the mouth of our river, where no one had even heard of a gold strike, and 212 rabid Americans tried to explain to the natives, who spoke only a mixture of low Spanish and African dialects, the pressing need for transportation across the isthmus.

"Panama!" they yelled. "Go Panama?"

"Sí," the natives nodded, with mouths agape.

"Which way? How? ¿Como?"

The natives pointed unhurriedly to their banana boats lying along the river playa. "Bungos."

Dubiously the Americans surveyed the rustic craft. They were made from single logs, usually guayacan, about 25 feet long and averaging 3 feet wide, hollowed out and covered with a canopy of thatched palm leaves to protect the banana cargoes from the sun.

"All right, let's go. Go Panama!"

"Sí," replied the natives. "Vamos."

"When? ¿Cuando?"

"Pronto."

"But how pronto?"

"Mañana."

"Manyanna hell. We vamoose right now."

The Americans dragged the natives toward their boats.

"We go Panama!" they shouted, shaking fists under Negroid noses. They piled in and found that the boats would accommodate four to six passengers in addition to the three or four boatmen. Resignedly the bungo boys cast off, in some cases with pistols against their heads.

There were not more than twenty bungo boats on the beach, which left half the Americans standing on the shore, gesticulating and shouting. But there were more boats up the river, the villagers assured them—twice as many. Some would surely arrive mañana.

A few of the lighter-burdened travelers, suspecting that mañana could mean the next morning or the next month, set out on the trail along the left bank of the river. The others accepted the hospitality of the huts to wait. Two days later the *Crescent City* arrived, followed at short intervals by the other ships. Soon about a thousand argonauts were chafing in the village.

Sleeping accommodations amounted to nothing more than straw-strewn lofts, dirt floors, and a few spare hammocks, all infested with lice. The twoscore huts of the village overflowed, and scores of travelers had to sleep outside. A few had pup tents; others unrolled their blankets under the tropic sky.

Upriver glided the jungle gondolas, making 10 to 12 miles per day against the strong current of the rainy season. They tied up at the villages along the bank while the locos Americanos went ashore for food and overnight rest, stimulating much curiosity and palavering among the natives.

Late on the third day the fastest of the bungos reached Cruces and unloaded their strange cargo. The boatmen stayed ashore long enough for a hasty meal, then they shoved off in their lightened boats for the restful downstream trip.

The bungos began to drift back singly, with the boatmen all smiles; they had received a dollar or more apiece from their passengers, and some of them had earned double fares for poling through the night in shifts. As each boat appeared at the river's mouth the waiting passengers argued, gambled, fought, and bid against each other for seats. By the time the last members of this first horde of gold seekers had scrambled into a boat, the fare had risen to $15. Then and there the banana-hauling business on the Chagres River quietly expired.

At Las Cruces inflation came as quickly. The first ones to arrive hired all available animals for the dawn-to-dark ride to Panama at a dollar each. The last ones paid a flat $10 for a riding animal and 10 cents per pound of baggage, take it or leave it.

The dozen hotels and pensiones in the capital overflowed. Many of the old aristocratic families, not above turning an honest dollar, let rooms. As the tide of argonauts continued to rise, sleeping space on the bare floors of the city's slums went at $2 a night. Scores of emigrants slept in the plazas.

Meantime the *California* had reached Callao, where the last of her handful of passengers had planned to disembark. But the fast-spreading gold fever had reached there. A hundred Peruvians piled aboard, and most of the the old passengers changed their minds and booked on to San Francisco.

When the *California* anchored at Panama 17 January 1849, all hell broke loose. She could take on 150 more passengers, at most; here were five or six times that many clamoring to get aboard. The Pacific Mail offices were a round-the-clock bedlam of shouting, fighting, outrageous bidding, attempts at bribery, and offers to do the clerks bodily harm.

Then somehow the Americans learned of the Peruvians on board the steamer.

"Throw 'em off!" they yelled, shaking revolvers in the face of Agent William Nelson, who refused to comply. The Peruvians holed up, leaving their cabins only for meals; not one set foot on shore during the two-week layover.

Nelson sent aboard the few men who held through tickets, then put the names of the others into a hat and drew out enough to fill the remaining vacancies. Immediately there were frenzied bids for the tickets; a few winners, unable to resist a quick profit, sold theirs for as much as $1,000 (price: $200) and bought passage on the sailing packet *Philadelphia* for $75.

The idea of allowing foreigners to supersede Americans on American ships, in going to seek gold in American territory, was too much for Major General Persifor Smith, U.S.A., who was en route to California to take command of the territorial garrisons. He charged the Pacific Mail offices and demanded that the Peruvians be ousted to make room for more U.S. citizens. Agent Nelson, who was also the U.S. consul at Panama, cited the law as to precedence on common carriers: first come, first served.

But this was different, boomed the general. If Nelson did not turn those berths over to Americans, he would take it up with Washington, and when he got to California he would order his men to exclude those Peruvians "and maybe all foreigners" from the gold diggings. This would be illegal, Nelson pointed out, and in any case it was none of the Pacific Mail's business.

Finally the general and the agent-consul compromised. For each foreigner who was on board, Nelson sent on an extra American. The Peruvians gladly doubled up.

Bunks were prepared in the hold and on deck, and the *California* sailed from Panama 31 January with 365 passengers—146 per cent of her registered capacity.

At sea an American was discovered stowed away in the bunkers, and the stoker who had abetted him was fined. At this the engine room mutinied, so Captain Marshall put in at Mazatlán and kicked off the ringleaders. Then the coal supply ran out. Spars, doors, bunks, decks were ripped out to feed the boilers, and after practically everything combustible on board had been sacrificed the *California* limped through the Golden Gate on 28 February with the first shipload of forty-niners.

The crew to a man joined the passengers in the rush for the gold fields, leaving Captain Marshall high and dry. It took him three months to corral enough hands to get up steam and resume his run.

The second Pacific Mail steamer to reach the isthmus was the *Oregon.* By then, 23 February, the town was bulging again with bungo passengers from Chagres, despite the departure of several jampacked sailing vessels which Nelson had chartered for the California run.

The *Oregon,* a sister of the *California,* had orders to take no more than 250 passengers, but the clamor in the office of Zachrisson & Nelson would not down; the agents finally sent out 50 more of the most insistent. She sailed 12 March for California, and three weeks later dropped anchor in San Francisco Bay alongside the embarrassed *California,* with forlorn Captain Marshall hanging on the rail.

Seeing his colleague's plight, Captain Pearson quickly posted a new payroll for his crew, which he made out simply by adding a zero to each rate on the previous schedule. In this way he kept enough hands to return to the isthmus, where he found the third Pacific Mail sister, the *Panama,* loading more frantic gold hunters. By June the three side-wheelers had ironed out a routine of monthly sailings at each terminal.

Meanwhile William H. Aspinwall, New York capitalist who had founded the Atlantic service, received permission to reduce the number of calls on his schedule in order to speed up the eastern leg. Then it was New York, New Orleans, Chagres, and back, as fast as the *Isthmus, Crescent City,* and *Falcon* could ply. The smaller *Orus* remained in the river after its second Caribbean run, to help with the unloading of larger ships and to become the first steamer to paddle up the Chagres.

The mail-line service was supplemented on both sides of the isthmus by every type of vessel that could make sail or get up steam: fishing smacks, schooners, whalers, harbor tugs, ferryboats, scows, from 15 tons up. The Gold Rush of '49 settled down from a sudden shock to a sustained frenzy.

The windjammers were working in a bad spot. Often they wallowed in the doldrums for weeks, within sight of the isthmus. Still they packed the passengers in, sometimes for as much as $300. The 500-ton schooner *Humboldt,* in which Julius Pratt paid $200 for passage from Panama to California in May 1849, had bunks in her hold arranged in tiers, so that each 6-foot cube of space held nine persons. Other passengers, bringing the total to 401, slept in the lifeboats and on deck. They suffered for 48 days on "this prison ship" before reaching Acapulco, with "our rotten and wormy provisions and our intolerably nasty water" almost depleted. Pratt and several others let the "new and fast sailing schooner *Humboldt*" proceed without them, and waited there for two months to be picked up by the *California.*

Life on the gold-rush liners may have been hard, but it was not dull. Thomas Warren found his fellow travelers "the roughest, most uncouth lot of desperadoes that ever climbed over a ship's side." Frequently the entire cabin-class dinner was seized in transit as it left the galley "and carried off in triumph by the steerage passengers." Loud oaths, brawls, seasickness were continuous, "while the Isthmus fever was making sad havoc among our number; day after day some poor fellow . . . was unceremoniously buried over the side." Drinking and gambling were "the order of the day." The long dining tables "were occupied by roulette, faro banks, and every known game."

Fares went highest in the first year: New York to San Francisco (cost of transiting the isthmus not included), $450 first class, $225 steerage. From there they fluctuated, with a general downward trend, until, for a few months in 1855, cutthroat competition brought out quotations for the same voyage of $50 and $10, *including* the trans-isthmian railroad fare of $25 first and $10 second class.

Many of the Panameños speculated in steamship tickets, buying them from the local agents far in advance of sailings. Then, when a long-awaited vessel finally dropped anchor, and it became obvious that hundreds would be unable to get berths, they auctioned off the tickets, often realizing five times their investment.

"Taking the gold-rush period as a whole," estimated Gerstle Mack, the fares averaged "$200 first class, $175 second class, and $100 steerage," plus the expense of crossing the isthmus.

XX: OVER THE HUMP

THE ISTHMIAN leg of the journey was an unpredictable adventure.

General Smith reported to the secretary of war that "No preparation was made . . . by the steamboat company for transporting passengers across the isthmus, or affording them any information or aid in relation to it. The roads are almost impassable for mules, and the number of boats in the river and animals on the roads are entirely insufficient."

But many others felt as did Bayard Taylor; he called it "decidedly more novel, grotesque, and adventurous than any trip of similar length in the world." It was "rough enough," he conceded, but "it had nothing that I could exactly call hardship, so much was the fatigue balanced by the enjoyment of unsurpassed scenery and a continual sensation of novelty. In spite of the many dolorous accounts which have been sent from the isthmus, there is nothing, at the worst season, to deter anyone from the journey."

"The voyage up the Chagres," wrote Joseph Gregory, "has been by some persons execrated in tolerably strong terms, not to say diabolical. As far as my own feelings were concerned, I never beheld more magnificent scenery, or luxuriant vegetation."

Charles F. Hotchkiss, who crossed in October 1849,

had boatman trouble. His party of four "concluded a bargain with two brawny natives to pole us through" to Cruces, and "took them before the alcalde to pay the fare and agree on the terms: they to feed themselves, four hours per twenty-four given for rest, and forfeit a flogging if they did not perform." Next morning "the rascals mutinied," refusing to go farther unless the passengers gave them food. "We took possession of the craft ourselves, shoved her off shore, and waited events. Four Yankees, with each a pistol . . . against two natives, stark naked, was considerable odds in our favor . . . They gave in, and at it they went."

Taylor saw the mutiny problem differently: "Many blustering fellows, with their belts stuck full of pistols and Bowie knives, which they draw on all occasions but take good care not to use, have brought reproach on their country by such silly conduct. It is no bravery to put a revolver to the head of an unarmed and ignorant native, and the boatmen have sense enough to be no longer terrified by it."

At Cruces, Hotchkiss found that "the demand for mules far exceeded the supply. Current price $10 to Panama—no reclamation on either side if he died on the journey." On the trail he noted a crude means of traffic control for the many long gorges which were too narrow for animals to pass: "On entering them from either end, a loud whistle or hoot of the man in charge of the train is given . . . The party omitting to give this notice, if met in the gorge, must back out."

The crossing by bungo and mule required five or six days normally, while many of the argonauts, feeling that all time gained was cheap at any price, hired extra boatmen and paid bonuses to keep moving day and night.

Such a forced draft, coupled with good weather, timely connections at the transfer point, and fast pack animals, might cut the time to three days.

Some of the travelers preferred to walk, refusing to believe that these forty crow-flight miles could take any longer afoot than by bungos against a swift, winding river, and the easygoing pack trains whose guides often themselves walked. After a day on the trail under blistering sun and drenching rain, and a night of mosquitoes and a hundred different crawling things, many of the walkers changed their minds. Then they had to leave the trail and wait on the riverbank to hail the passing boats.

Most of the chartering parties ignored them, but sometimes they stopped, if only because a fellow argonaut might be in serious trouble. The hiker, if he could talk himself on board over the charterers' ire at the prospect of reduced speed, had to pay the boatmen double fare for the extra work and extra caution of poling an overloaded vessel.

Some of the walkers kept to the trail as far as Gorgona or Cruces, thinking to hire a mount and take a rest on the overland leg of the transit. They soon learned that traveling over Panama's steep-sided mountains gave a rider as much work to keep his seat as it gave a hiker to keep his feet. A few hardy souls "stuck it out by Shank's mare all the way to the Pacific Ocean," where they dangled their aching feet in the salt water for hours. This type of crossing required, as some of them remarked, "one hell of a week."

While the New Granadan government collected a head tax from each transient, the jungle took toll of each shipload in lives. The year-round threat of yellow fever increased during the rainy months, and in '53, '55, and

'56 mounted to epidemic severity. Cholera spread in '48; the following year it raged in every town and village on the route, reducing the native population by a fourth; it flared again, less seriously, in '50.

"The great secret" of rapid transit up the river, advised Gregory, "is to get off early in the morning, and be liberal to the men that work the canoe. You can coax better than drive them." At Gorgona "it is tempting to stay, but should you go on shore there, you will experience great difficulty . . . in getting your boatmen into their canoe again. This is their worst fault generally."

The Gorgona mule owners "will advise you to take the road to Panama from that point. *Pay no attention,*" he warned, "for that road is totally impassable for nine months in the year. Push on without delay to Cruces, and if you arrive there in the morning, you will hardly be able to get on the Panama road before the next morning. Meanwhile you can call at Funk's [or] Pleise's, where they forward baggage by mules to Panama. Ascertain their charge . . . *but let no promises induce you to leave your baggage to be forwarded after you, but see it start at least.*"

J. D. Borthwick, a Britisher who crossed the isthmus late in '49, found that "Most of the principal houses [in Panama] had been converted into hotels . . . kept by Americans." While "all foreigners were spoken of as *los Americanos* by the natives, they were," he noted, "men from every country in Europe. The Frenchmen were the most numerous, some of whom kept stores and very good restaurants. There were also several large gambling saloons . . . always crowded."

Auctioneers did a thriving business each morning,

selling U.S. real estate for argonauts who had gone broke at the gambling tables the night before. Since the sales were "sight unseen," and the titles questionable even when the sellers could show apparently authentic deeds, the prices paid were very low. Oftentimes the buyers later suffered reverses at roulette and had to sell in turn; many an eastern-state farm changed hands again and again, as individual owners came and went but ownership remained on the isthmus.

When steamers arrived at Chagres, the boatmen charged $2 to land each passenger and his baggage. In rough weather the fee was well earned, for the larger steamers would not attempt to pass the treacherous rocks that had wrecked four of Morgan's ships. They anchored outside in the open sea, and often pitched about for days, waiting for the weather to settle enough to permit unloading. Sometimes the bungos were swamped in the rolling sea, drowning boatmen and passengers.

During the rainy season the bungos continued to Cruces, 45 river miles from Chagres and 18 trail miles from Panama. In the dry months they could get no higher than Gorgona, 5 river miles below Cruces and 20 trail miles from Panama. From Gorgona there was a 10-mile unpaved stretch leading to the ancient cobblestones of the Cruces trail; it was passable only in dry weather. While a change of season brought a change in the trail distance and a compensating change in the river distance, it did not affect the fares charged by either of the carriers.

Boat fares rose steadily to a peak of $50 a head to Gorgona or Cruces in November 1851, when the Aspinwall-Gatún section of the Panama Railroad was completed. This took 10 miles from the bungo distance, and thereafter Chagres boat fares fell every time the railroad line reached another station on the riverbank. When the railroad reached Cruces, and eliminated boat travel entirely, the bungo fare dropped to $3.

Judson Ames from Baton Rouge arrived at Chagres in January 1850, with the most cumbersome piece of luggage that ever made the bungo-mule transit: a 1,200-pound Washington hand press (R. Hoe & Co., New York; serial no. 2327). He hired a barge and eight natives; together they loaded the press and shoved off with their poles. When they reached midstream the barge suddenly tilted, and the press slid off and settled out of sight in the sandy bottom. Ames borrowed a grappling hook from a steamer, and with this and a towing rope the party dragged the press back almost to the bank. There for half a day the natives tried to raise it onto the barge; finally Ames jumped into the water and, according to Horace Bell, "set it on the raft without help, while the natives looked on as if he were a brother to Samson."

At Cruces he paid $200 to hire the two strongest mules that he could find, and strapped the press across their mattress-covered backs. Somehow they got it to Panama.

Ames had to accept a booking to San Francisco three months away. To occupy his time he set up the press and began to publish the Panama *Herald*. When his steamer arrived, he sold his subscription list and accounts to the Panama *Star*, which thereby became the Panama *Star & Herald*, as it has since remained. The press was the first to arrive in America's new western territory, and stands today on display in the office of the *Independent*, of Independence, Inyo County, California.

The bulk of the cargo that was transshipped up the Chagres consisted of gold-mining equipment. The next most important item was cats—huge latticed crates which squirmed with layer upon layer of scrawny felines. They were sorely needed by California prospectors, to keep rats from eating the precious stocks of food in their shanties. In New York and New Orleans, speculators paid moppets a few cents apiece for alley cats, boxed them up by the dozen, and attached high-smelling cartons of fish with printed instructions to freight agents for feeding them. Sometimes the crates broke apart at sea, creating merry moments when all hands turned to recapturing them. Those which busted during loading or unloading in the bungos were a total loss, for the cats scampered off into the Chagres jungle and added another breed to the tigres that already lived there. But those which held out to San Francisco brought handsome profits; the mousers sold there for as much as $25 a head.

The *Orus,* a 250-ton side-wheeler owned by Howland & Aspinwall, was the first of the gold-rush river steamers to begin working the Chagres. It came down from New York packed with 150 argonauts, and arrived at the mouth of the river two weeks after the *Falcon* had anchored there on her initial voyage.

The rains were drawing to a close; already the stage of the Chagres had dropped several feet. To shorten her draft as much as possible, the captain hired a string of bungos and loaded them with baggage and freight from the hold; then the *Orus* chuffed up the river with the boats in tow. But she had made only twenty miles when the gravel bars began to rasp along her bottom. The captain tied her up at Bohío Soldado and announced that the passengers would have to hire boatmen to pole them on to Gorgona in their bungos.

The passengers reminded him that they had paid $10 a head for transportation from Chagres to Gorgona, and contended that they were entitled to have their bungo fare paid or at least to receive a rebate for incompleted contract. But the captain argued that he had agreed only to carry them "to Gorgona or as near there as the *Orus* can go." As usual, it was the traveling public that paid.

On learning that the river would be low for the next three months, the captain took the *Orus* back to New Orleans and brought another load of argonauts to the isthmus before beginning a fairly regular service from Chagres toward Gorgona one day and return the next. In May he reached Gorgona for the first time, and there he turned several bags of U.S. mail over to a muleteer, with a promise that he would be paid for carrying them to Panama by the captain of the next Pacific Mail steamer. When the native arrived in Panama there was no P.M. boat in the harbor, so he hawked the bags to the highest bidder. It caused a furor in Washington, but that particular consignment of first-class matter was never recovered.

Getting the mail across the Chagres valley continued to be a problem until 1 January 1852, when the Panama Railroad Company, despite the fact that its railway was still far from complete, began a contract to carry them for a flat $100,000 a year. There was no further trouble, and the contract remained in effect until the Union Pacific began its transcontinental service in 1869.

In September 1849, the *General Herrán*, one of those newfangled stern-wheelers, which had been designed especially for service on the Chagres, began a schedule which supplemented that of the *Orus*. For the next few months the argonauts had the convenience of daily steamship departures at each end of the run. While the steamers carried only a fraction of those who were clamoring to get aboard, they temporarily drove the bungo fare down to $6. But the teredo worm promptly went to work on the exposed hulls, and before the rainy season was over the *Orus* had to churn to New Orleans for repairs.

This led Howland & Aspinwall to order an iron-hulled boat, specifying a 12-inch draft, and the following 29 June the *Raphael Rivas* steamed into the mouth of the river. Her captain announced that she would proceed to Gorgona as soon as a load of passengers could climb aboard.

But it turned out that the 12-inch draft was what the boat had had before her iron sides were added. She now drew thirty inches, and so had to tie up at Palenquilla, eleven miles below Gorgona. Still, she was faster than the other two, making three net miles per hour against the current, and her passengers easily reached Gorgona by bungo that night.

The *Rivas* was the biggest steamer that ever plied the Chagres waters: 110 feet long, 23-foot beam. She carried 450 passengers, which was greater than the combined capacities of the *Orus* and the *Herrán.*

A month later the 46-foot *Harry Gleason,* an old Mississippi side-wheeler out of New Orleans, appeared in the river, and shortly afterward the similar *Swan.*

Before the end of the year the *Gorgona,* an iron-hulled steamer belonging to the Panama Railroad, began hauling construction materials and tools to the various sites along the river that had been selected for railroad way stations. Work on the iron road was being pushed, and the *Gorgona* had orders to waste no time attempting to carry passengers, even on the empty downstream trips.

The last of the Chagres steamers, the *William H. Aspinwall,* was built on Manzanillo Island by Howland & Aspinwall mechanics, and placed on the river 6 February 1851. She was a little smaller than the *Rivas* and almost twice as fast. Her four hundred passengers "actually had room to walk about" on the run to Gorgona, which took her 7½ hours; the return trip was an easy 3 hours. The *Aspinwall* was the only steamer to give daily service both ways.

Allowing for maintenance layovers, the combined steamship facilities on the Chagres then provided for the daily transport of about a thousand passengers each way. But the tide of gold seekers continued to rise. So Captain Abraham Banker quit his job as shipping-news reporter for the New York *Herald* and organized a unique service to supplement that of the steamers and the bungos.

His Isthmus Transportation Company bought fifty spanking new lifeboats from New York and New Orleans ship chandlers, rigged them up with canvas canopies, and initiated a de luxe paddle-and-pole fleet. The Isthmus Transport raided the Panama Railroad construction gangs to fill out its crews, using the double suasion of higher pay and pleasanter work. The imported boats carried a dozen or more passengers, and still were easier to handle than the crude bungos.

The higher pay possible with these advantages led many of the native owner-operators to sell their bungos and take jobs with the Isthmus Transport. It maintained high standards, instantly discharging boatmen who were guilty of baggage pilfering, cheating, tardiness, drunkenness, insolence, or indifferent poling.

When in 1853 the gold rush showed no sign of abating, the Panama mule-dealing firm of Hurtado y Hermanos organized an ocean-to-ocean service which took a passenger from a newly arrived ocean liner at either terminal and put him on board a liner at the other. The through ticket cost $30, out of which the Hurtado brothers paid the New Granadan government's transit tax, the fees for landing and loading at each port, and the railroad, river, and trail transportation between.

The Yanqui firm of Garrison & Fretz, which previously had confined itself to the operation of a Panama gambling casino, imported a hundred Kentucky mules and initiated a similar service. Then the isthmian outposts of the old-line American express companies, Wells-Fargo and Howland & Aspinwall, which had specialized in baggage and freight, began to handle passengers on the same basis.

By co-ordinating schedules at the transfer points, so that the travelers literally climbed out of steamboats onto mules and railroad cars, these agencies reduced the over-all time for transiting the isthmus so efficiently that in 1854 the Pacific-to-Atlantic crossing often was completed within seven hours. The Atlantic-to-Pacific transit, with its river travel against the current, was accomplished in twelve hours.

XXI: ONE MAN'S JOURNEY

Of all the argonauts who published accounts of their emigration by the Panama route, Bayard Taylor, world traveler and author from Pennsylvania, kept the most detailed account of his adventures on the isthmus. He also recorded graphic, if at times flowery, impressions of the Chagres before a stupendous work of man gave to it an even greater grandeur.

Taylor crossed in July 1850, after sailing down from New Orleans with a boatload of "tall, gaunt Mississippians and Arkansans, and Missouri squatters who had pulled up their stakes yet another time, and an ominous number of professional gamblers, including some new varieties of the American: long, loose-jointed men with large hands and feet, and limbs which would still be awkward whatever the fashion of their clothes, faces lengthened in an expression of settled melancholy, the corners of their mouths curving downwards, giving that cast of destructiveness peculiar to the Indian."

These men "chewed tobacco at a ruinous rate, and spent their time either in dozing at full length on the deck or going into the fore-cabin for drinks." They each "carried enough arms for a small company, and breathed defiance."

Their first glimpse of the isthmus was the headland of Porto Bello, "a bold, rocky promontory, fringed with vegetation and washed at its foot by a line of snowy breakers . . . The Andes of Darien towered high behind the coast." Turning west, they "followed the magnificent sweep of hills toward Chagres, passing Navy bay, the Atlantic terminus of the Panama railroad," where construction was just beginning. "The entrance is narrow, between two bold bluffs, opening into a fine land-locked harbor, surrounded by hills." Somehow Taylor failed to mention the Black Swamp.

"Chagres lies about eight miles to the west of this bay, but the mouth of the river is so narrow that the place is not seen till you run close upon it. The eastern shore is high and steep, cloven with ravines which roll their tropical vegetation down to the sea."

The ruins of San Lorenzo he found to be "similar to the Morro Castle at Havana, and equally impregnable." (If Taylor had known the history of the castle on the Chagres, he would not have called it impregnable.) "Its brown battlements and embrasures have many a dark and stirring recollection, [but] it now looks harmless enough, with a few old cannon lying lazily on its ramparts." From their anchorage they could see "only the tops of some huts among the trees."

The deck was soon covered with luggage, since "everybody was anxious to leave first." The ship's officers went ashore while the passengers organized groups for the river trip. "An immense dug-out canoe, manned by half-naked natives," came out with agents for the bungo men, and all boats were quickly engaged.

The returning purser "was assailed by such a storm of questions—the passengers leaning half-way out over the bulwarks—that he could not make himself heard." When the clamor subsided, he told them that the next Pacific

Mail steamer would sail from Panama 1 August. There would be no river boats before tomorrow, for Captain Notestein had engaged all the ready ones to carry a consignment of gold-mining equipment to an agent in Gorgona for forwarding.

They took their gear below, resigned to another night on board, and soon rejoiced that they had not been able to start, for with darkness came a sudden storm. Taylor was entertained by "broad, scarlet flashes of lightning, surpassing any celestial pyrotechnics I ever witnessed. The dark walls of San Lorenzo, the brilliant clusters of palms on the shore, and the green, rolling hills of the interior leaped at intervals out of the gloom."

They went ashore at dawn, "rounding the high bluff on which the castle stands and finding beyond it a shallow little bay on the eastern shore of which, on low ground, stand the cane huts of Chagres." They piled their luggage on shore and looked around for their crews, but "without a single exception, the natives were not to be found, or, when found, had broken their bargains. Everyone ran hither and yon in great excitement, anxious to be off before everyone else, and hurrying the naked boatmen, all to no purpose." The boats that had come down the river during the night had been beached and the men were "leisurely engaged in re-thatching their canopies."

In the doors of the huts Taylor noticed "men and women, each in a single cotton garment, composedly smoking their cigars, while numbers of children, in Nature's own clothing, tumbled about in the sun." He breakfasted with a native family on "some pieces of pork fat, bread, and a draught of sweet spring water from a cocoa shell," which was spread on a hen coop beside the door. Pigs and dogs surrounded them "to offer their services, but maintained a respectful silence, which is more than could be said of pigs at home."

During the morning several bungos arrived from upriver. Among their passengers was a homeward-bound argonaut with $20,000 worth of dust and a four-pound nugget, the sight of which maddened the emigrants. "Life and death were small matters compared with immediate departure from Chagres. Men ran up and down the beach, shouting, raving, gesticulating, cursing the deliberate habits of the natives, as if their arrival in California would thereby be at all hastened." The boatmen remained cool. "They had not seen six months of emigration without learning something of the American habit of going at full speed."

Taylor and three friends paid $15 each to engage a boat to Cruces, stood insistent over the boatmen until they had finished refitting it, and helped to push it through the mud and shoal water to the riverbank. When they had stowed their luggage they turned and found that the crew had disappeared, along with all the others. They "waited the pleasure of the dusky gondoliers, while the sun blazed down on the swampy shores, and visions of yellow fever came into the minds of the more timid."

As they sat waiting, little native boys brought out "bottles of fresh water, biscuits, and fruit, presenting them with the words 'Bit!' or 'Picayune!'" Taylor was "much diverted by seeing one of our passengers issue from a hut with a native on each arm, and march them resolutely down to the river."

Their boatmen ambled out toward noon, each with a bag of rice, a supply of dried pork, and an armful of sugar cane. "A few strokes of their broad paddles took us from the excitement of the landing-place to the seclusion and beauty of the river." Their chief boatman was Ambrosio Mendez, a mestizo; his assistant, Juan Crispin Bega, was "almost entirely Negro—a strong, jovial fellow who took such good care of some of our small articles as to relieve us from all further trouble about them.

"This tendency," Taylor noted, "is common to all of his caste on the isthmus."

Another native, a runaway soldier from the Colombian army who had just paid the subalcalde a fine of three bottles of liquor for having stolen the same, was aboard to work his passage, but they were scarcely out of sight of the town when he demanded $5 a day for his labor. "We refused, and he stopped working." They threatened to set him ashore, so he picked up his paddle again, but only hindered with it. They decided to let him be until they got to Gatún.

While Juan sang "Oh, Susanna!" which he had learned from his previous fares verbatim with no idea of the meaning of the words, the passengers relaxed to enjoy the scenery.

"There is nothing in the world comparable to these forests. No description conveys an idea of the splendid overplus of vegetable life . . . The river, broad, and with a swift current of the sweetest water I ever drank, winds between walls of foliage that rise from its very surface. All the gorgeous growths of an eternal summer are mingled in one impenetrable mass so that the eye is bewildered. From the rank jungles of cane and gigantic lilies, and the thickets of strange shrubs which line the water, rise the trunks of the mango, the ceiba, the cocoa, the sycamore, and the superb palm. Plantains take root in the banks, hiding the soil with their leaves, shaken and split into immense plumes by wind and rain. The zapote, with a fruit the size of a man's head, the gourd tree, other wonders attract the eye on all sides. Blossoms of crimson, purple, yellow, of forms and magnitude unknown in the north . . . Flocks of paroquets, brilliant butterflies circle like blossoms blown away . . . A spike of scarlet flowers thrusts from the heart of a convolution of unfolding leaves . . . Creepers and parasites drop trains and streamers of fragrance from boughs that shoot halfway across the river."

Each turn of the stream "disclosed another, more magnificent vista of leaf, bough, and blossom. All outline of the landscape is lost under this deluge of vegetation. No trace of the soil is to be seen; lowland and highland are the same; a mountain is but a higher swell of the mass of verdure. The sharp, clear lines of our scenery at home are here wanting. What shape the land would be if cleared, you cannot tell. You gaze upon the scene before you with a never-sated delight, till your brain aches with the sensation, and you close your eyes, overwhelmed with the thought that these wonders have been here from the beginning, that year after year takes away no blossom or leaf that is not replaced, but the sublime mystery of growth and decay is renewed forever."

In the afternoon they reached Gatún and found that the earlier boats were tied up there; the boatmen, it seemed, had a working agreement which transcended the desires of their passengers, and they had decided to stay there overnight. Taylor's party bodily removed their sponging passenger against "passive resistance," and engaged another boatman to finish the trip for $8. "I shall never forget the forlorn look of the ousted man as he sat on the bank beside his bag of rice, and the rain began to fall."

Ambrosio engaged hammocks for the night, at $2 each, in a one-room hut. Under the pyramidal thatched roof was a loft, gained by a notched pole; up there went several late-arrivers, to be "stowed away on a rattling floor of cane, covered with hides." After supper of pork and coffee, Taylor began to make his day's notes by the light of a "starveling candle stuck in an empty bottle," but gave it up when his paper became covered with fleas. Meantime the host had swung his hammock, so Taylor turned in to avoid any contest for possession of it.

"To lie there was one thing; to sleep another. A dozen natives were crowded round the table, drinking their aguardiente and disputing loudly; the cooking fire was on one side of me, and everyone who passed to and fro gave me a bump. My weight swung the hammock so low that all the dogs on the premises were comfortably rubbing their backs under me." Just as he dozed off the señora and a boatman opened an argument, standing to each side of his hammock so that their gestures grazed him time and again. Knowing little Spanish, it seemed to Taylor that "my own head, and not the reckoning, was the subject of contention."

They were to have started at midnight, but by the time they had roused and mustered their boatmen it was two o'clock. They glided silently up the river until dawn, when, at Dos Hermanos, they overtook two rival boats which had been all night on the river, trying to gain a slight lead. With the sunrise the clouds began to gather, and a short time later, as they neared the rancho Palo Matilda, "a sudden cold wind came over the forests, and the air darkened. We sprang ashore and barely reached the hut, a few paces off, when the rain broke on us as if the sky had caved in. A dozen lines of white electric heat ran down, followed by crashes of thunder which I could feel throbbing in the earth under me. The rain drove into one side of the cabin and out the other, but we wrapped ourselves in India-rubber cloth and kept out the wet and chilling air."

The river rose rapidly, forcing them to hug the bank, running under trees and drawing themselves through the swift current by low-hanging boughs. But the flood quickly fell. Thereafter Juan kept time with his paddle to his Spanish-accented interpretations of the songs that he had picked up from the emigrants, "looking round from time to time with a grin of satisfaction at his skill." Taylor preferred the native songs, "which the boatmen sing with a melancholy drawl on the final syllable of every line, giving a peculiar but not unpleasant effect." One of them which Taylor liked especially ran:

> Ten piedad, piedad de mis penas,
> Ten piedad, piedad de mi amor.
> (Have pity on my sufferings, have pity on my love.)

Between songs Juan guzzled Taylor's brandy, and after each drink dipped his coco shell in the river and took a long draught. "This is a universal custom among the boatmen, and the traveler is obliged to supply them." Ambrosio told Taylor that they served no one well who treated them badly. "If the Americans are good, we are good; if they abuse us, we are bad. We are black, but muchos caballeros" (real gentlemen).

The second night they spent at Peña Blanca, where the party slept in the bare loft of a hut, "in the midst of the family and six other travelers." They started at sunrise, hoping to reach Gorgona that night, but soon ran upon a sunken log and were detained. Ambrosio finally released them by jumping into the river and swimming ashore with a rope in his teeth.

After they had passed the ranchos of Agua Salud, Barro Colorado, and Palenquilla, another river storm overtook them. "We could hear the roar and rush of the rain as it came towards us like the trampling of myriad feet on the leaves." They shot under a sycamore, made fast to the boughs, and waited under their rubber ponchos until the storm passed.

As they proceeded, "the character of the scenery changed somewhat." Taylor noted that the banks grew bolder and steeper, with "more signs of cultivation, where the forest had been lopped away to make room for fields of maize, plantain, and rice. But many were the long and lonely reaches of the river where we glided between piled masses of bloom and greenery." At one spot, "from the crest of a steep hill to the edge of the water, descended a flood, a torrent of vegetation. Trees were rolled upon trees, woven into a sheet by parasitic vines that leapt into the air like spray from the topmost boughs. When the wind agitated the leaves, and the vines were flung like a green foam on the surface of the river, it was difficult not to feel that the flood was about rushing down to overwhelm us."

They stopped four hours short of Gorgona at San Pablo, the hacienda of Padre Dutaris, priest of the interior parish. Ambrosio led them to the house across a rolling sábana, dotted by immense palms and acacias. "Herds of cattle and horses were grazing in the short, thick-leaved grass of the rancho, which commands a beautiful view up and down the river." When Ambrosio recommended the party as buenos caballeros, the padre offered them "a splendid supper of fowls, eggs, rice boiled in cocoa milk, chocolate, and baked plantains for bread." Usually there was difficulty getting food here, the boatmen told them, since the priest often had been cheated by Americans.

The party slept better than on the previous nights, but was up at four o'clock to make haste for Gorgona. "The current was very strong, and in some places it was almost impossible to make headway. Our boatmen worked hard, and by dint of strong poling managed to jump through very difficult places. Their naked, sinewy forms, bathed in sweat, shone like polished bronze." Ambrosio soon gave out, but Miguel, the new recruit, "flung himself on the pole so that all the muscles of his body quivered as the boat shot ahead [around] the foot of Monte Carabali, a bold peak clothed in forests and crowned with a single palm—the only hill in the province from which both oceans may be seen at once."

The party had heard reports of the cholera epidemic at Cruces. As they neared Gorgona the boatmen began chanting: "Cruces—mucha colera." Clearly they were hoping that their passengers would elect to try the Gorgona trail instead of continuing upriver.

At Gorgona Taylor "climbed the bank and called at the store of Mr. Miller, the only American resident, who informed me that several passengers by the Falcon had already left for Panama, the [Gorgona] trail being reported passable." At the alcalde's house nearby, Taylor met "Mr. Powers, who had left New York a short time previous to my departure, and was about starting for Panama on foot, mules being very scarce."

As the party was deliberating whether to go on to Cruces, Ambrosio beckoned Taylor into a nearby hut, where "the owner, a very venerable and dignified native, received me swinging in his hammock. He had six horses which he would furnish us the next morning, at $10 the head for riding animals and $6 for each hundred pounds of freight . . .

"Now came the settlement with our boatmen. In addition to the fare, half of which was paid in Chagres, we had promised them a *gratificación* provided they made the journey in three days. The contract was not exactly fulfilled, but we thought it best to part friends and so gave them each a dollar. Their antics of delight were most laughable. They grinned, laughed, danced, caught us by the hands, vowed eternal friendship, and would have embraced us . . .

"Half an hour later I met Juan, in a clean shirt and white pantaloons, with a heat in his eye . . . which readily explained an incoherence in his speech. '*Mi amigo,*' he cried, '*Mi buen amigo!* Give me a bottle of beer!' I refused . . . 'But we are friends; surely you will give your dear friend a bottle of beer.' 'I don't like my dear friends to drink too much,' I answered . . . As a last resort, he placed both hands on his breast and, with an imploring look, sang: '*Ten piedad, piedad de mis penas* . . .' I burst into a laugh at this comical appeal, and he retreated, satisfied that he had at least done a smart thing."

During the afternoon several more boats arrived. As it grew dark, "the sound of wooden drums in the village proclaimed a fandango. The aristocracy of Gorgona met in the alcalde's house, while the natives assembled on a level sward before one of the huts. The ladies were dressed in white and pink, with flowers in their hair, and waltzed with a slow grace to the music of violins and guitars. The alcalde's daughters were rather pretty, and at once became favorites of the Americans, some of whom joined in the fandango and went through its voluptuous mazes at the first trial, to the great delight of the natives."

The Señora Catalina, "a rich widow of pure Andalusian blood," caught Taylor's fancy. "She danced charmingly, her little head leaned coquettishly on one side, while with one hand she held aloft the fringed end of her crimson scarf, which rested lightly on the opposite shoulder. The dance over, she took a guitar and sang, the subject being 'Los Amigos Americanos.' "

Meanwhile the plebeians indulged in "half-barbaric orgies in the pure and splendid light pouring on the landscape from a vertical moon. The only accompaniment to the wooden drums was the *ña, ña, ña* nasal monotone of the women. Those who danced longest and most voluptuously had the hats of all the others piled upon them in token of applause."

At daybreak their guide was at the door with the horses, "tough little mustangs which I could almost step over." The party left their baggage "to the honesty of our host, who promised to send it the same day. A servant of the alcalde escorted us out of the village, cut us each a good stick, pocketed a real, and then left us to plunge into the forest."

The trail at the outset was "rough enough," but as the woods grew deeper and darker "it became finally a narrow gully, filled with mud nearly to our horses' bellies. Descending the steep side of the hills, they would step or slide down almost precipitous passes, bringing up all straight at the bottom, and climbing the opposite side like cats. So strong is their mutual confidence that they invariably step in each other's tracks, and a great part of the road is thus worn into holes three feet deep and filled with water and soft mud, which spirts upward as they go, coating the rider from head to foot."

In the party since leaving Gorgona had been "a lank Mississippian, whose long face struck me at first glance as being peculiarly cadaverous." He had attached himself without ceremony, leaving his own party behind. Soon he announced that he had felt symptoms of cholera during the night, and was growing worse. They insisted on his returning to Gorgona at once, but he refused, saying that he was "bound to go through."

At the first rancho they found a traveler prostrate on the ground, attended by a friend who "seemed on the point of taking the epidemic from his very fears." The sight seemed to operate on the ailing Mississippian, for "he soon became so racked with pain as to keep his seat with great difficulty. We were alarmed; it was impossible to stop in the swampy forest, and equally impossible to leave him, now that all his dependence was on us."

The only medicine they carried was a bottle of claret, which was, as Taylor observed, "an unusual remedy for cholera," but he insisted on drinking it.

As they trekked, the mountain range became irregular. "Above us spread a roof of transparent green, through which few rays of sunlight fell. The only sounds in that leafy wilderness were the chattering of monkeys cracking palm-nuts and the scream of parrots flying from tree to tree."

In the ravines "spent mules lay dead, and high above them, on the large boughs, the bald vultures waited silently for us to pass. We overtook many trains of luggage, packed on the backs of bulls and horses, tied head-to-tail in long files." Whenever they came upon a rancho they asked for refreshments, but "all the natives could furnish us was a cup of thick, black coffee."

After ascending for several hours, they came to a "level table-land, covered with palms." When the horses "went down the other side through clefts and gullies which seemed impassable," the party supposed that the worst of the journey was behind them, "but this was a terrible deception. Scrambling up ravines of slippery clay, we went for miles through swamps and thickets, urging forward our jaded beasts by shouting and beating. On a precipitous bank, washed soft by the rains, my horse slipped and made a descent of ten feet, landing on one side and I on another. He rose quietly, disengaged his head from the mud, and stood flank deep, waiting till I stepped across his back, and went forward, my legs lifted to his neck."

At dusk they ascertained from their guide that Panama was four hours away. "We pitied the poor horses, but ourselves more, and determined to push ahead." When they reached the Cruces trail, Taylor "looked forward to sighting the Pacific, but every ridge showed another ahead, and it grew dark with a rain coming up. Our horses avoided the hard pavement and took bypaths through thickets higher than our heads."

The poor Mississippian, in no wise helped by the claret, "implored us, amid his groans, to hasten forward. Leaning over the horse's neck, he writhed on his saddle in agony, and seemed on the point of falling at every step."

In their hurry they got ahead of their guide and lost the way several times in the darkness. When at last the Indian overtook them, washed his feet in a mudhole, and put on a pair of pantaloons, "it was a welcome sign." Soon they smelled the salt air of the Pacific, and began to distinguish huts on each side of the road. "These gave place to stone houses and massive ruined edifices, overgrown with vegetation. We passed a plaza and magnificent church, rode down an open space fronting the bay, under a heavy gateway, across another plaza and through two or three narrow streets, hailed by Americans all the way with: 'Are you the Falcon's passengers?' . . . 'From Cruces?' . . . 'From Gorgona?' . . . till our guide brought us up at the Hotel Americano."

Taylor found the city "already half American," with the native boys whistling "Yankee Doodle" and the "señoritas of the pure Castilian blood" singing the plantation melodies of Virginia to their guitars. The hotels were doing a thriving business, although "the fare and attendance were alike indifferent. We went to bed immediately, so that our clothes might be washed before morning, as our luggage had not arrived." But the venerable native at Gorgona had not betrayed their confidence; next morning his mule was at the hotel, laden with their trunks and valises.

Among the *Falcon's* passengers were several women argonauts, who had made the crossing in male attire. They were "obliged to sport their jackets and pantaloons several days before receiving their dresses." Many of the travelers were forced to remain in Panama because, "notwithstanding the formal contract of the alcalde of Gorgona, their luggage did not arrive before the sailing of the steamer."

The next day practically all the *Falcon's* passengers came in, and reported that there had been a heavy rain across the divide the night before, so that the Gorgona road, "already next to impassable, became actually perilous. A lady from Maine, who made the journey alone, was obliged to ford a torrent of water above her waist, with a native on each side to prevent her being washed away." A Frenchwoman who had been washed from her mule at the same crossing "only got over by the united exertions of seven men."

What became of the cholera-stricken Mississippian? Taylor neglected to say.

XXII: FRONTIER TO THE SOUTH

TAKE a movie set of a Pacific coast mining camp in America's Wild West of the 1850's. Remove the hitching racks and other signs of horses. Ring in some tropical foliage. There you have a suggestion of how the rip-roaring, Yankee-dominated, international frontier town of Chagres looked in those days.

Pity that no Bret Harte, no Bob Service chanced to pass that way. Such a place deserves a teller of tales, a singer of songs; rather, the world deserves that minstrels should capture for posterity the flavor of such a place. It is a sorry turn when a riographer, whose river down through the ages has a story as lurid as any could be, finds that no one has preserved any integrated picture of what undoubtedly was the gamiest interlude of all.

Scraps there are: a sentence here, a phrase there, in newspaper items, magazine articles, and books written by diary-keeping argonauts. But all these men were in transit; their eyes were on their destinations and on their own problems and adventures. The town of New Chagres was merely one of the several layover points; few of those who happened along seemed to see anything there except a place of nuisances where it was necessary to wait to make travel connections.

The town had a small permanent population: express agents, steamboat crews and mechanics, innkeepers, bartenders, gamblers, cooks, waiters, barbers, prostitutes—probably well over two hundred all told. But none of them seems to have published any memoirs. There are a few old-timers in Panama, whose grandfathers arrived there during the gold rush and for one reason or another decided to stay; they recall snatches from family conversation.

A distillate of available facts, sized with judicious inferences, produces something that needs a little liberality to be called history:

When the *Orus* arrived, early in January 1849, to make the first steamer run up the river, the need of wharfage became apparent. The captain, or some other Howland & Aspinwall official, arranged for the construction of a wharf on the opposite bank of the river's mouth from the native village. Next a small building, of Georgia pine lumber loaded at Savannah, went up behind the wharf to serve as an office and tool shed.

When the tide of argonauts continued to rise, and other steamers came to take up the Gorgona run, the dock facilities were expanded. The jungle was cut back, and two hotels were built, with more Georgia lumber. Around this nucleus mushroomed a shantytown, owned, operated, and patronized by aliens—mostly Americans, with a sprinkling of French and other nationalities.

The place received matter-of-fact mention in the pamphlets that were sold by New York and New Orleans magazine stands to aid adventurers who were about to set out for the gold fields by the tropical route. The cautiously written *Gregory's Guide for California Travellers via the Isthmus of Panama* gave it the most space: "The Steam Ship Company provide for the landing of the passengers and their baggage, using the ship's quarter-boats for the former, and the launch of the Steamer Orus for the latter, conveying the whole to the Orus, which vessel lands the passengers on what is called the American side of the river. Three or four taverns are kept at this landing by white men, one or two of whom are Americans."

What was thus unimaginatively called "the American side of the river" had a more succinct designation by the natives on the opposite bank. "Yanqui Chagres," they called it, with perhaps a sneer. The dirty-aproned bartenders of Yanqui Chagres, when asked by transients about the clump of huts across the water, showed the same degree of disdain; "Native Chagres," they sniffed into their handle-bar mustaches.

The two principal hotels were the Californian and the Crescent City. They were rambling, two-story frame structures, with wide piazzas going completely around both floors. Their huge rooms were filled with cots, in barracks style, at $4 each the night; during overflow times there were hammocks swung between the posts, for $2. One of the rooms usually was reserved for women travelers, but if space was pressing the management put the ladies in rooms with men and provided a pretense at privacy with screens of woven palm fronds, blankets, or sheets.

The other buildings were squat clusters of packing boxes, pieced out with scrap lumber left over from the construction of the hotels and the repair of steamers. Many of them, if not all, were without flooring. They extended in an irregular line along the riverfront, behind a sidewalk which oozed ankle-deep in mud during the rainy months.

Besides the dining rooms in the main hotels, there was an Eagle Café & Restaurant, with perhaps other eating places. The fare, like that in Panama's pensiones, was terrible; refrigeration was impossible, and so the menus were pretty much restricted to dried meat, beans, bread, tropical fruits, and coffee. Out of the Black Swamp flew clouds of cockroaches to share the food, sometimes even while the diners sat. Prices for meals were more reasonable than for lodging and other accommodations; this was the result of competition from the native huts on the other side, where one could eat about as well; at mealtimes bungos skimmed across to pick up travelers who were dissatisfied with the Yanqui fare, or who wanted to "see how those poor devils live."

The hotel bars were supplemented by a Silver Dollar Saloon and others. Bar liquor cost $1 a drink, better grades on up—about seven times the then prices in New York. At Chagres many a grizzled prospector, with a fortune in his jeans, slaked a thirst that had grown through months of panning along the California mountain streams and weeks of seasickness on the return voyage to Panama. On days when bungo arrivals were light, the town was shot up a bit; only when a river steamer came down loaded was the town shot up thoroughly.

It was an anarchic community. Titular sovereignty remained with New Granada but, since none of her citizens lived there, Bogotá saw no need to police the place. The American firm of Howland & Aspinwall had leased the site, and it sublet ground space to the other colonists; it assumed no responsibility for the maintenance of order. The steamship agents, who handled vast amounts of cash daily, carried arms, but they were not policemen; so did everyone else. There was no sheriff, no law enforcement of any kind; indeed, there were no laws. That is, except for the unwritten laws of the faraway Golden West, such

A VILLAGE ON

THE CRUCES TRAIL

as no swindling at cards and smiling when you say that, stranger.

Deaths, attributable to yellow fever, cholera, malaria, dysentery, typhoid, and gunshot wounds, were common, but there is no record of a cemetery. Presumably all corpses were dropped into the Chagres to be carried out to sea. No questions were asked when men died; there was no one with authority to ask any.

The transient population, both east- and westbound, certainly averaged higher than a thousand, with each individual visitor remaining about a week. Fluctuations in the total from day to day were not great, for by the time the town had grown up the homeward migration was almost as voluminous as the outward stream. Boats which carried travelers up the river came back down with replacements. Liners from New Orleans carried away about as many as they brought.

Nearly everyone who came to Chagres had plenty of money; the westbound travelers had their grubstakes, and the returning ones had struck it rich, for otherwise they could not have afforded the journey; prospectors who had gone broke either stayed in California or straggled home across the mountains and plains.

Some of the free-flowing cash was spent in the Emporium (Gents' Furnishings), but most of it was raked in by the croupiers of the Monte Carlo Casino and other gambling houses. There were tables for roulette, faro, blackjack, trente et quarante, casino, poker, and craps; $2 floor, no ceiling.

The hostesses took another large slice, charging $2 for a dance ("Once around the room, Tex; my time is money"), other favors in proportion. When offered a drink they always ordered a Blue Moon, which consisted of colored water; it cost $1, and the house credited the girl with 50 cents. (The system continues in vogue on the isthmus; cabaret girls at Madam Kelley's tonight will order Blue Moons, for which the waiters will openly hand them small metal checks to be redeemed later.) There was a House of All Nations, run by a French couple. Its extravagant title was supported lamely by an assortment of white, brown, black, and blended Panameñas, some Americans (mostly New Orleans mademoiselles), and a few second-rate Parisiennes.

Since there was no bank, the femmes de joie changed their receipts into big bills and secured the wads in the usual places; then, since there was no police protection, they wore their side arms even in the throes of plying their trade. "Disconcerting as hell," commented a Briton. "All the time she kept one hand on her blasted six-shooter."

There were other services for the transients: a hasty shave cost $1, or $1.50 if clippers had to be used first, and an indifferent haircut $2; laundry was 25 cents per garment, large or small. There was no library, and no church.

The town held the spotlight on our stage for longer than two years. Then, in November 1851, the railroad reached Gatún, eliminating the necessity of river travel between there and the mouth. The express companies moved their hotels and other buildings seven miles eastward along the coast to the new terminal on Manzanillo Island, and the hangers-on followed. Now the beaten track of the argonauts by-passed the mouth of the river, which promptly returned to its former somnolence.

Soon the insatiable jungle had digested every trace of Yankee Chagres.

The Pacific Mail side-wheelers out of San Francisco brought large shipments of gold and smaller ones of silver, to be transshipped from Panama to Chagres and the eastern mail packets. By 1853 there was a steady flow down the river of $8 million in gold and $2 million in silver every month. For the seven-year period between the strike at Sutter's mill and the completion of the Panama Railroad, the isthmus express agencies handled some $280 million in gold and $85 million in silver, by mule train and river steamer.

Brigandage was to be expected. Since New Granada made no effort to provide police protection, the wonder is that losses to bandits were not greater.

The first important robbery came in August 1850, when a Howland & Aspinwall train was attacked by a band of masked men on the Cruces trail and relieved of $30,000.

Promptly Henry Tracy, agent for Wells-Fargo, wrote to his home office in New York to report the incident and to requisition the following: "One (1) doz. Colt revolving rifles. One (1) doz. prs. revolvers, dragoon size. One (1) doz. prs. revolvers, police size. Two (2) doz. Bowie knives. Two (2) buck shot guns. Ample powder and ball for Above."

He added these comments: "Robberies have just commenced, and there are about a hundred as precious villains on the Isthmus as ever went unhung . . . There will have to be bloodshed . . . I am determined that there shall be none stole from your trains except there be several funarls."

The following December a Zachrisson & Nelson train was robbed of $120,000 on the Cruces trail. The so-called Derienni, the "land pirates of the Isthmus," were limbering up.

Several weeks later the *Northerner* brought $2,600,000

in gold express and five hundred opulent prospectors from California. The express agents and the passengers gathered together all the public animals on the isthmus, and formed one vast convoy for mutual protection. They made a formidable array as they set out from Panama in a line that extended for almost a mile.

Near the Gorgona fork, at the signal of a pistol shot, the masked horsemen appeared from widely spaced concealments along the trail with guns drawn.

"¡Arriba!" they commanded. The travelers understood well enough to comply.

Unerringly the leader singled out the gold-carrying mules, and turned them over to a group of his men, who led them away on to an unfrequented cross trail. Then the bandits made the mistake of beginning a search for personal pouches.

It is difficult to cover several men while frisking one. A quick-drawing Californian shot the leader through the head, and instantly gunplay flared all along the line. Four of the bandits bit the dust; others plunged into the covering foliage; a few dropped their guns and raised their hands. A troop of prospectors spurred their mounts and set out after the gold, which had had only a few moments' start.

At the sound of the shooting, the bandits leading the mules had begun to shift the loads to their horses. When the Americans approached, the bandits spanked the mules into the brush and made off with what gold they had transferred. With their faster mounts they easily outdistanced the pursuit in an ineffective hail of lead. The prospectors turned back to find the express mules gathering again on the trail; only $120,000 of the rich shipment was missing.

The late bandit leader was identified as a Chilean. He had worked as a muleteer, as had two of the other outlaw casualties. Agent Tracy's resolve had been kept; there were several funerals.

In ensuing months lesser robberies occurred all along the Cruces and Gorgona trails. Murders were commonplace. Bungo boatmen, who had learned from the Yanquis about the advantages of carrying knives, massacred whole boatloads of passengers along lonely stretches of the Chagres, and tossed their bodies into the jungle. The circling zopilotes in the sky showed where they were, but no one bothered to investigate. What could be done?

The American, French, and British consuls reported the incidents to their governments and urged them to send marines to police the route. Diplomatic representations were made in Bogotá, but New Granada well knew that certain countries seemed never to get around to evacuating a territory once they had occupied it. She demurred, and continued to restrict her activities along the Chagres to the collection of the transit tax.

The greatest single loss of the gold-rush era came in the following September, when a pack train was robbed of $250,000 near the Gorgona fork. Two of the muleteers were killed.

At this the officials of the Panama Railroad Company, looking into the future when it would be operating steam trains along the route, demanded authority to provide its own police force. Reluctantly, Governor Urrutia Añino signed a secret conveyance to the railroad of absolute police power on the isthmus, including the right to impose death penalties without trial or accountability. Then the railroad began to look around quietly for a man to act as its private sheriff. Here was one of the rarest things in all history: the voluntary assigning of complete dictatorial power to an alien, by a land which, technically at least, was at peace.

Some weeks later a small, unobtrusive man, scarcely turned twenty-one, weighing a scant 135 pounds, but withal a veteran of service in the Texas Rangers, took rooms at a small pension in Panama.

"Headed for the gold diggings?" another American asked affably.

"Just looking around," answered the stranger, brushing an unruly lock of chestnut hair from his forehead.

In the next few days he was seen to enter the offices of the several consuls and the transportation agencies. Then he bought a string of mules. Soon small advertisements began to appear in the newspapers:

"Runnels Express Service. Panama-Gorgona or Ocean-to-Ocean. Prompt, Safe. Ran Runnels, Prop."

A motley string of Chileans, Peruvians, Mexicans, and Isthmians of all shades tramped into Runnels's private office in the rear of his mule stables, looking for jobs as drivers. From among them he selected forty men and swore them secretly into his Isthmus Guard. For weeks their only assignment was to loiter in the markets and plazas of Panama, Cruces, Gorgona, and Chagres, along the waterfronts and in the dives, with eyes and ears open and mouths closed. As they reported whatever they picked up to Runnels, he expanded his file of information.

Banditry continued unchecked, and the railroad officials grew impatient at the seeming lack of action. Then, one night in January 1852, the quiet little man from Texas struck.

Next morning, from the ramparts that had cost the

king of Spain a fortune, the Panameños discovered thirty-seven corpses hanged by the neck. All the races on the isthmus were represented; several, in the good old Wild West tradition, were respectably prominent businessmen. No questions were asked, no explanations were offered. Silently the citizenry looked at the spectacle and went on about its business.

Runnels's strategy had been masterful. If he had begun his campaign by putting his guards into uniforms and sending them out with the gold trains, to give battle only when the robbers attacked, the net effect would have been little more than an increase in casualties on both sides. As it was, he had cleaned out the bulk of the Derienni in a single stroke.

For three months all was quiet. The secret international committee began to breathe easy. But Runnels continued his undercover operations, keeping track of surviving suspects and suspicious newcomers. Then seven Americans who had left Panama as a party were found murdered near Gorgona, and that night the Isthmus Guard rode again. This time there were forty-one victims, and Runnels added variety by stringing them up to the gallowslike timbers that projected from the concrete face of the Sea Wall.

Now the false whiskers came off. Runnels sold his express business and began to police the gold route openly with his heterogeneous corps. Isthmian wits spoke of "Ali Runnels and his forty ex-thieves," which no doubt was partially true. Each guardsman was his own judge, jury, and executioner. Runnels was the only ranger chief on the American frontier who could admit publicly that his orders to his men were "Shoot first, then investigate."

Often the guards escorting the mule trains clashed

with outlaw bands. In the three more years that it took to complete the transisthmian railroad and put the bandits out of business, the corpses of more than a hundred highwaymen were left hanging from trees along the banks of the Chagres.

At least one U.S. citizen turned badman in the Chagres valley. Runnels learned of it through his operatives, and decided on a lenient course of action. He accosted the man in a bar on Avenida Norte.

"Jim Holmes," he said softly, "take the next steamer, and don't ever come back to the isthmus." Then he turned and walked out.

Holmes went on to California, and within a few months found himself in San Quentin Prison serving a sentence for robbery. From there he sent word to the Hon. John Bigler, California's "beer-drinking governor," that he alone knew the location of a $200,000 cache of California gold on the isthmus. Bigler pardoned him in March 1856, and sent an agent with him to recover the alleged treasure.

When they arrived at Panama, Holmes bowed to his escort and said:

"Tell Governor Bigler with my compliments that I will lay for him the next time his Excellency crosses the isthmus going east."

The California deputy had no authority on foreign soil. He went to the U.S. consul, who referred him to Runnels, who disliked having his banishments disregarded. Holmes was toasting freedom with a champagne cocktail at the Shades when a pair of Runnels's guardsmen arrived and marched him away to a lifetime of labor in the mines of Veraguas.

Perhaps Jim Holmes really had a fortune in gold buried somewhere in the Chagres valley. If he did, it is very likely still there. ¿Quién sabe?

Throughout the years of the gold rush an undercurrent of hatred ran between the Panameños and the argonauts, who wanted nothing of the isthmus except to get across it fast. Banditry along the renascent Gold Route spread into the cities at its termini. The isthmian press often carried items of news such as this one from the *Herald:*

"On Tuesday last an American was found dead in his room at the Pension Gonzalez. It is believed that he was murdered."

A serious outbreak came in May 1850, when an American chased and caught a Negro boy who had snatched his wallet in a crowded Panama street. The natives organized to rescue the youth, and the sojourners rallied in opposition. A battle royal ensued, in which two Americans and several Isthmians were killed. Lesser riots were common.

The worst of the racial disorders came on 15 April 1856, when one Jack Oliver picked up a slice of watermelon from a fruit stand near the Sea Wall and walked away. The vendor followed, shouting that the Americano had failed to pay. While a mixed audience gathered, Oliver handed the Negro a coin and told him to be off. But the huckster's dander had riz; he used fighting words, and drew a knife. At this Oliver pulled his pistol, and a bystanding Negro grappled with him. The gun went off, wounding an onlooker and setting off the "Watermelon War."

At the time there were three thousand California-destined Americans in the city, plus nine hundred eastbound passengers who had just landed from the S.S. *Golden Gate*. Disorders flared all over town. The enraged blacks invaded the hotels. Americans were beaten, their baggage carried off, their rooms looted. By nightfall hundreds of them, including about sixty women and children, had taken refuge in the railroad terminal, and a mob of natives was railing at the barred doors and windows.

"All the arms in the office," according to the official report of Amos B. Corwine, special investigator for the U.S., dated 18 July 1856, "were a double barrelled gun, a pair of pistols, a sabre, and fourteen old flint muskets. [These] were given out and loaded."

Police Chief Garrido turned out the local garrison. Shots from the mob were peppering the station when the constabulary came up on the run with bayonets fixed. The mob parted, and the fire of the besieged Americans killed one of the soldiers. At this the police "joined the people and commenced firing on the Depot."

The mob seized Governor Añino and threatened him with instant death if he did not turn over the keys to the arsenal. The governor shook himself free and replied, like a brave Castilian:

"I know that you would murder me. I know that you have long wished for a chance to do so. But listen, all of you: before I would issue arms for any purpose except to disperse this infamous mob, I would suffer myself to be torn limb from limb."

The rioters released him and returned to the attack. As they charged the building the Americans inside picked them off through cracks in doors and windows.

Colonel Garrido "sent on board the Taboga," the railroad's steam tender which was waiting to ferry passengers out to the *Golden Gate* as soon as the tide came in, "disarmed the passengers, and [carried] away the ship's gun."

In the waiting room of the station stood a rusty mortar from old Panama, which had been kept as a relic of the days of derring-do. Joe Stokes, freight agent, and Bob Marks, depot watchman, filled it with rivets and trained it on the door. When the bars seemed about to give, most of the defenders ran up the stairs while Stokes and Marks lit the fuse.

The blast killed one of the attackers and wounded several. But it also removed the door. The enraged natives poured through, caught and killed the two railroaders in the telegraph room, then killed several men and women who had tried to hide in the downstairs offices. But when they surged up the steps they were met by fire from above. Moving out of range, they cut the telegraph wires and were preparing to set fire to the staircase when Ran Runnels arrived with a posse of guardsmen, white Panameños, and Jamaica Negroes. The rioters found themselves besieged in turn.

After exchanging a few shots, they came out waving white flags and quickly dispersed into the crowd, which gave sympathetic refuge; only a handful were taken into custody.

When Corwine arrived at the scene some minutes later "a horrid sight presented itself, many dead and wounded, horribly mutilated, lay all about; the floor was covered with blood . . ."

The official figures were fifteen Americans killed and sixteen wounded. (Estimates of the mob's casualties ran from forty to as high as two hundred.) Corwine charged that the attack was "deliberately planned by the police and Mob," and urged "immediate occupation of the Isthmus, from Ocean to Ocean, by the United States [unless] New Granada [provides] proper protection and [makes] ample atonement."

Accordingly on 19 September a force of 160 U.S. Marines landed and occupied the railroad station. Three quiet days later they withdrew, ending the first "armed intervention" on the Chagres route. Washington based its action on the Treaty of 1846, with its guarantee that "free transit from the one to the other sea" be not "interrupted or embarrassed." The clause concerned "neutrality of the isthmus," but the United States had now interpreted it as a right to intervene against internal disorders as well. It was to become a far-reaching precedent.

Diplomatic haggling continued for nine years. On 18 August 1865, Bogotá signed an acceptance of full responsibility, and paid to the United States indemnities totaling $412,394.17.

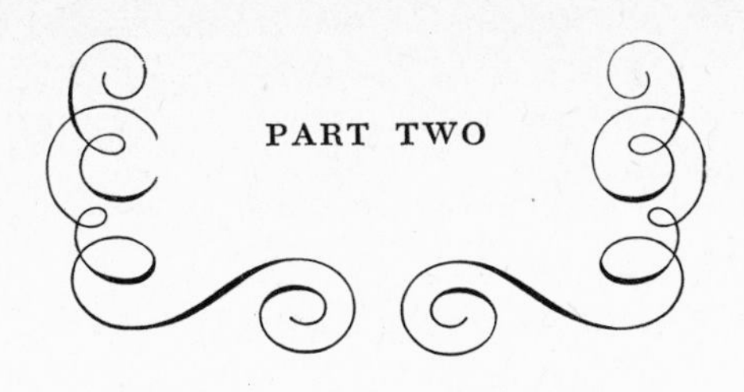

PART TWO

Ferrocarril

XXIII: *YANQUI* TOOTLE

SOON after the nineteenth century argonauts began their hell-raising on the sixteenth century gold route through the Chagres valley, another kind of tumult arose nearby in the jungle: a handful of Yankee engineers and native laborers started across the isthmus with the world's first transcontinental railway. The Panama Railroad was destined to be the costliest per mile, in both lives and dollars, and yet the most profitable railroad investment the world has ever seen.

John L. Stephens was the Roy Chapman Andrews of his day. He had gone to Central America in 1839 at the request of President Martin Van Buren to examine the various routes that had been proposed for an interocean canal. He had incidentally explored the Mayan ruins in Chiapas and Yucatán, and had written two volumes on Maya archaeology which are still the definitive works. He had also fallen in love with the Chagres river (which he recommended to the president as the best of the proposed routes) and had built himself a dream cottage on its banks a few miles above Bohío; it was there that he had done most of his writing.

William H. Aspinwall, New York capitalist of the early shoot-the-works era, had been laughed at in Wall Street for sinking his fortune in the Pacific Mail line. The discovery of gold in California had turned the laughter into a sickly grin. When he and Stephens called for a million-dollar subscription to finance their Panama Railroad Company, the wise money cried to get in, and even before the concession was negotiated the shares were selling at a handsome premium. The company was incorporated under the laws of the state of New York in April 1849.

As a poet, Stephens must have shuddered at the idea of a railroad running past his back door. But as a practical Yankee, he saw that the disturbance of his idyllic retreat could have compensations in the form of regular dividend checks. He accepted the presidency of the corporation and went to Bogotá to iron out the details of the concession.

With his knowledge of the Spanish language and temperament, Stephens was able to negotiate a very favorable treaty—what else would you call it?—under date of 15 April 1850, with these principal provisions:

(1) The company would be allowed eight years for building a railroad across the isthmus, with the southern

terminal at the city of Panama and the northern terminal wherever the company chose to locate it.

(2) The company would have access to all public land on the isthmus during construction, and afterwards would be allowed to select 250,000 acres, to which New Granada would give it permanent title.

(3) The terminals would be free ports.

(4) The company would be allowed to set such tolls as it saw fit.

(5) The treasury of New Granada would be paid a royalty amounting to 3 per cent of each dividend paid to the stockholders.

(6) New Granada would have the option of purchasing the railroad 20 years after the first dividend was declared, upon payment to the company of $5 million; after 30 years for $4 million; 40 years, $2 million. After 49 years title to the entire property would pass willy-nilly to the government, without reimbursement to the company.

(7) The company would put up $120,000 as security, to be refunded with interest upon payment of the first dividend and to be forfeited if the road remained unfinished at the expiration of the construction time limit.

(8) New Granada agreed not to allow the construction of an improved highway, a railway, or a canal anywhere on the isthmus to compete with the company, without the consent of the directors, for the life of the contract.

Now the company had the capital, and it had the monopoly. All it had to do was build the railroad. . . .

George Law, another Wall Street wolf who had founded the steam-packet service between New York and Chagres, attempted to muscle in with a clever bit of speculation. To help him apply the squeeze, he engaged an American soldier of fortune known as Colonel Zwingle, who had figured in several of the recent revolutions in the banana republics. Zwingle appeared at Porto Bello with a satchel full of greenbacks and in a few hours bought up all the land along the waterfront between the Black Swamp and the far end of the harbor; then he and his wife settled down in the choicest cottage on the beach as caretakers of the estate, while Law confronted the railroad directors with what he thought was a corner in real estate for the Atlantic terminal.

It is not known what price he demanded for his land, but it must have been high, for the directors elected instead to take the road across the swamp. Certainly they had no conception of what they were asking of their contractors when they determined that the Atlantic terminal would be at Manzanillo Island. On the map it looked good enough, being a few airline miles closer to Panama than was Porto Bello; and the Black Swamp was public land, which would cost the company nothing. No one had thought of trying to scalp the company on the real estate there, and homesteading would have been impossible anyway. The crocodiles, scorpions, tarantulas, cockroaches, and mosquitoes were the only claimants. The discomfited Law sold his property back to the natives at a considerable loss, and Colonel Zwingle returned to the revolution circuit.

Colonel George W. Hughes of the U.S. Army Topographical Corps arrived at Chagres early in '49 at the head of a group of military and civil engineers to begin the preliminary survey. By the end of May the job was done; Captain John J. Williams had discovered a hitherto unknown pass in the Cordillera which was only 275 feet above mean sea level, and had driven a stake among the mangroves in the soppy surface of Manzanillo Island to mark the beginning point.

The army engineers commented, in their reports to the secretary of war, on the feasibility of a canal. Hughes called it "more than problematical, unless the consideration of cost be disregarded." He was compelled, he wrote, "to largely increase" previous estimates: "It will not be very extravagant to place it at . . . $50,000,000." Captain Edward W. Serrell was even gloomier. "The very considerable length through the base of the water-shed," he wrote, "together with the fact that no adequate sources exist for the [water] supply of a summit level and lockages . . . must forever preclude the possibility of connecting the two oceans at this point by water communication." (He had seen the Chagres only during the brief dry season, and apparently envisioned a summit level much higher than the 85 feet of the present canal.)

The contractors were George M. Totten and John C. Trautwine, who had had previous experience at tropical engineering on the project known as El Dique—the canal from Cartagena to the Magdalena River at Calamar. On a May morning in 1850 they chartered a string of bungos at Yanqui Chagres, ushered aboard a handful of American assistants and a dozen Indians with machetes, and paddled coastwise toward the projected terminal. Gingerly they stepped ashore on the narrow coral rim around the 650 sunken acres of Manzanillo, as the nearby crocodiles submerged in the ooze and came up at a safe distance to watch the invaders. Instantly a cloud of mosquitoes formed around each man, darkening face, neck, and hands. The newcomers slapped until their exposed areas were coated with dead insects, and then set to work.

While the Indians hacked away at the underbrush, Trautwine and his assistant James L. Baldwin stood knee deep in the mire and plied their axes into the trunk of the nearest coco palm. Soon there came a half-joking shout of "Timber!" as the stately tree crashed onto the beach. Then another, and another, and the Indians began to take up the cry. (Today, half a world from the North Woods of Paul Bunyan, the native slang of the isthmus includes the word for use as a warning of any kind.)

The party had brought along several tents, expecting to pitch them and live on the island. But there was not a dry spot. Even the thin band of beach was covered when the slight tide of the Gold Coast rose. So the men piled into the boats at dusk and paddled back to the American village at the mouth of the Chagres. There the engineers hit upon a simple solution to the problem of quarters:

Close by the landing pier languished a leaky 200-ton brigantine, so old and weather-beaten that name and nationality were indeterminate. Her captain and crew had followed her last billet of passengers up the Chagres toward California. Many a reclaimed hulk, having brought a load of argonauts this far, had been thus abandoned. Most of them had been dismantled to provide wormy timbers for the building of the gold-rush settlement at Chagres, but this vessel had another fate in store. The party plugged her leaks and laid in a supply of food; next morning the *Orus* interrupted its river run to tow her to Manzanillo.

The men sharpened the tallest coco trunks and drove them into the mire for piling. Across the butts they laid rough planking, and atop this they erected a large shack in the hope of moving ashore. But spiders, lizards, and tarantulas entered the shelter in such numbers that it could not be occupied. The nameless brig, anchored in the lee of the island, provided the only quarters of the working party for several weeks.

Every few days Totten chartered the *Orus* for a recruiting run to Cartagena. On each trip he brought back scores of laborers, but most of them deserted after a week or two and went to work for the California Transit. At the end of June he had a total of forty-one workmen on his rolls. So he doubled his rates.

By now the ancient brig was so badly infested with insects below that all hands were forced to sleep on deck, in the continual rain of the deepening wet season. Many of them remained violently ill all night, due to the constant motion of the vessel. As more recruits arrived, sleeping space on the open deck shrank until the men had to lie across each other's legs.

Then a decrepit steamboat, the *Telegraph*, was abandoned at Chagres, and soon found itself anchored beside the brig. This relieved none of the men's hardships except the crowding; and by the end of July there were a hundred workers, so they were as crowded as ever. But the clearing of the island went on apace, reducing the number of insects and forcing the reptiles to withdraw to the mainland. By the end of August it was possible, after an all-out campaign of slaughtering bugs and spiders, to occupy the shack. Others were built around it.

The force had grown to four hundred, and the island was practically clear. Mosquitoes were fewer, but they had had their day; now the men began to come down with the fevers that had been planted in their blood. The labor crews alternated between a week of work and a week of babbling prostration on the bare floors of the shacks. There were no doctors, no medicines; convalescents carried food and water to the acute cases. The death rate was one in five per month, or, as the Census Bureau would express it, 2,400 per thousand per annum. Little wonder that the workmen continued to desert in droves, despite announcements of pay increases almost weekly. The paymaster began to dole out money for immediate needs (rum, tobacco, mamacitas), holding the bulk of each man's earnings as collateral to be forfeited if he should desert.

The contractors watched the soaring wage rates and saw that they would be broke even before the clearing of the mainland had begun, so they petitioned the company to release them. An amicable settlement was reached; the company retained the contractors on salary and pursued construction by spending its own capital.

Steamers carried part of the labor force, including fifty newly arrived Irishmen, up the Chagres to Gatún, and they started working back through the swamp toward Manzanillo. The directors sent down a doctor, who built hospitals at both places. Soon they were overflowing; rarely did as many as half the workers answer to roll call even during their on-week. Disease and death thus continued to dog the builders through the five years that it was to take to build a roadbed less than fifty miles in length. But the ill wind at least brought the hospitals a neat profit, from shipping cadavers in wholesale lots to medical schools all over the world.

Totten barnstormed the Gold Coast again and again, and by December had more than a thousand workers on the rolls. Docks went up around the island, and steamers began to arrive daily with construction materials, machinery, food, medicines, and recruits. Grass-roofed shacks grew into a solid line around the four-mile perimeter of Manzanillo. Stores and saloons opened. When a shipload of dusky whores arrived from Cartagena, and then another from Havana, the town had all the essential aspects of the average tropical fleshpot.

Baldwin was in charge of the running of lines and the locating of track on the mainland. He carried his lunch in his elephant hat, and at noon raised his insect veil to eat it, standing waist deep in the fetid ferment of the swamp amid envious crocodiles and snakes. The great reptiles occasionally attacked workers who got too far from the group, hence many of the men carried revolvers as well as machetes. The combination of feverish blood, swamp air, nagging insects, and tropical fatigue was not conducive to patience and sweet reason; the men quarreled with each other over nothing, and sometimes settled it with their six-guns. There was nothing that Baldwin could do about it, except to draw a pencil line through another name on his grimy payroll.

During December a shipment of pile-driving equipment arrived, and work began on the building of a roadbed into the swamp. Progress was by inches, with the bog swallowing up unbelievable amounts of ballasting material. For weeks the working party stood immobile a few yards inland from the coral strand that marked the shore, while an endless chain of carts dumped rocks into the mire with no apparent effect. Finally the foreman, an Irishman, went to Baldwin and announced that he was ready to quit.

"What's wrong?"

"Well, the first sounding showed solid earth at 180

feet. I've dumped three thousand tons of material there, and it still tests 180 feet. I was afraid you wouldn't be satisfied with the progress I am making."

"Nobody's dissatisfied," replied Baldwin. "Getting the roadbed up above the water is my job. Your job is to keep throwing stuff down there until I tell you to quit. Go back and get to work."

In February a Philadelphia-built locomotive and several open cars were unloaded, and the laying of rails was begun. The train shuttled from the pier to the end of the track with loads of crushed rock, dumping its freight off the end until it had built up enough bed for the track crew to lay another section of rail. It took a month of this to reach the low ridge that rose two miles inland from the edge of the swamp. The first high ground that the rail layers reached they called Monkey Hill, because it seemed to be the simian metropolis of the Chagres valley. There they built the official cemetery of the Panama Railroad, which was named Mount Hope.

Across the ridge was the Black Swamp again, and the dumping of ballast was resumed for another four miles. More rolling stock arrived; spur tracks on the shore were laid, and the volume of dumped materials multiplied. One locomotive with dump was assigned to the job of building up the surface of Manzanillo, and another went to work filling a causeway to the mainland. Soon there was a link of solid earth, and Manzanillo was no longer an island. Now the daily funeral train ran direct from the hospital across the artificial isthmus and through the jungle to Monkey Hill, where a crew of carpenters and painters worked full time at turning out white crosses.

In April the double line of steel emerged from the swamp and entered the newly built station house at

Gatún. The celebration of the event was informal: an Irish section foreman and his crew of Negroes and Indians got soused on native rum and cheerfully shot up the village with a rusty arquebus they had found in the ruins of San Lorenzo.

It had cost more than the entire original million dollars of capital to clear Manzanillo Island and lay seven miles of track across the swamp to the eastern bank of the Chagres at Gatún. The directors in New York called for another stock subscription to provide more capital, but Wall Street knew the situation on the isthmus; the new issue went begging, and the earlier certificates soon were being offered at ten cents on the dollar with no takers. Aspinwall and Stephens had to keep the project going on their personal credit.

The flow of materials ebbed; employment rolls were reduced, and work slowed to a snail's pace. The wolves of Wall Street laughed again. But not for long.

In October two side-wheelers, the *Georgia* and the *Philadelphia,* lost several lives while trying to land passengers at Chagres during a storm. Then the weather grew even worse, and forced them to run into Navy Bay for shelter. When the passengers saw the construction trains shuttling into the swamp toward Gatún, they set up a clamor to ride them.

Totten was sorry, he had no passenger coaches. But that made no difference to the argonauts. Totten then objected that he had received no orders as to the rates that should be charged.

"All right," said the passengers, "we'll pay you double whatever you think would be the highest fare that your directors could ever dream of."

Expecting to get rid of them, Totten finally announced that he would transport them to Gatún at their own risk for 50 cents a mile plus $3 per hundred pounds of baggage. Before he could change his mind the eleven hundred travelers piled their mining tools onto a string of flatcars and clambered aboard. As the first Golden Gate Special of the Panama Railroad huffed over the causeway, Totten looked after it unbelievingly with some seven thousand dollars of U.S. currency piled in his sun helmet.

Thereafter all steamers landed at Manzanillo, and Yanqui Chagres sank into oblivion. Passenger coaches were rushed down from the States, and trains were run to connect with all steamers. The seven completed miles of road began to yield a small fortune in revenues almost daily. The news reached Wall Street, and Panama Railroad stock began to perk up. When the directors proffered another $4 million of stock to finance the remaining construction, the wolves snapped it up.

By the following March the track reached Bohío Soldado, the second station on the east bank of the Chagres, eight miles above Gatún. On the 15th a daily service of freight and passenger trains was inaugurated from Manzanillo to Bohío, first class fare $5. From there the bungos charged $3 to Gorgona.

There were big doings on the erstwhile island of Manzanillo 21 February 1852, when the cornerstone of the first brick building was laid. Railroad officials, the consular corps, and isthmian leaders assembled. The orator of the day was Victoriano de Diego Paredes, New Granada's minister to the United States, who pointed with pride to the bond of friendship between the two countries etc., praised the acumen and energy of the road's founders etc., predicted prompt completion despite the tremendous obstacles etc., and wound up by suggesting that the terminal city which was growing up where he then stood be named in honor of that great financial genius, etc. etc.

The directors liked the idea, and so the terminal city on Manzanillo, which previously had been known only as Otro Lado (Other Side), was christened Aspinwall. Notices were sent out, postal guides were amended, steamship offices were advised, seamen's charts were brought up to date, and Aspinwall took its place among the cities of the world.

But when the government at Bogotá heard about it, there was hell to pay. The hotheaded envoy was recalled, his suggestion was repudiated, and an order was issued naming the new city Colon in honor of the island's discoverer. The railroad directors objected, pleading fait accompli and contending that they should be able to name their own terminal whatever they pleased. Bogotá replied, truly enough, that the town was still under New Granadan sovereignty. Very well, said the railroad, you call it Colon, and we'll call it Aspinwall.

For years there was exasperating confusion. Mail was addressed variously to Aspinwall, Colon, Colon-Aspinwall, Aspinwall-Colon, Colon (Aspinwall), and Aspinwall (Colon). Some maps said one thing, some said another.

There was one tragicomic result. A Dutch shipmaster on his first voyage to the new port piled his vessel up on the rocks just east of the mouth of the Chagres, with the loss of several lives. At the investigation he produced his charts, which showed "Aspinwall-Colon."

"I vass zailing vestvard for de port of Colon," he related. "I zailed past dis Aspinvall, vich I could zee vass de name on de port buildinks. Unt now look blease at dis chart; iss not Colon after Aspinvall? I zailed on for dis Colon, unt instead it iss rocks!" His insurance was paid.

In the 1870's the squabble reached high government levels. The U.S. Department of State, having espoused the cause of the railroad, commissioned a consul to the port of Aspinwall. But the minister from Bogotá refused to grant him an exequatur, saying that there was no such town in his country. Irked, Secretary of State Hamilton Fish changed the appointment from "consul" to "commercial agent," for whom no exequatur was needed.

Finally in 1890 the government at Bogotá issued an order to its department of posts that any matter addressed to Aspinwall or any variation thereof be returned to sender. Aspinwall, said Bogotá, did not exist, and Bogotá set out to prove it. The railroad, facing huge confusion in its mail service, had to knuckle under, and Colon it has been since.

At the time it ceased to be Otro Lado, Colon was a bustling city of some three thousand men and a few dozen women of various hues. The railroad and the port were the principal industries, with the hospital, the hotels, the undertakers, and the prostitutes close behind.

The harbor did not offer adequate protection from the frequent storms, and many a vessel was broken up on the rocky coast before the railroad got around to building the breakwater that extends today from Toro Point. The built-up land of Manzanillo was not much safer for the rolling stock; it settled here, and sank there, so that a locomotive dump had to be assigned permanently to the job of filling the holes. The yardmasters were careful not to let a string of cars stand very long in one spot.

The best hotels were the Howard, the City, and the

Aspinwall, which charged $3 a day for first-class passengers. There were a dozen smaller ones with lower rates for second-class travelers. "It is well," advised Otis in his handbook, "to have the terms well understood beforehand."

All the land on which the town stood was the property of the railroad; it leased the areas which it did not require for its own use at an annual rental of $18,000.

The town had no convenient source of fresh water (a pipe from the Chagres at Gatún was being laid), and so the buildings had huge catch basins rising above them; the rain reservoirs had to be large enough to hold a four-month supply, to tide the town over the dry season. These open-topped wooden tanks became lushly inhabited by wigglers, frogs, insects, and a variety of water plants. No one was ever free of intestinal disease.

The American mechanics and the better-paid railroaders of other nationalities restored themselves periodically from the wastage of the fevers and the foul water by going on a regimen of champagne cocktail, using quinine for bitters. These binges served also to lighten for them by several shades the color of the women, who occupied tiny verminous stalls along Bottle Alley and employed barkers to stand in the ankle-deep mud of the street, describing their charms and propelling passers-by through their saloon-type swinging doors. In time the bottles that had been tossed into the street formed a solid surface beneath the mud, and when the pavement-laying crews arrived years later there was no need for them to put down a gravel base.

A queer incident occurred in May 1852, when a group of French workers at Bohío Soldado mutinied, raised the tricolor over the newly built station house, sang "La Marseillaise," and refused to discuss their grievances in any other language than French.

President Stephens happened to be at his cottage, which stood only a short distance down the Chagres from the village. He climbed into the cab of the locomotive that had stopped to bring him the news, and ordered the engineer to back it all the way to Bohío. He announced to the mutineers (in English) that he would be glad to hear their troubles, but only after they had taken down their flag and replaced it with the Stars and Stripes.

The Frenchmen made no move to comply, so Stephens climbed back onto his train and went home, sending orders to the commissary that no food be sent to the strikers until they went back to work. A few hours after the next day's ration train failed to arrive on schedule, a passing dump engine noticed that the American flag was back and the mutineers were hammering away at their jobs. Stephens prudently let the sleeping dog lie.

But, since the Frenchmen declined to talk about the matter in English, no one ever found out what was eating them.

That summer, as the track inched southward along the Chagres toward the Gold Road rest station of Tabernilla, cholera swept the isthmus. Besides hundreds of laborers, it took the lives of fifty-one Americans—almost the entire roster of planners and supervisors. President Stephens was among the victims. Work stood still for weeks until replacements arrived from the States.

In September the workers reached Barbacoas, 23 miles from Colon, where the plans called for the railroad to cross the Chagres. Since the situation was disorganized anyway, the directors decided to try the contract system again, and signed Minor C. Story to build the Barbacoas bridge and complete the line to Panama for $3,500,000.

Story imported a shipload of Irishmen from County Cork, and soon had the bridge almost complete. Then a freshet carried away one span, and the entire structure collapsed. Next the fevers wiped out almost all of his labor force. He brought in more Irishmen, and they started afresh, but by now his resources and credit were exhausted; when his twelve-month contract expired the bridge was still unfinished. Stephens's successor, William C. Young, with nothing to show after a year in the saddle, resigned.

The railroad again took up the work on its own. It chartered cattle boats and sent agents all over the world to recruit labor; Irishmen, Englishmen, Welshmen, Scots, Frenchmen, Germans, Hindustanis, Malaysians, Chinese came in by the shipload—more than seven thousand in all. Using timbers from the piny woods of Georgia, this great force built the vastest wooden-trestle bridge the world has ever seen: more than 600 feet long and 50 feet above normal stage of the Chagres. The first engine crossed our river 26 November 1853.

But by now the mosquitoes had done their work, and the new laborers began to sicken and die. Only a few dozen of the Europeans survived, and the hardy Asiatics fared only a little better.

The Chinese contingent suffered worst of all. In December, as the track neared Matachín, their opium supply ran out. The railroad, which had agreed to provide it in addition to their food, had failed to order new stocks against future needs. With half their fellows already dead of the fevers, and with the comfort of their drug denied them, the coolies resorted to mass suicide. They strangled themselves with their queues, hanged themselves from trees along the river, threw themselves on their machetes, weighted their clothing and jumped into the Chagres, paid the Malaysians to shoot them.

The railroad rushed a handful of morose survivors to Jamaica, where the Chinese colony welcomed them. It offered a lame defense of its neglect by pointing out that the laws of the state of New York, under which the company was chartered, forbade the unlicensed dispensing of habit-forming drugs.

Because of this occurrence, amateur etymologists have theorized that the name of Matachín station came from a contraction of the Spanish for "dead Chinaman," but they are wrong. Matachín also means "butcher," and the village is so named on prerailroad maps of the Chagres valley.

The cattle boats made more recruiting voyages, this time to Caribbean islands and ports. The work went on, with dark-skinned Jamaicans, Cubans, Haitians, Cartagenans, and local talent. In January 1854, the track crossed the continental divide, 37 miles from Colon and 11 miles from Panama. In that month a shipload of equipment and laborers was sent around the Horn to Panama, and soon another track began to inch its way northward from the Pacific terminal toward the Chagres.

The two crews met a year later at a point some five miles north of Panama. At midnight of 27 January 1855, under a pelting rain, the last rail was laid. Next morning a Philadelphia-built locomotive crossed the Chagres neck from sea to sea—the world's first crossing of a continent by a railroad train.

On the return journey from Panama, with the consular corps and prominent Isthmians on board as guests of the railroad, the train jumped the track after passing Emperador. The distinguished party walked the ties to Obispo, and arrived very late at Aspinwall for the special dinner that had been prepared.

Canal Zone folks tell visitors today that every tie of the original Panama Railroad cost a life. This is an exaggeration. A literal-minded employee in 1860 spent his vacation walking the track to count the ties, and came up with a total of 94,326. (Other counts have varied somewhat from this, according as they included spurs and terminal yard trackage.) The railroad's official estimate of deaths during construction was 6,000. The actual figure, based on an average of calculations by several impartial authorities, was about twice that.

XXIV: AN ODYSSEY OF ULYSSES

In the rainy season of 1852 the 4th United States Regiment of Infantry, en route to its new station in the territory of California, disembarked at Aspinwall with all its equipment, including wives and children. Cholera was raging on the isthmus; the regimental surgeon warned everyone before they went ashore not to eat or drink native products nor to associate with the local people.

The regimental supply officer arranged with Superintendent Totten for special trains to carry them to the end of the track, which then lacked about a mile of reaching the future bridge site at Barbacoas. There he organized all available bungos and set in motion a shuttle service which took two days to ferry all personnel and equipment up the surging Chagres to Gorgona. During this time many of them began to feel the dreaded abdominal pains.

The main body of soldiers set out from Gorgona to march overland in single file to Panama, while the supply officer, the surgeon, and a detachment of guards and orderlies remained behind to shepherd the women, children, and sick men upriver by bungo to Cruces. There the supply officer contracted with the mule transport agencies to carry the party on to Panama at 11 cents per pound. But individual travelers, who were paying from 16 to 20 cents per pound for the service, also were waiting; the mules that had been promised to the army failed to materialize. The thwarted officers went on a quiet drunk.

On the third day at Cruces, the suspected cholera cases began to enter the acute stage, and other members of the party developed early symptoms. While the supply officer haunted the transport agencies demanding mules, the surgeon paddled down to Barbacoas, hiked to the end of the track, and from there pumped himself on a handcar back to Aspinwall, to trace his medical supplies which had not been forwarded as promised. Superintendent Totten gave him a special train to carry them back, but when he arrived at Cruces he found five of his charges already dead of cholera. He and the supply officer, between rounds of native rum, discussed the transportation agencies of the isthmus in specific terms.

Five days they held at Cruces, while a dozen more deaths occurred; finally the supply officer went out to round up mules at any price, intending to force the contractors to pay the difference. The two officers, aided by an occasional bracer, worked from daybreak one day until noon the next dispatching the party.

The movement to Panama was "a straggling one," chronicled Captain Charles S. Tripler, the surgeon, because "the moment a rider or a cargo is placed upon a mule's back that moment he must set out, or the muleteer strips his mule and carries him off." Once mounted, each ailing man made his own way. The women and children traveled in a makeshift convoy, with the two officers bringing up the rear. Three deaths occurred on the Cruces trail.

At Panama they found the main body long since arrived and nursing its own newly sick men at a bivouac on the waterfront. The surgeon went to work on his new patients while the supply officer paddled out to the *Golden Gate,* which had contracted to transport the entire regiment on to California. But the captain refused to take aboard any person with the slightest symptoms of cholera or other tropical disease, nor would he carry any women or children at army rates; it wasn't in the contract. The supply officer argued, to no avail, and the *Golden Gate* sailed 3 August with only 450 officers and men aboard. Again the surgeon and the supply officer were left behind to care for the stragglers and get them on to California as best they could.

The surgeon set up an infirmary in the U.S. consulate, with wards for cholera, dysentery, and yellow fever, and for days on end did not take off his clothes. Military funerals were held almost hourly, while the supply officer tried to find a ship that would transport his charges; he was treated like a leper. Finally, after a week of appealing to patriotism and human kindness, he persuaded the captain of the *Northerner* to take them all.

The regiment had lost eighty officers and men, plus an unrecorded number of dependents, in its brief stay on the isthmus. Little wonder that the two rear-guard officers drank heavily on shipboard all the way to San Francisco.

When the Union Pacific Railroad's transcontinental route was completed seventeen years later, the necessity for army travel via the Chagres valley was eliminated. And no one in the whole United States was happier about it than President Ulysses S. Grant, former supply officer of the 4th U.S. Infantry. Grant had seen firsthand the crying need for a waterway between the oceans. And while the nations squabbled over how and where, he showed again the tenacity that had brought him victory at Appomattox: he declared himself for a canal to be owned and operated exclusively by the United States. The principle became the keystone of our foreign policy until its realization.

XXV: THE RAIL ROUTE

THE TRANSIT of the isthmus, which had taken the Indians, the Spaniards, and the early argonauts at least four days, now required less than four hours. But it had lost little of its former picturesque variety, and had added a few noteworthy novelties.

Along the western shore of Manzanillo was the native market place, El Mingillo, where Negroes and Indians sold fish, cassava, bananas, plantains, coconuts, oranges, and other produce from bungos lined up on the beach. Customers of all races crowded around large steaming kettles of sancocho, the meat-and-vegetable stew that is the national dish of the Panameños. Nearby stood the railroad employees' clubroom, with billiards and other games and a library of "several hundred volumes."

On the Avenida Central of Aspinwall (Colon) were colorful shops operated by Chinese, Turkish, Syrian, and East Indian merchants in addition to the larger enterprises run by Yankees and Europeans.

A noteworthy business was the Boston & Panama Ice Company, whose branches at each of the termini had brought to the Chagres country its first sight of frozen water since the Ice Age. In its special refrigerator ship, the company dispatched cargoes of 700 tons of ice from Boston and considered itself lucky if it delivered 200 tons to its isthmian retail establishments. The ice sold at first for 50 cents a pound, but as volume increased the price dropped to 10 cents. In 1862 we find the enlightened isthmus receiving ample supplies of "natural ice from Sitka, in Russian America," at 1 cent a pound.

Beyond the business district were the railroad yards, maintenance shops, wharves, and warehouses, fringed on the oceanfront with vessels of sail and steam from all the ports of the Atlantic. Snipe, plover, teal, heron, and pelican, noted Otis's handbook, "abound along the shore."

From Aspinwall the trains clattered across the artificial isthmus and plunged into the Black Swamp, with its queer animals, colorful birds, and profuse vegetation. A few minutes later the traveler saw, rising from the watery jungle, the grassy pate of Monkey Hill with its thousands of white crosses. There the old-timers among the engineers were wont to whistle a long blast as a salute in passing.

On reaching "the seventh mile-post," Otis narrated, "you emerge from the swamp and come to Gatún station, on the eastern bank of the Río Chagres, at this point about fifty yards in width, and here makes a great bend, opening beautiful vistas through the dense forests up and down its course. Gatún station, like all the others on the line, was a two-story frame house with wide verandas all around, providing quarters for the division superintendent and his crews of track workers and fuel-wood gatherers. It had "a little garden in front, where roses and peonies, pinks and pansies of our northern clime challenge comparison with the orchids, fuchsias, and passifloras of the tropics." On the opposite bank of the river sprawled the native village of Gatún.

"From there the road lies along the base of an irregular line of high lands that rise up from the eastern side of the Chagres valley, and crosses the Río Gatún, a tributary, by an iron truss-girder bridge of 97 feet span. Close on the left are Lion and Tiger Hills, [so called because their] thousands of monkeys made the nights miserable during construction days." Which was no mean accomplishment.

After passing the next station, Ahorca Lagarto (Hang the Lizard!), the trains entered a dense forest of cedro trees, with a sprinkling of mahogany, lignum vitae, and other valuable varieties, all covered with orchids. Bohío Soldado was next, and a mile beyond it was a freestone quarry which supplied ballasting materials for the maintenance crews. Half a mile farther stood the remains of Poet-Railroader Stephens's cottage.

"The Chagres winds like a great serpent along this tortuous valley" as the trains followed it past the native village of Buena Vistita to Frijoles station, where scarlet and purple passion flowers dominated the landscape.

Next came the crossing of the Chagres over the great boiler-iron bridge at Barbacoas, and half a mile farther up the west bank of the river stood San Pablo station, where the land was originally broken and worked by the Jesuits two centuries before. Just past there yawned a quarry of volcanic rock, then the trains entered Mamei station near the native town of Gorgona. Here the road "turns from the river bank through a deep red-clay cut, sweeps around a hill, and enters the meadow-lands of Matachin, where the Chagres appears again, broadened now by the tributary flow of the Obispo." (Otis was led by his flowing words into a technical aberration: he was traveling upstream, and so had passed already any broadening of the Chagres which the Obispo may have caused.)

At Matachín station, roughly halfway across the isthmus, was a system of sidetracks by means of which trains passed each other in opposite directions. There the natives operated stores in their huts, selling fruits, cakes, and dulces to the trainloads of waiting passengers. There was also a saloon which offered "English beer and French claret."

From Matachín the road entered the Obispo valley, crossing the stream twice within a mile, passing Obispo station and continuing along the riverbank through a rolling woodland of mango, zapote, nispero, and guava to Emperador station (twisted by the Americans into Empire). Next came Summit, or Culebra, boasting "three hotels which were imported ready-made from the States," where more than a thousand men and women often were "promiscuously accommodated for the night." It was here, before the road was finished, that "travelers mounted mules and floundered on through heavy sloughs, along deep ravines, over precipitous mountains, in drenching rain and scorching sun, often plundered by bandits, for the remaining twelve miles to Panama."

Beyond Culebra the trains passed through a 40-foot cut almost half a mile in length, which represented man's first nibble into the natural saddle between the two oceans. Then it began the descent toward Panama.

A mile from the summit the road passed along the base of a huge balsatic cliff, whose great crystals averaged a foot in diameter and twelve feet in length, lying at about forty degrees from the perpendicular "as they are in the Fingal's Cave at Staffa and along the Palisades of the Hudson."

Three miles farther stood Paraíso station. Thence the road continued around hills and through ravines to Río Grande station, passing through the shadow of the Cerro de Buccaneros, where Morgan bivouacked the night before he attacked Panama. "Then around the base of bald Mount Ancón, and a mile further into the Pacific terminus, with the city of Panama to the east."

Along the railroad's 500-foot waterfront at Panama mingled a hodgepodge of seagoing craft from the tropical, temperate, and frigid ports of the Pacific, similar to those which crowded the docks of Aspinwall. Among them steamed several 100-ton launches, owned and operated by the railroad for assistance in servicing vessels of too great a draft to reach the wharves.

Thus, in the 1860's, ran the Chagres valley's unequaled overland link between East and West.

Like all but a handful of the medical men of that day, Dr. Otis took no stock in the theory of mosquito-borne diseases. "It is not known that a single case of sickness has occurred during or in consequence of the transit since the entire opening of the road in 1855." The diseases that "previously had raged across the Chagres valley were of a purely malarious character . . . always found resulting from great exposure and fatigue . . . unavoidable while transit was performed upon mules and in open boats, [taking up to] five days, the traveler frequently obliged to live upon the vilest food, and sleep upon the wet ground or in the but little less comfortable huts of the natives; the comfortable railway carriage, and the passage from ocean to ocean reduced to *three hours*, having fully demonstrated a *perfect* immunity to the traveler from all those varieties of sickness long popularly recognized under the head of *Chagres Fever*."

The good doctor, as might be surmised, was an official of the Panama Railroad at the time he wrote this premature clean bill of health for the Chagres neck.

XXVI: MIDAS ON WHEELS

DAILY railroad service each way across the Chagres valley was inaugurated 15 February 1855. The governor of Panama declared a three-day fiesta, with fireworks, free bullfights and horse races, special trains, and banquets.

The right of way was open, but the road was far from finished. For months there was trouble along the route; cars and engines continually jumped the track, because the roadbed was soft in many places and the weight of each passing train shifted the track slightly. Once a dumping crew left its train standing in the Black Swamp and ran into the foliage in pursuit of a passing school of marmosets; when they returned an hour later with several captured pets, they found that the swamp had opened up and swallowed their engine, tender, and six dump cars. Landslides frequently blocked the tracks.

Construction crews were maintained at full strength for four more years, ballasting soft places with rock, replacing timber trestles with bridges of iron on abutments of stone, replacing soft pine ties with termite-proof lignum vitae (so hard that it had to be drilled and bolted to the rails instead of spiked), reducing grades and straightening curves. A 450-foot pier was built at Panama, wharves and stone warehouses went up, and the temporary structures that housed the maintenance shops at both ends of the road were replaced with brick buildings. Across the Chagres valley, on poles set in concrete alongside the tracks, stretched the wires for one of those newfangled Morse electric telegraph inventions.

These improvements and additions were made without the issue of new stock, by spending the $2,125,232.31 that the road had taken in for part-way travel before the line was completed. The construction account was closed as of 1 January 1859, showing expenditures by the company of $8 million. But the road had actually cost considerably more, for it had bankrupted two private contractors whose losses did not show on the company's books.

As of the same date, the gross earnings of the road totaled $8,146,605.91. After operating costs, the net balance was $5,971,728.66. This from a railroad whose overall length was 47 miles 3.02 feet.

The first outrageous fare of 50 cents a mile had continued in effect while the road was under construction, and was raised slightly for the complete transisthmian journey to $25 gold. (Children under 12, half price; under 6, one-fourth price.) Personal baggage, 5 cents a pound. For travelers who could not afford to pay such rates, the railroad offered steerage passage in cattle cars for $10 gold, and extended the privilege of walking its tracks from sea to sea for $5.

Freight rates were equally unbelievable. Cattle $7 each, horses $40 each, at owner's risk. Coconuts, 1 cent each. Express, $1.80 per cubic foot. Gold (dust, nuggets, ingots, or coins) and jewelry, 25 cents per $100 of value. Coal (owner's load, unload, and risk), $5 a ton. Rosin and pitch, $1 per barrel. Etc.

THE UNEQUALED

OVERLAND LINK

For the next fifteen years the Panama Railroad was the most important link between the United States and its western frontier. Each year it carried twenty thousand passengers each way across the Chagres valley. In the five years ending with 1859 it transported more than $300 million of California gold and 100,000 bags of U.S. mail without loss.

The postmaster general paid the railroad a flat $100,-000 a year to carry the mail. The general freight business was equally lucrative. In 1860 a visitor in the stone freight depot at Colon noticed "bales of quina bark from the interior, piled many tiers deep; indigo and cochineal from Salvador and Guatemala, coffee from Costa Rica, cacao from Ecuador, sarsaparilla from Nicaragua, ivory nuts from Porto Bello, copper ore from Bolívia, silver bars from Chile, boxes of hard dollars from Mexico, gold ore from California, hides from the whole range of the north and south Pacific coast, bushels of glistening pearl-oyster shells from Panama fisheries, North American beef, pork, flour, bread, cheese; English and French goods, a train of cattle cars on which huddled a hundred meek-looking llamas from Peru, en route to Cuba, among whose mountains they are used for beasts of burden as well as for their wool."

Three months after the right of way was opened, the directors met in their offices in New York's Tontine Building (88 Wall Street) and declared a 6 per cent dividend. Three months later came another. As they followed again and again, thus yielding 24 per cent per annum, the stock climbed until it was the highest on the New York Stock Exchange. Four years later, when the construction account was closed, the directors decided to compensate the stockholders for the road's expenditure of revenues for capital improvements by declaring a 40 per cent stock dividend. The announcement reached the floor of the exchange while the stock stood at 250. It dropped immediately, under fear of a watering manipulation, but the next day the subdivided shares were selling at the same old price.

After a decade of astronomical earnings, the directors bethought themselves of the clause in the original contract with New Granada (which meantime had restyled itself the United States of Colombia in 1863) whereby that country would be able to take over the property in 1875 by paying $5 million to the company. Since this amount represented less than a fifth of the then value of the road, Colombia would be sure to exercise its option, and so the directors ordered Superintendent Totten to go to Bogotá and negotiate a new contract on the best terms that he could secure.

Bogotá drove a hard bargain. In return for releasing the company from its option and granting a new lease of 99 years (beginning 7 July 1867), the railroad had to (1) agree to carry the Colombian mails and government employees free; (2) assume the payment of an annual subsidy to Colombia of $250,000 in addition to its 3 per cent royalty on each dividend; (3) undertake millions of dollars' worth of improvements at both oceanfronts; and (4) pay to Colombia a cash bonus of $1 million.

Soon every Colombian with political connections had a lifetime pass as a "government employee," and thereafter the annual total of deadheads often exceeded the number of paying passengers. The politicos sent their farm and mine produce and even their livestock across the Chagres valley by first-class mail. In effect the company was giving Colombia free railroad service at great expense and at the same time was paying a hefty assessment for the honor. The revenues of the road in those days came almost entirely from its interocean trade.

But the Golden West continued to boom, and the road's profits, despite these new burdens, continued to climb. For its first fifteen years the dividends never dropped below 6 per cent per quarter, and often ran higher. The rosiest year of all was 1868, when the 31 December dividend brought the total for the four quarters to 44 per cent. In the following week the stock rose to 348, which was double the quotation for New York Central, the next highest on the board. Each dollar invested during the ten-percent-of-par construction days now represented a redemption value of $48.72, in addition to the $50.40 it had earned in dividends.

Four months later (10 May 1869), at Promontory Point, Utah, the last tie of the Union Pacific's transcontinental route was laid. The hammer that drove the famous gold and silver spikes echoed three thousand miles to southward across the Chagres valley, sounding the death knell of the greatest prosperity that any railroad has ever known.

XXVII: MEN WANTED

EVEN though it was paying double the Stateside wage rates and providing free maintenance and medical attention, the company had great difficulty in keeping its workers longer than a few weeks. Every California-bound steamer carried dozens of erstwhile railroaders who had succumbed to the gold fever.

The road required a record high proportion of man-hours per car-mile. The line had a total of 176 waterways, most of them less than ten feet across. The fills, cuts, and bridges had to be inspected and repaired after each freshet. The track required so much attention that permanent maintenance crews were assigned to each four-mile section. The U.S.-built rolling stock had to be repaired constantly, for its lumber rotted quickly in the tropics. (In time the original wood of the coaches and freight cars was entirely replaced with hardwoods found along the right of way. Visitors marveled at the opulence of a railroad whose boxcars were of solid mahogany.) The timber cutters also had the job of replenishing the stacks of wood alongside the track at each station; even at high wage rates it was cheaper than importing coal for fuel. Labor and materials for upkeep and operation averaged higher than $20,000 per mile of track per year.

To help maintain its army of workers at full strength, the railroad bought ten stern-wheelers and established the Brig Line (New York-Aspinwall), which operated for fifteen years without a major mishap except that its *Magdalena* was caught and burned by the Confederate prowler *Alabama*. The Brig steamers carried recruits to the isthmus with the understanding that they would be entitled to free passage on to California by Aspinwall's Pacific Mail after six months of working on the railroad. Thus the road's personnel, except for a few key men, remained in constant flux. Thousands of forty-niners got to California by virtue of a stint of railroading in the Chagres valley.

One day Superintendent Totten strolled into the employment offices at Colon and stood by while a shipload of workers, newly arrived from New York, filed past the interviewing desks to get their assignments. One of the recruits bulked larger than the rest, with massive shoulders and heavy, gnarled arms. Totten caught his eye and beckoned him out of the line.

"Name?"

"Tom Sharp."

"Read and write?"

"Enough."

"Prizefighter?"

"Somewhat."

"Ever been licked?"

"Not hardly."

"Want a better job than the ones they're passing out over there?"

"Sure."

"Then listen. At Frijoles the trackmaster is Sean Donlan, the toughest Irishman on the isthmus. I have fired him several times, but he won't quit. And whenever I send a man over there to relieve him, Donlan beats him to a pulp and piles him on the next train back here. If you can lick him, you can have his job. Four dollars a day. You hire and fire."

"I'll try it."

"Here's my pass. Good luck."

Donlan was in the station when the train stopped and Sharp got off. He eyed the newcomer suspiciously.

"Looking for trouble?" he asked hopefully.

"Looking for a job."

"You look stout enough. I'll put you on."

"I'm here to put myself on."

"Eh?"

"It's your job I'm looking for."

"Oh!" The Irishman rubbed his hands in anticipation. "You know you have to lick me first?"

"So I hear."

The Irishman took him cordially by the arm and led him outside to a circular clearing which had been fenced off for a flower garden.

"What style?" he asked, as they stripped off their balbriggans.

"Any way you like."

"London Prize Ring?"

"London Prize Ring it is."

"That takes seconds, and a referee, and such."

"We'll let that part go, eh?"

"Right."

The Irishman bowed the visitor over the low pickets, and stepped in after him. They shook hands, took stances toe to toe, pumped their arms like piston rods, and began to smash each other with their hamlike fists. Within a few minutes the polyglot station crew had surrounded the ring, shouting encouragement in Chinese, Hindustani, Spanish, English, and several African dialects.

Soon both men were bleeding at nose and ears. The audience, volunteering as seconds, brought buckets of water and set them down by the fence.

"Time?" asked the Irishman between labored breaths, without lessening his blows.

"Reckon so."

They dropped their arms and stepped backward. Each one picked up a bucket of water and drained it, then raised another and dumped it on his head.

"Time?"

"Reckon so."

They toed up and went at it again. Each one went sprawling into the dirt several times. Their faces grew unrecognizable; blood caked on their bodies; their tired arms began to flag. Lower dropped the Irishman's guard, until the American saw his opening. Summoning the last of his strength, he crunched his fist into Donlan's chin. The Irishman spun round and crashed through the railing into a mango trunk, face first. His arms flopped around the tree, and after a moment he slowly crumpled to the ground.

The American rolled him over and dashed a bucket of water in his face. The Irishman opened his bloodshot eyes, and motioned feebly to get up.

"Out?" asked Sharp.

Donlan tried a second time to marshal himself, but could not stir.

"Bejesus," he whispered, and closed his eyes.

An hour later the afternoon freight pulled up, and Totten swung from the caboose to the ground. In the station he found Sharp and Donlan, washed clean and coated with arnica.

"Come in, colonel," said the Irishman, "and meet the new trackmaster of Frijoles." The superintendent shook Sharp's swollen hand.

"Meet my assistant," said Sharp, waving toward Donlan.

"But he's fired," said Totten. "That's what I sent you out here to take care of."

"Sure he's fired, by you. But don't I hire and fire on my gang?"

"Certainly."

"Well, he's hired again, by me."

Totten pondered for a moment and shrugged. "Hired it is," he said. Then he turned and walked out to the train, signaling to the engineer as he stepped aboard.

BOOK FOUR

WESTWARD PASSAGE

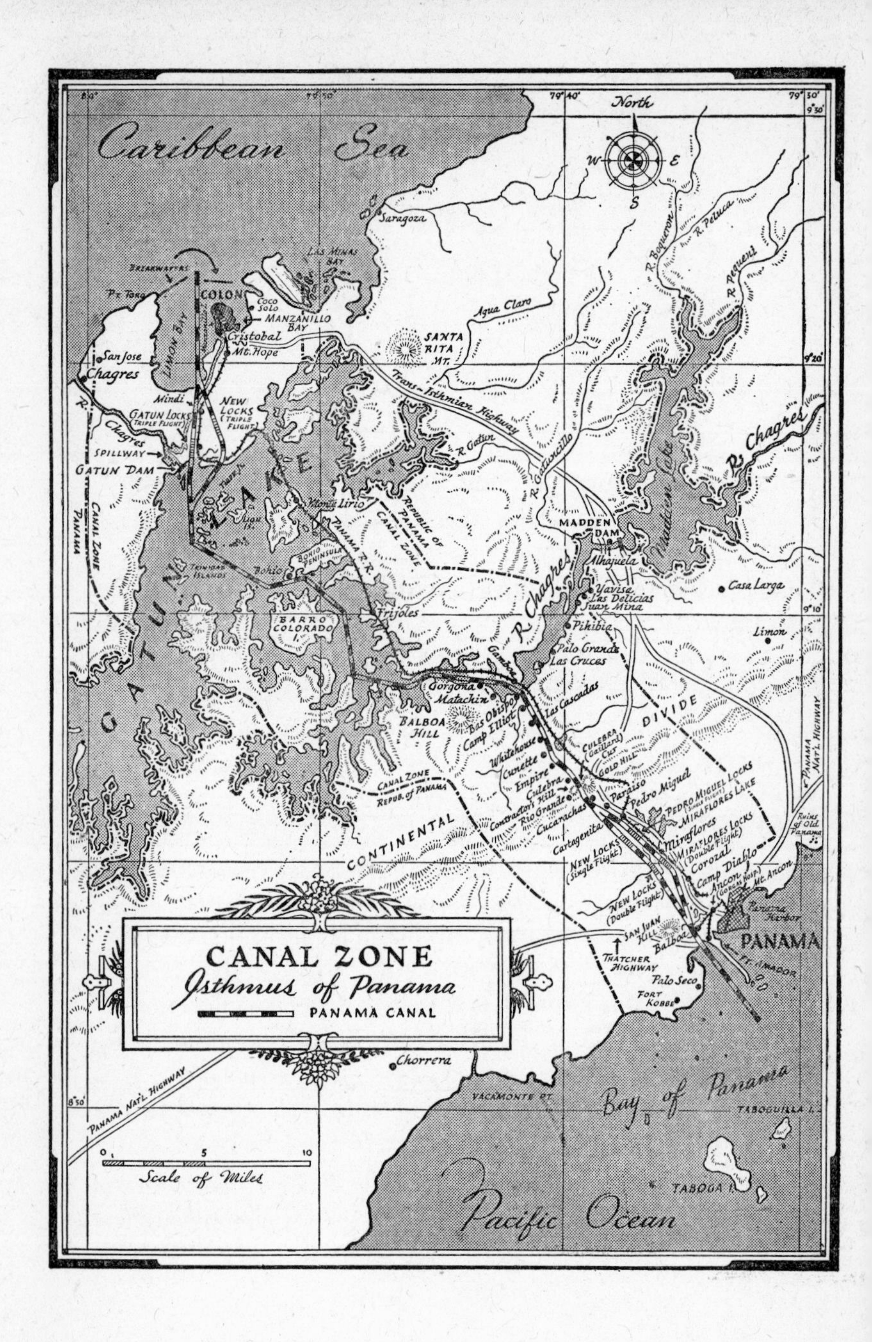
CANAL ZONE
Isthmus of Panama
PANAMA CANAL
Caribbean Sea
Pacific Ocean
Bay of Panama
Scale of Miles

XXVIII: DAWN OF THE DIGGING DAYS

COLUMBUS had dreamed of a Westward Passage. After him Spain had surveyed and debated a canal across the isthmus of America. After the Spanish hold on the new continent had been broken by Simón Bolívar, all the seafaring nations of the world had continued to discuss and negotiate.

A close approach to a final contract by the United States came 14 January 1869, when diplomatists of Washington and Bogotá signed a convention providing for a cut across the Chagres neck, inside a zone twenty miles wide which would be subdivided into lots fronting on the canal and "equally distributed between the two Governments" so as to alternate in sovereignty. The concession was to run for a century and then revert to Colombia without compensation. But the Colombian senate rejected the treaty before the U.S. Senate could bring it to a vote. This elicited from Panama a threat to secede, whereupon Colombia offered a revised contract; it was rejected by the United States.

Colombia turned to dickering with the other Latin-American countries for a co-operative pool to build and operate a Chagres canal, but got only verbal encouragement. Meantime President Grant reopened the question of the best site; he ordered the navy to make new surveys of all the proposed locations, from Tehuántepec to Urabá.

The navy's surveying party, headed by Commander Edward P. Lull, studied the Chagres route from every angle, but could see nothing in our river, canalwise, except a hindrance. The only solution they could suggest was to take the ships across the Chagres at Matachin, through a colossal overhead viaduct, 1,900 feet long, which would be supported by twelve massive culverts. The summit level would be 124 feet above the sea, with twelve locks on each side.

The navy's first choice was the San Juan River. And so, after its reports were in, the U.S. Interoceanic Canal Commission on 7 February 1876 decided unanimously on the Nicaragua route. A canal on the Chagres, it commented, "would probably be subject to land-slides, from which the Panama Railroad has suffered seriously, and . . . would be exposed to serious injury from floods. The cost [would] exceed by nearly fifty per cent that of the Nicaragua route."

Washington was still debating the merits of the commission's opinion a year later when a surveying party from Paris, representing the newly organized Société Civile Internationale du Canal Interocéanique du Darien, arrived at Colon. In charge was Lucien Napoleon-Bonaparte Wyse, a lieutenant of the French navy and natural son of Princess Laetitia.

One trip across the Chagres valley in a railroad coach was enough to sell Wyse. He left his assistants to work on topographical details while he made a record-breaking dash to Bogotá: by sleeping and eating in the saddle he reached the Colombian capital eleven days after his arrival at Buenaventura. On 20 March 1878, he received a concession similar to that held by the railroad; it allowed three years for surveys, two years for organization of a working party, and twelve years for construction; the diggers would deposit 750,000 francs with Colombia by 31 December 1882, to be forfeited if the canal was not completed within the time limit; Colombia pledged 500,000 hectares (about 1,235,555 acres) of public land; the builders agreed to indemnify the Panama Railroad to the satisfaction of its directors, and to pay an upsliding scale of royalties to Colombia, beginning with 5 per cent of the gross receipts for the first 25 years of operation, minimum $250,000 a year. At the end of 99 years the entire property would revert to Colombia without compensation.

Wyse hastened to New York to negotiate with the railroad directors, and was offered three choices: (1) a contract to provide all transportation necessary for construction, at the end of which the road would be sold outright to the canal company; (2) a lease of the entire railroad property during the work, followed by sale; or (3) a sale of controlling interest in the road at $200 per $100-par share.

From there Wyse went to Washington to invite the U.S. government to send delegates to an organization meeting in Paris. He was encouraged by President Hayes and Secretary of the Navy Richard W. Thompson, but was coolly treated by Secretary of State William M. Evarts.

"I had a difficult interview," wrote Wyse. "M. Evarts, believing that he could detect the hand of the French government . . . and not understanding that, on account of my relationship to the imperial family, I actually had to bear the [republican government's] ill will, obstinately refused to appoint two commissioners . . . Thereupon I rose and told him firmly that I really cared very little about [U.S.] participation . . . M. Evarts [finally] promised to send two official delegates."

In the end Washington sent eleven representatives, headed by Admiral Daniel Ammen. "You will take part in the discussions," instructed Secretary Evarts, "[but] you are not authorized to state what will be the decision of the Government of the United States . . . or the line of action it will pursue."

The Congress International d'Etudes du Canal Interocéanique opened 15 May 1879 in Paris, with Count Ferdinand de Lesseps, the builder of the Suez Canal, presiding. De Lesseps was, as Mack observes, "neither an engineer nor a financier. He was a promoter—a promoter whose ambition was not the accumulation of wealth but the accomplishment of tasks called impossible by lesser men."

De Lesseps had led a storybook life. In 1869 he had emerged victorious after a ten-year battle against nature and international politics at Suez, during which the world had laughed at him for undertaking an "impossible" task. Ten years before that he had saved the Empress Eugénie from a mob at Tuileries. As a widower of 64 years and five sons he had wooed and won the 21-year-old Louise Hélène de Bragard, one of the most beautiful women of France, who bore him nine more children. He was le grand Français of the century.

His eldest son Charles had tried to reason with him: "What do you expect to gain at Panama? Money? You will concern yourself with it no more at Panama than you did at Suez. Glory? You have acquired so much that you can afford to leave some for others. All of us who have worked at your side are entitled to a little rest. Certainly the Panama project is a magnificent one [and] I believe it is practicable . . . but what risks those who direct it will have to run! Remember that the Suez canal, during the ten years required for its construction, was almost daily on the verge of bankruptcy . . . You [won out] by a miracle; should not one be satisfied with one miracle in the course of a single life . . . ?"

Still, it is easy to understand how de Lesseps, having cut through the great land mass of the East, would want to round out his abundant life with a final blaze of glory, to gain an untouchable niche in history, by cutting through the great land mass of the West.

In his opening address, de Lesseps asked that the assembly proceed "in the American fashion, that is, with speed and in a practical manner, yet with scrupulous care."

He formed the 136 delegates, representing 23 countries, into committees and subcommittees, and they set about evaluating the several proposed routes, estimating construction costs and probable revenues, and considering the most effective type of organization to undertake the task.

The Chagres came in for discussion, pro and con. The Americans, who still clung to Nicaragua as the best route, held that a sea-level canal at Panama would never overcome the disruption of sudden floods. A French engineer, Godin de Lepinay, came surprisingly close to the eventual solution; he wanted to dam the Chagres near Gatún and the Río Grande near Panama to create a vast intershed lake about 80 feet above sea level, in which the anger of Chagres floods would be dissipated. He thought that six locks on each side of the lake would be enough.

But the committee decided that "the construction of such [locks and] deep excavations of highly dubious stability, as well as the measures designed to restrain the Chagres, present [too] many difficulties and unpredictable contingencies," and so de Lepinay and the Americans were overruled. The congress resolved (far from unanimously) on 29 May "That the excavation of an interoceanic canal at sea level, so desirable in the interests of commerce and navigation, is feasible; and that, in order to take advantage of the indispensable facilities for access and operation which a channel of this kind must offer above all,"—meaning perhaps the existing railroad—"this canal should extend from the Gulf of Limón to Panama Bay."

Promptly the Compagnie Universelle du Canal Interocéanique de Panama was formed, and the société was paid ten million francs for the Wyse concession. Amid wild enthusiasm and applause, de Lesseps announced that "I have accepted the leadership of the enterprise."

In his closing address the conqueror of Suez remarked:

"Two weeks ago I had no idea of placing myself at the head of a new undertaking. My dearest friends tried to dissuade me, [but] if you ask a general who has just won a battle whether he will try to win a second, he cannot refuse."

And so it fell to the French to make the first dirt fly.

Word of the great things to come arrived in the Chagres country when Superintendent Totten was requested by the compagnie to head an engineering commission in a detailed survey. The group spent several weeks on its task late in 1879, and estimated a cost of $168,600,000 (exclusive of overhead, interest, and the price of the railroad) and a construction time of eight years for a sea-level cut, with a diversionary dam above Gamboa to take care of the Chagres.

Then on 30 December the French stern-wheeler *LaFayette* steamed into the harbor at Colon, carrying Count de Lesseps, his wife, three of their daughters, and a party of engineers, contractors, and news reporters. Aboard swarmed a welcoming delegation of consuls, Colombian officials, and Yankee railroad men for a gala reception in the saloon "with plenty of champagne."

Railroader Tracy Robinson was amazed at de Lesseps' energy at his advanced age. He described the great promoter as "a small man, active and vigorous . . . French in detail, with winning manners and . . . magnetic presence. When he spoke, the hearer would not fail to be convinced that whatever he said was true."

De Lesseps discussed the canal enthusiastically, but made only general comments whenever specific difficulties were pointed out by the receptionists. His standing reply to such questions was a firm "The canal will be made!"

One M. Le Blanc, a French merchant who had lived for years on the isthmus, told the count bluntly:

"If you attempt to build a canal here, all the trees of the Chagres jungles will not provide enough wood for the cemetery crosses that will be needed."

"Never mind," replied de Lesseps. "The canal will be made!"

That night the party came ashore for a stroll along the beaches and streets of Colon. As de Lesseps first set foot on the soil of America, the Panama State Band struck up "La Marseillaise" and fireworks arced out over the bay from atop the icehouse. The virtually naked native children gave him the same reception that distinguished-looking newcomers get today: they crowded around his feet, somersaulted, turned cartwheels, did intricate rumba steps, and sang "No tabaco, no papel, no dinero, damn it to hell!"

De Lesseps laughingly tossed them a handful of coins; as usual, the gang immediately doubled in size and redoubled its efforts to entertain.

Along the streets fluttered "the flags of all nations, with," noted the *Star & Herald*, "the notable exception of that of the United States."

Next morning the party boarded a special train for Panama, with the de Lessepses occupying the luxurious president's car. At Barbacoas they saw the reason why the delegation from the isthmian capital had not been on hand the day before: a sudden flood had undermined the great iron bridge across the Chagres, rendering it unsafe for heavy loads; on the other side idled the special train from Panama, with its delegation gathered beside it.

The Colon party minced across the bridge on foot, with de Lesseps himself boldly taking the lead. Midway he paused and glared down at the swollen Chagres as it swirled angrily among the girders.

"A flood like this," observed Robinson, "would play hob in your canal."

"True," nodded the count. "We shall have to divert this torrent into the Atlantic well above the canal line. It can be done," he shrugged, "at no great cost." Then, as he beckoned the tie walkers on, he added sternly:

"The canal will be made!"

On the left bank de Lesseps embraced Presidente Damaso Cervera, and there was more champagne all around.

At Panama an even more elaborate welcome had been prepared. A borrowed circus tent stood near the railroad station, to keep the Chagres sun from wilting the starched whiteness of an elite Colombian regiment and from overheating the cushions of the six-horse open carriages that were to carry the party. When the train whistled from beyond Mount Ancón, the guard of honor poured out of the tent and formed ranks. The soldiers presented arms, and the newcomers clattered off through the arch of the Plaza Santa Ana, underneath a banner of flowers which read: "Colombia Salutes Ferdinand de Lesseps," down flag-lined Avenida Central with its crowds of cheering Panameños to the Grand Hotel, where a lavish banquet had been laid. The speeches and toasts (each followed by an interpreter) lasted well past midnight. There was dancing in the streets, and fireworks sizzled continuously skyward from the cathedral plaza.

The first dirt was about to fly.

The formal inauguration of work on the canal interocéanique was held the following afternoon; always a showman, de Lesseps had scheduled his trip so that the occasion would fall on New Year's Day of a new decade.

At the Sea Wall waited the railroad's steam launch *Taboguilla,* with champagne on ice in the cabin. The party came on board betimes, but there was engine trouble. Everyone sat around and sipped champagne; finally they sailed, two hours behind schedule, for the point on the bay (near the future site of Balboa) where the French engineers had decided to place the Pacific entrance of their canal.

On the way de Lesseps called his entourage together and spoke:

"Under the authority of the United States of Colombia, with the blessing of Monseigneur the Bishop of Panama"—count and bishop exchanged bows—"in the presence of the members of the Technical Commission for the Final Study of the Universal Interoceanic Maritime Canal"—Colonel Totten returned the count's bow for his group—"Mlle. Ferdinande de Lesseps"—his seven-year-old daughter, nicknamed Tototte, stepped forward and made her best curtsy—"on this first day of January, 1880, will give the initial blow of a pickax on the point which will mark the entrance of the canal on the side of the Pacific Ocean. All present will then successively strike a blow in sign of the alliance of all the peoples who contribute to the union of the two oceans for the good of humanity."

Parenthesized cynic Robinson: "Great applause and more champagne."

But by the time the delayed launch neared the proposed scene of ceremony, the tide had started out, and there was not enough depth to reach the beribboned stake.

De Lesseps had a handy solution to the problem. Chronicled the New York *World* correspondent: "He [again] called the audience together (a difficult task indeed, seeing that cognac and champagne had been freely distributed for two hours), and said that . . . the whole thing [would] be done right there on board."

With a little help from one of the railroad men, Tototte swung a gold-plated pickax, which had been brought from France, into a box of sand on the deck.

The others followed suit, the bishop blessed the undertaking, and there were "speeches and more champagne" on the return voyage.

Thus, in a manner of speaking, did the first dirt fly.

First dirt of actual excavation flew ten days later, when the same party detrained near the point where the railroad crested the Cordillera. To the usual accompaniment of speeches and popping corks, Mme. de Lesseps set off a dynamite charge which blasted several chunks of rock from the saddle between Gold Hill and Contractor's Hill. (Robinson the belittler could not resist the chance for a prophetic anticlimax; "The blessing had been pronounced, and the champagne, duly iced, was waiting," he wrote; "there the crowd stood, breathless, ears stopped, eyes blinking . . ." Then he did violence to the facts: "But there was no explosion! It wouldn't go!")

After six weeks on the isthmus, during which he traveled by bungo up to the projected damsite at Gamboa and down to the mouth of the Chagres, de Lesseps took his family aboard the *LaFayette* and sailed for New York, leaving his technicians to lay plans for the digging. On the voyage, de Lesseps the optimist looked over Totten's estimate, decided that it was too high, and offhandedly reduced it to $131,720,000.

The French challenger of the American isthmus cut a wide swath across the United States—from New York to San Francisco (via Philadelphia and Washington) and return (via Chicago and Boston). Receptions given in his honor by social and scientific organizations drew as many as eight thousand guests. He rode on the new elevated steam railways, visited marvelous skyscrapers in which "as many as six elevators were in constant operation," saw model police and fire departments called out for drills and mock rescues. "One minute and 47 seconds after the alarm was turned in," a French correspondent cabled his Paris newspaper, "the first engine arrived at a gallop."

But the country was cool to the idea of an American canal to be controlled from Europe. While Washington society was lionizing le comte, President Hayes sent a special message to Congress reiterating that "the policy of this country is a canal under American control." He pointed out that European control would involve armaments which the United States could not tolerate on its southern doorstep. The French promoter promptly cabled his Paris offices: "The message of President Hayes assures the political security of the canal."

De Lesseps announced that he had "reserved" $30 million in canal stock for U.S. investors, but Wall Street (undoubtedly under pressure from Washington) declined to broker the issue.

In April de Lesseps returned to Paris to supervise the final organization of his compagnie, which was capitalized at $60 million. As president (at $25,000 a year), he made his son Charles the subdirector of the company and seated a brother and another son on the board of directors. He also (it was disclosed in the French government's probe a decade later) authorized the distribution of 5 per cent of the first year's budget of $6,448,355.80 to the Paris newspapers which formerly had condemned his canal scheme. The scathing attacks turned overnight into paeans of praise.

Stock was offered throughout Europe, but the French press was the only one that had been subsidized; sales outside France were negligible. By the following March there were more than a hundred thousand French stockholders, of whom 99 per cent were owners of less than fifty shares each; sixteen thousand of them were women. The life savings of a tenth of the families of France had been tapped.

When the vital matter of closing out negotiations for control of the Panama Railroad came up, it transpired that the Wyse options were invalid. And a Wall Street syndicate headed by Trenor W. Park had quietly amassed a majority of the outstanding stock by small purchases at an average price of $125 per share. Now it demanded $250 per share. The compagnie was forced to pay some $18,900,000 for control of a road which at the time was worth, at best, no more than half that.

The railroad company, of course, remained a New York corporation, with a Yankee board of directors (elected by the compagnie) running things from Wall Street.

At whatever cost, de Lesseps at last had the men, the money, the tools, and the franchise. Soon the dirt of the Chagres valley would fly in earnest.

XXIX: *LE TEMPS DE LUXE*

THE TECHNICIANS whom de Lesseps had left on the isthmus pushed on with the final survey, and in their explorations they stumbled upon a moss-covered brass plate atop Cerro Grande, the highest mountain within sight of the lower Chagres. Grinding away the green mat with their boot heels, they uncovered a legend which is still decipherable:

"Dusommet du Cerro Grande, on aperqoit les deux Océans."

(It had been embedded there, 1,050 feet above the sea at a point from which both oceans could be seen, by their compatriot Napoleon Garella, who had surveyed the Chagres country in 1844 for another canal syndicate.) The new engineering party used it as their base triangulation point.

The stakes driven, they rounded up several hundred swarthy Isthmians for the job of cutting back the jungle from the line. On 1 February 1881, Chief Engineer Armand Reclus sent home a cablegram which was used verbatim by most Paris newspapers as the next morning's banner headline: "WORK BEGUN."

At first the laborers received 60 cents (U.S.) per work day, plus 30 cents, work or holiday, for subsistence. But they came off the line each Saturday for a weekend binge in Panama or Colon, and spent their Mondays nursing hangovers. So the superintendent ordered the Sunday food allowance withheld unless the workers spent that day in camp; promptly the entire force struck. Reclus withdrew the order so readily that the workers struck again almost immediately for a 50 per cent raise. This time he allowed two workless, payless days to pass before yielding, and there were no more strikes for a while.

Much of the route paralleled at close hand the railroad's right of way, and hence was more or less open, but much was still virgin Chagres forest; it took until the end of April to clear an unbroken strip across the isthmus to an average depth of eight yards on each side of the center line.

As French steamers unloaded thousands of U.S.-produced prefabricated buildings on the Gold Coast, warehouses and machine shops went up at Panama, Culebra, Gatún, and Colon, and construction villages mushroomed all along the line. The new French sector of Manzanillo was christened Christophe (now Hispanicized into Cristobal), and the largest canal settlement on the Chagres, near Gatún, was titled Lesseps City.

At year's end there were two thousand laborers, mostly Isthmians, on the rolls. On 20 January 1882, was held a second formal inauguration of digging in Culebra pass, accompanied by dynamite explosions, speeches, and champagne; the presidente proclaimed a valley-wide fiesta, with fireworks.

Laborers poured in, from Cartagena, Cuba, Martinique, Jamaica, and other Caribbean lands. Several hundred U.S. Negroes filtered down via New Orleans, and a shipload of native-born Africans came over from Senegal.

A few Chinese migrated from California, but soon quit the digging gangs to open restaurants and laundries.

The compagnie bought the Grand Hotel de Panama and remodeled it for use as administrative headquarters. The other hotels and rooming houses of the capital overflowed as they had during the California gold rush.

The opposite end of the line became again the beehive that it had been two decades before; a special correspondent of the Paris *Bulletin* wrote that Colon "is no longer recognizable . . . Its harbor is [crowded] with steamers coming and going . . . It is easy to find work, but difficult to find lodgings . . . There are three French restaurants, and an excellent new hotel [the International] catering to French tastes, with a French chef imported from New York."

European and United States engineering firms reaped staggering profits under a system of cost-plus contracts. Since higher costs raised rather than lowered their earnings, they bid recklessly against each other for the available labor; some say that they deliberately fomented strikes for better wages. The basic day's pay for unskilled labor finally leveled off at $1.80, with skilled workers receiving up to $5 plus maintenance.

Money flowed like water. The engineers and office workers, receiving unprecedented salaries, joined the dark-skinned laborers in spending all they made in the wide-open casinos of Panama and Colon, where one Edouard Reloise found that "*all* varieties of entertainment could be had." The wine and the women were "outrageously high-priced," he confided in a letter to friends at home, but the greatest money absorbent was gambling.

"Ah, cette roulette!" moaned Edouard. "How it bleeds the canal workers!"

The compagnie, observed the Chamber of Deputies committee following the probe, "always spent money as if it had too much." The investigators were particularly irritated by "immense stables which sheltered no fewer than a hundred thoroughbred horses," providing luxurious transportation about the terminal cities for officials and their friends.

Henri Maréchal, owner of a large block of canal stock who voyaged to Panama for a look around, wrote in 1884 that compagnie officials had used its funds and labor to build for themselves "a miniature Bois de Boulogne" on the banks of the Chagres, where they "entertain at charming picnic parties and make daily pleasure excursions on the company's horses . . . Ladies, possibly too swarthy but not too strictly virtuous, render these jaunts more pleasant and are repaid . . . by being carried on the . . . payrolls as laborers." If such a rustic retreat ever existed, no trace of it can be found today.

Critics of the French effort still take delight in telling about the "palace" that was built on Ancón Hill as the residence of director-general Jules Dingler; it cost slightly under a quarter million francs, but some references give the figure as a quarter million dollars—more than five times as much at the then exchange rate.

Undoubtedly M. Dingler lived well on the isthmus; besides his mansion, the company provided him with a specially built Pullman car (the old presidential coach was too shoddy) for his tours of inspection; he drew a hundred thousand francs a year in addition to full maintenance for himself and family and an annual all-expense vacation of three months in Paris. But he found nothing but sadness in his opulence. One by one his three children and then his wife succumbed to the fever; he went home in 1884 a broken man, and died in an insane asylum. (Years later, the U.S. canal builders sold the mansion on Mount Ancón for $25, on condition that the buyer remove it.)

The less scrupulous minor executives of the compagnie and its contracting firms paid their gambling debts and rewarded their dusky mistresses with luxurious furniture, which they acquired by requisition and then wrote off as destroyed. Because any friend of any acquaintance of any contractor, engineer, or canal official could get a railroad pass, the conductors found it futile to check their passengers for tickets; they gave it up, and the whole isthmus rode across the Chagres valley whenever it liked, at the expense of French peasants. It was almost as easy to borrow a horse and carriage with liveried driver for an afternoon or night. The people of Panama still refer to the French digging days as "le temps de luxe."

Shortly after midnight of 6 September 1882, the earth of the isthmus quivered, and its people scrambled out of their houses in terror. Within a few moments the plazas of the cities were "black with people." Twice more before dawn came lesser shocks. "While nobody was afraid," wrote Wolfred Nelson, a sojourning physician from Montreal, "the sociability was intense."

In the morning they found an irregular fissure, varying up to six inches in width, across Manzanillo, and another running southward along the right bank of the Chagres for three miles; its bottom in some places could not be reached with 200-foot sounds. Every village of the valley had suffered damage, and the Panama Railroad was disabled for weeks: the track from Colon to the divide was twisted and buckled; the roadbed in places had sunk and in others had risen; the great Barbacoas bridge was thrown out of line.

Hundreds had been injured by collapsing walls and roofs, but the only deaths seemed to be of a few elderly people whose hearts had failed. The ancient church at Las Cruces, in which Francis Drake had impounded the garrison before sacking the town, was a pile of rubble, and several historic arches in the terminal cities had fallen.

For the next four days there were occasional vibrations. No one dared to sleep under a roof; the entire population camped in the plazas of the cities and in the clearings along the canal line. Digging stopped short, and the laborers thronged the waterfronts begging the shipmasters for immediate passage (destination immaterial). About five hundred left.

The cable connections had been broken, so it was several days before the world knew what had happened. When the news reached Paris the price of Panama Canal stock on the Bourse dropped sharply, moving de Lesseps to issue a statement promising that there would be no more earthquakes at Panama.

After a week of outdoor vigil, the people decided that the disturbance was over. Life slowly returned to normal, and work on the canal was resumed. But for months afterward every household kept an upended beer bottle poised on the edge of the highest shelf, so that the slightest tremor would send it crashing down.

Man-made troubles came in the spring of 1885, when Rafael Aizpuru, a former president of Panama, staged a coup. For two weeks intrigue and bloodshed reigned on the isthmus; finally Pablo Arosemena, the current presidente, resigned his office and took refuge on a British warship in the bay. On 1 April, Aizpuru proclaimed himself chief of state.

Meanwhile another insurgent, a Haitian mulatto named Pedro Prestan, took advantage of the situation to seize control of the city of Colon. His gang of three hundred hoodlums looted homes and warehouses, tore up rails and canal-digging equipment, and forced members of the foreign colony to make sizable "loans to the cause." When the steamer *Colon* arrived with a cargo of rifles, Prestan demanded that the arms be turned over to him. The Pacific Mail agent refused, so Prestan jailed him, along with the U.S. consul, the railroad superintendent, and two officers from the U.S.S. *Galena,* and sent word out to its commander, Theodore F. Kane, that he would hold them until the arms were surrendered. If Kane should attempt to land a force, Prestan warned, he would shoot his prisoners "and every other American in the city." For answer Kane seized the *Colon* and hauled her away from the dock; then he brought up the *Galena,* landed a hundred Marines, and raised barricades around the railroad property.

Prestan was preparing to make good his threat when word came that a train full of soldiers was on the way from Panama. He led his men out to Monkey Hill and derailed the train, but the advantage of surprise was not enough; the soldiers poured from the coaches and drove the rebels back toward the city. Prestan, seeing that hope was gone, set fire to the town and disappeared into the Black Swamp. Nothing burns like Georgia pine; in a matter of hours Colon was a glowing heap of ashes. The conflagration left eighteen dead and ten thousand homeless.

Within a few days seven U.S. warships steamed into

Limón Bay, and three hundred Marines landed to guard the transit.

Three uneventful weeks later the Marines pulled out, with a great piece of news to report: only one man had died of yellow fever. The naval surgeon, F. M. Gunnell, had ordered "mosquito nettings for each man," as protection not from insects but from "the miasmic night air." He had hit upon the answer to Chagres fever without knowing the cause.

After three months of hide-and-seek with Colombian soldiers in the jungle, Prestan was captured and tried by court-martial. On 18 August the man who had caused twenty million dollars' worth of damage was hanged, in front of the Colon police station which he had used for his headquarters.

Political turmoil on the isthmus was one of the major causes of the French failure. Rafael Núñez, president of Colombia in 1883-1884, himself admitted that "the maintenance of public order was the exception, and civil war the rule." The hatred of foreigners that had flared into the Watermelon War continued to beset the canal builders. There was no "canal zone"; Colombian courts had jurisdiction, and they always found in favor of the native merchant and the native laborer against the foreign company.

Another prime factor in the fiasco was the problem of sanitation and health, over which the French had virtually no control.

"Colon," wrote a correspondent of the Paris *Journal de Débats*, "is a foul hole. [By comparison] the ghettoes of White Russia, the slums of Toulon, Genoa, Naples, and old Stamboul . . . deserve prizes for cleanliness. There are neither sewers nor street cleaners . . . toilets are quite unknown, all refuse is thrown into the swamps or onto rubbish heaps. Toads splash in the liquid muck . . . Rats infest the solid filth . . . [snakes] hunt both toads and rats; clouds of mosquitoes swarm into the houses . . . Need I say that the canal company has no authority at Colon?"

In the adjoining canal settlement conditions were far better, but the cleared strip between the towns (which had saved the French sector of Manzanillo in the burning of Colon) was not wide enough to protect it from disease. The Christophe hospital was as crowded as the others.

Panama was cleaner than Colon only because there was less rainfall. Between her flagstone sidewalks stretched boggy streets which received the refuse of the city. There was no sewerage. Moss-covered carts squeaked about town selling, at a penny a quart, water from a series of deep wells which Dr. Nelson found to be "receiving the drainage of one of the largest cemeteries."

Facing such handicaps, the compagnie did its utmost; it built infirmaries at each village, a vast general hospital in the shadow of Ancón Hill, and a convalescent sanitarium on Taboga Island where the standard fare included truffles, mushrooms, and rare French wines. Even Dr. Nelson, who had little respect for de Lesseps and his organization, conceded that they were "without doubt the finest and most perfect system of hospitals ever made within the tropics." Colonel Gorgas found them "very much better" than any in America "at the same period carried on by a firm or corporation."

But les médecins unwittingly turned their institutions into infection centers. They placed the legs of the hospital beds in pans of water, to keep ants from annoying the patients. The pans became breeding places for the mosquitoes which the world at that time did not suspect of carrying disease. Victims of fractures or dysentery usually developed the fever before they were dismissed; the death rate from yellow Jack and malaria among patients who had been admitted for other causes was double that of the force as a whole. The nurses (sisters of the Order of St. Vincent de Paul) and doctors, among whom the fever rate also was disproportionately high, shook their heads and opened the unscreened windows wider to dispel the "bad air" which they believed was the cause.

"If the French had been trying to propagate yellow fever," wrote Gorgas, "they could not have provided conditions better suited to the purpose."

During the eight years of operations by the compagnie, with a daily average of 10,854 employees (peak 17,615 in 1884), there were 5,527 deaths, of which about half were due to malaria or yellow Jack. The excellence of the French hospitals is attested by the fact that the death rate (calculated by Gorgas as 63.1 per thousand for the entire period) was less than one-fourth that of the railroad construction days. This despite the fact that there had been no material advance in medical knowledge of the Chagres fevers.

The sea-level project offered, theoretically at least, a far simpler over-all engineering problem than a lock canal. The idea was simply to dig along the line the surveyors had staked out, and keep digging until the ditch was deep enough to connect the oceans. The attendant complication of diverting the Chagres was left for the final phase, on the theory that it would help the excavators by washing tons of soil down to the sea. De Lesseps never accepted as final the contention by some of his engineers that a tide lock on the Pacific side would be necessary.

There is no question that such a canal could be made, at Panama or anywhere else, given enough money and enough time. It is easy to understand the Great Frenchman's desire to make a finished job of it, to create a Strait of Panama, through which the ships would steam under their own power, without the delay and expense of locks. Such a canal could be widened and deepened at small cost as the world built larger ships, while the largest locks would in time become obsolescent; once completed, a sea-level ditch would require comparatively little maintenance, and far less operating equipment and personnel. De Lesseps had as much right as Columbus to dream of a wide-open Westward Passage, and he was indifferent about expenditures because he was sure that his canal, once made, would bring in such a flood of money that its initial cost, however high, would fade into insignificance. The cost per cubic yard of excavation meant little to him, so long as each yard of earth removed brought him closer to his shining goal.

His great mistake was in grossly underestimating the magnitude of the task. Had he planned from the first on a lock canal, he would have avoided the waste of millions that went for digging a channel which today lies useless at the bottom of Gatún Lake. Or, had he called for ten billion francs in the beginning, the nation (or perhaps the world) that idolized him might have provided it (his first stock issue was apportioned at one share for each five requested). With careful expenditure, it might have been enough to build a temporary lock canal, which could have been carried down to sea level in leisurely fashion by using a fixed portion of its revenues for the purpose.

As it was, de Lesseps found himself obliged each year to revise upward his estimate of cost, to set back again his predicted opening date, to explain another time why progress had not measured up to his promises. Inevitably, public confidence waned; as the clamor to buy Panama securities changed into an avoidance of them, de Lesseps began paying "special commissions" to the manipulators on the Bourse and making extravagant claims in the well-paid press:

"A certain hill must be removed in the ordinary course of excavation; it is a gigantic mound of rock, but, far from being a hindrance, [it] is one of [our] best assets; for we are [assured] by our geologists that [it] is full of gold [and] that the ore from this place alone will be worth more than will be the total cost of the canal construction; that is, [the canal] will accrue to its stockholders as a *by-product* [of] one small part of the necessary excavation."

As the French steam shovels bit deeper into the saddle of the Andes, the soft earth crumbled from the hillsides again and again to refill the gap. The slides not only reduced the excavation gains; they buried shovels, engines, cars, and buildings, injuring and killing workmen. By the end of 1884 the diggers had removed forty million cubic yards of earth from the line, and its summit level still stood more than 250 feet above the sea. No gold had been found in Culebra Pass, but one of the knolls that today looks down on the finished canal is still known as Gold Hill.

Realizing that the compagnie would need far more

money than it could expect to receive from the sale of ordinary securities, de Lesseps petitioned the government for authority to sell $160 million in lottery bonds. The question divided French politics for three years, and brought about the resignation of several cabinet ministers; it finally became law 8 June 1888, but the position of the compagnie was by then precarious. It had been forced to borrow millions at usurious rates, and the situation was known on the Bourse.

As a last-ditch measure, when he still did not know whether his lottery bill would be enacted, de Lesseps had approved (October 1887) a revision of plan, providing for a temporary lock canal of five flights with a summit level of 161 feet. Philippe Bunau-Varilla, the engineer in charge of digging in the Culebra section, is credited with the idea, which called for the lock basins at each stage to be separated by their combined width. Once in operation, the canal would provide revenues with which the center-line summit level would be excavated to the level of the next lower stage, and thus that flight could be abandoned. In time all locks would in this way be eliminated.

For the building of these locks deLesseps engaged Gustave Eiffel, whose famous 300-meter tower in Paris was at that time the world's highest structure. The contract was so drawn that Eiffel received some $25 million, of which at least a fifth was clear profit, without completing a single lock. (Later the Deputies committee, in ordering him to refund $600,000, commented that "The negligence of the . . . company [here] shows up most blatantly . . . It is . . . obvious that [the] principal object was the purchase in a disguised form of the great engineer's name."

But Eiffel's name was not enough; less than half the

lottery issue was sold. On 13 December 1888, the compagnie petitioned for a 90-day moratorium on its current and bonded indebtedness. At a special session of the Chamber the petition was denied, and on the following day the compagnie went into the hands of receivers.

Desperately de Lesseps tried to organize a new company, but his erstwhile incomparable prestige was gone; underwriters could not be found. On 4 February 1889, the courts dissolved le Compagnie Universelle du Canal Interocéanique, and appointed a liquidator.

The news plunged the Chagres valley into chaos. When isthmian banks refused to honor French drafts, all canal work ceased; bills and payrolls were defaulted; merchants refused credit; riots flared in the construction towns. The imported laborers (who had been guaranteed repatriation) wandered about footloose; the crime rate soared. The British government rushed vessels to Colon and evacuated ten thousand of its dark-skinned subjects to their West Indian homes at $5 a head. Washington sent army and navy transports to rescue several hundred stranded U.S. citizens. Chile, needing immigrants to develop the country, offered free passage (one way) to Valparaiso for all comers; for months each southward sailing steamer carried away from Panama hundreds who had never dreamed that they would end their days as pioneers in the Chilean Andes.

Broken in mind and spirit, de Lesseps retired to his château, La Chesnaye, and spent the remaining six years of his colorful life in a wheel chair, oblivious of the great "Panama Scandal" that rocked the French nation, led to a parliamentary probe, caused duels, mental breakdowns, and suicides by the dozen, and sent many of the principals (including his son Charles) to prison.

The Chagres valley grew quiet. A handful of maintenance men stayed on to give indifferent care to the countless dredges, shovels, engines, and dumpcars that stood rusting along the lifeless line. Squatters, mostly former canal laborers, moved into the abandoned villages, settled down, and began raising crops.

"One of the most pathetic sights at the Isthmus," observed Fullerton L. Waldo, an American engineer, "is the decaying French machinery . . . steam shovels . . . rotting in the jungle on tracks that are mere wisps of rust . . . little top-heavy Belgian locomotives disgorging orchids at their cab-windows . . . [One] can poke his finger through the iron-rust in many a place."

While the Chagres flowed on undisturbed, the diehard advocates of the Panama route struggled to salvage something from the mess. Little was going on within the valley commanded by our river, but this was the most crucial period in its history: the 12-year construction limit was almost up, and the line across the Chagres neck was barely scratched; Washington was making ready to connect the oceans across Nicaragua; something akin to a miracle was in order.

Wyse, who had withdrawn when de Lesseps failed to give him what he considered a fitting position in the compagnie, stepped forward now in a spirit of self-sacrifice: "Only in me, the original grantee, are combined all the qualities needed for negotiating with [Colombia], and my special position is no less vital to the organization . . . which will complete the canal . . . I so completely personify the work . . . that its execution would perhaps be impossible . . . if I did not devote [myself] to it." He journeyed again to Bogotá, and secured a 10-year extension of his old franchise, to run from 28 February 1893. Then the liquidator, Pierre Gautron, wangled a further and final extension which allowed the ten years to begin 31 October 1894, on condition that a new company be organized by that date.

Meanwhile Bunau-Varilla tirelessly ground out books and pamphlets extolling the Panama route, and scoured the United States and Europe in search of backers; in March 1894, we find him in the Kremlin—about as far from the Chagres Theater as he could go—trying unsuccessfully to enlist the aid of Czar Alexander III.

It remained for Gautron to produce the miracle. He pushed through the Chamber a special law which empowered him to levy capital for the new company, in amounts approximating their anticipated fines, from the indicted officials, contractors, and financial manipulators who had profited hugely at the expense of the old. Everyone benefited. The courts were relieved of a maze of complex, protracted trials; the defendants saved their faces ("I emphatically assert," asserted Eiffel emphatically after "subscribing" ten million francs, which was one-sixth of the entire capital of the new company, "that my co-operation was spontaneous and voluntary"); the old stockholders saw a glimmer of hope for, if not profits, at least lighter losses.

The Compagnie Nouvelle du Canal de Panama was incorporated 20 October 1894, under a twelve-man executive board of whom "not one," it was careful to point out, "held any official relationship to the old Company." Later it created an advisory council of thirteen engineers representing six countries; the two Yankees were Brigadier

General Henry L. Abbot and Alphonse Fteley, chief engineer of the New York Aqueduct Commission.

The new board decided on a canal of four stages on each side (two locks at Bohío, two at Obispo, one at Paraíso, two at Pedro Miguel, one at Miraflores) with a summit level of 101 feet, and two dams across the Chagres (at Bohío and Alhajuela). It estimated the net cost at $102,400,000, and since the capital available for all expenditures (including interest and overhead) amounted to less than a tenth of this amount, it is obvious that the purpose was only to keep the concession alive while the directors tried to figure out what to do with it. In February 1895, a fresh engineering party headed by Maurice Hutin arrived on the isthmus and set about resuming the Sisyphean labor.

Their first preoccupation was with the horde of squatters on canal property. Under Colombian law, they had acquired limited rights by virtue of long unopposed occupancy, and it was necessary to negotiate settlements with 1,287 homesteading families before the line was clear enough to accommodate a new labor force. By the end of the year things were humming again, but on a soberer note and with a smaller volume. Le temps de luxe were over.

The new company at no time had more than four thousand employees, and it paid modest wages—so modest that it had occasional strikes even while there was a surplus of labor on the isthmus. It did import a few hundred workers from the West Indies, and one shipload from Sierra Leone. The latter group developed beriberi, which at that time was believed to be contagious, and dozens of them died within a few weeks of arrival; Isthmians, fearing that the disease might take root in the Chagres country, made such a fuss that the company shipped the survivors back to Africa.

The Compagnie Nouvelle built no palaces, kept no racing stables, let no fat contracts. Its activity was confined almost entirely to caring for acres of equipment and digging in Culebra Pass, which would be of value to either a sea-level or a lock-type canal. During ten years of operation it excavated 11.4 million yards, bringing the total for the entire period of French control to 72 million yards.

XXX: *INDEPENDENCIA*

When its franchise was half run, the directors of the Compagnie Nouvelle du Canal de Panama realized that the task of making a Westward Passage was too immense for any private corporation. And they knew that the United States would never permit its transfer to any Old World government. So they sent a delegation to lay before President McKinley a proposal for outright sale of concession, equipment, and work already accomplished.

The representatives of the bogged-down Chagres canal faced heavy handicaps as they arrived in Washington 2 December 1898. True, the Yankees were in a canal-building mood; earlier that year the battleship *Oregon* had consumed sixty-nine days in steaming at forced draft from San Francisco around the Horn to join the Atlantic squadron for the victory at Santiago. But Panama was still an international paradigm for graft, corruption, inefficiency, disease, waste, failure, scandal; again, the terms of the French concession would not admit of its sale to a foreign government without Colombia's consent. (Such consent was not likely; when the current and final extension expired, Bogotá would acquire the partially dug canal and all equipment without cost.) To cap it all, Washington was far along in negotiations for ditch-digging rights across Nicaragua.

The rival San Juan River route offered several advantages: there were natural lakes; the pass was only 143 feet high; it was closer to the eastern and western seaboards of the United States. There were also disadvantages: the isthmus at that point was over three times as wide, meaning much more excavation for a salt-water ditch despite its lower summit level; there was not enough railroad to provide the sinews for canal-building operations; several active volcanoes belched occasional smoke rings on the sky line around the San Juan valley.

It was the indefatigable labor of William Nelson Cromwell, New York attorney (Sullivan & Cromwell) who had been retained by the French company as its general counsel in the United States, that discomfited the advocates of Nicaragua and focused Congressional attention again on the Chagres route. Cromwell subsidized a group of prominent American engineers; forth poured a stream of newspaper and magazine articles extolling the Panama site. ("Far from being a menace," wrote General Abbot, "the Chagres is a most useful friend . . . It supplies all the water that can ever be demanded by any probable traffic for centuries to come, and yet with judicious regulation no annoyance from currents will ever be experienced by shipping on any part of the route. Nothing better could be desired to subserve the object in view.") Cromwell haunted Congressional lobbies and swelled the legislators' mail with reprints of his propaganda.

Then Bunau-Varilla arrived from Paris to enter the fracas. One of his more spectacular stunts was to buy up from New York philatelists every available specimen of a Nicaraguan issue which pictured Mount Momotombo, the largest of the San Juan volcanoes, in full eruption, and distribute them to the ninety U. S. senators. "Nicaragua now claims officially that her volcanoes are long since extinct," he commented. "Could anything be more official than her own postage stamps?" Later (14 May 1902) Momotombo obligingly clinched his point by erupting again, causing an earthquake which destroyed a wharf on Lake Managua.

Congress rejected pending legislation which would have committed the United States to Nicaragua, and on 3 March 1899, created a new canal commission, which again reopened the question of site. The commission surveyed yet another time, and, in a report dated 16 November 1901, estimated the cost of a San Juan canal at $189,-864,062 against $144,233,358 to complete the Chagres cut.

The Compagnie Nouvelle was asking $109,141,500. When the commission hinted that it would recommend the purchase if the offer was low enough to undercut the Nicaragua project, the compagnie did a quick arithmetical subtraction and reduced its price to a round $40 million.

Now Bogotá disrupted things by stepping in with a demand for an indemnity (reputedly $20 million) from the compagnie for its consent to the transfer. At the same time Colombian diplomatists in Washington began to dicker with the State Department over various proposals, all involving large initial payments and annual rentals for a Chagres canal zone. There ensued a tangle of agreements, abrogations, repudiations, recalls, and revisions which seemed to have no particular pattern except that whenever Washington yielded a point Bogotá decided that the advantage should be increased by holding out. Secretary of State John Hay repeatedly called attention to the fact that the United States still could turn back to Nicaragua, but Bogotá regarded this as a bluff.

President Theodore Roosevelt afterwards documented

his contempt for such vacillation: "To talk of Colombia as a responsible power [is] a mere absurdity . . . You could no more make an agreement with the Colombian rulers than you could nail currant jelly to a wall—[the failure] is not due to the nail; it is due to the currant jelly."

Finally, on 17 March 1903, the U.S. Senate ratified the laboriously devised Hay-Herran Treaty, which called for an initial payment of $10 million to Colombia and an annual rental of $250,000 on a zone six miles wide over which the two countries would maintain joint judicial and military control. The lease would run for one hundred years, indefinitely renewable; Colombia would be allowed free transit of the canal for her ships and free transportation by the railroad for her military and civil employees and property; the United States would have fourteen years to complete a lock canal, with a 10-year extension should it decide to dig on to sea level.

For months the treaty gathered dust in Bogotá, while Colombia wondered whether she might squeeze another inch of advantage. On 4 May, U.S. Minister Arthur M. Beaupre wrote to Hay that "It is entirely impossible to convince these people that the Nicaragua route was ever seriously considered." In due time Dictator José Marroquín called a special session of the Colombian Congress. After protracted debate, the legislators rejected the treaty on 12 August; then they set up a committee to work on another draft, and on 14 October the committee recommended that canal negotiations be suspended until "a later date." The Congress adjourned 31 October, leaving the matter in greater confusion, if possible, than when it convened.

Several prominent Panameños, anticipating just this turn of events, had quietly organized a secessionist junta in June and, on 1 September, Dr. Manuel Amador, chief of the Panama Railroad's medical service, had arrived in the United States—ostensibly on railroad business but actually to solicit aid for a revolt.

Amador encountered Bunau-Varilla in New York, and the Frenchman gladly took over the mission. On 9 October the engineer disclosed the plot to President Roosevelt, who grinned noncommittally and passed him on to Secretary Hay. Hay also was cagey, but a few days later he advised Bunau-Varilla that several U.S. warships of both oceans had been alerted for a quick concentration at the isthmus "to protect the free and uninterrupted transit" guaranteed by the Treaty of 1846. This the engineer interpreted as a promise that Colombian troops would not be allowed to land if revolutionists were in control—not to aid the revolt, but to keep the peace.

"He had no assurance in any way," wrote Roosevelt later, "from Hay or myself, or from anyone authorized to speak for us, [but] it was his business to find out . . . what our Government would do. I have no doubt that he was able to make a very accurate guess."

Thus obliquely encouraged, Bunau-Varilla returned to New York and worked through the night in his hotel room. Next day he handed to the departing Amador a complete plan for the revolution, including an outline of military strategy, a secret code, a ready-written Declaration of Independence, and even a national flag which Mme. Bunau-Varilla had hurriedly stitched up according to her husband's pencil sketch. He also guaranteed to advance $100,000 of his personal funds as soon as the revolt began, and to secure prompt recognition by Washington for the revolutionary government. The mild Isthmian medico, overwhelmed by such thoroughness, promised to Bunau-Varilla the post of minister to Washington and assured him of action within three days of the Colombian Congress's adjournment.

Unbeknownst, detectives hired by the minister from Bogotá were watching every move.

The revolt for independencia brought on a fast-breaking series of double deals, with dollars usually tipping the scales, such as would do credit to any comic-opera librettist.

The junta had not been idle on the home front. Governor José Domingo de Obaldía was in league with the rebels, and he controlled the Panama police; in order to be of maximum value to the cause, he was to maintain an appearance of loyalty to Bogotá. General Esteban Huertas, commander of the regular garrison on the isthmus, had pledged his co-operation for an honorarium of $50,000. With the key men of the civil and military power in line, and with American warships believed available to prevent a landing of hostile forces, the local situation seemed well in hand.

That is, except for that Captain Béxar Tascón; although Tascón had agreed on his price, Huertas suspected him of incipient loyalty to Colombia, for when the general had come upon him in the act of writing a message in the cable office Tascón had retreated in disorder. Huertas stationed a censor at the office and told Obaldía of his fears. Together they worked out a neat ruse: next day, as Huertas and Tascón chatted at headquarters, Obaldía excitedly entered with a forged dispatch to the effect that troops from Costa Rica had invaded the westernmost province of Chiriquí. Huertas ordered Tascón to set out immediately for the border with a company of infantry. As soon as the undisloyal officer had marched off the scene to chase imaginary Costa Ricans out of the country, the chuckling plotters whimsically sent a cablegram to Marroquín reporting the "invasion" and the action that had been taken to repel it.

Through his spy ring, Marroquín had known for weeks that a revolt was brewing, and he wondered whether this might be some sort of shenannigans. Evidently not, he decided, for it gave him a ready-made excuse to send reinforcements to the isthmus; that would be the last thing the rebels would want. Moreover, the unsettled boundary between Colombia and Costa Rica had been causing wrangles intermittently for years; he could not afford to disregard the report. So he notified Obaldía that Colombia's crack battalion of riflemen, nicknamed Los Tiradores (The Sharpshooters), with Generals Juan Tovar and Ramon Amayo in command, was sailing immediately from Barranquilla for Colon in the transport *Cartagena.* He also ordered the governor to send the warships *Padilla* and *Bogotá,* which were then at anchor in Panama Bay, under full steam to Buenaventura to pick up additional troops for the imminent campaign.

Then, because he was not sure of Obaldía himself, Marroquín ordered one of his followers, General Pompilio Gutierrez, to proceed quietly to Panama and relieve Obaldía as governor. Utmost secrecy, he cautioned, for if the junta should get wind of the move it would try to keep Gutierrez from landing.

The problem of reinforcements from Buenaventura was easily solved: when the Colombian vessels in Panama

Bay sidled up to the railroad-operated bunkering station, the Yankee foreman said he was sorry. All out of coal. Expecting some any day now.

The gunboats were helpless.

But the junta could do nothing to stop the shipload of troops that was on the way from Barranquilla. The Tascón stratagem had backfired. Hastily thumbing his code book, Amador framed a cablegram which summarized the crisis: FATE NEWS BAD POWERFUL TIGER URGE VAPOR COLON. In Washington, Bunau-Varilla deciphered the message and hurried over to the State Department to inform them that Colombian troops were scheduled to land five days thence at Colon and that there might be hostilities along the isthmian transit. As usual, he got no assurances, but his attention was casually invited to a newspaper story to the effect that the U.S.S. *Nashville* happened at that moment to be in Kingston harbor. The *Nashville*, an aide remarked apropos of nothing, was capable of a sustained speed of ten knots. Quickly Bunau-Varilla divided this speed into the distance from Jamaica to Panama, and cabled back: VAPOR EAGLE COLON LADDER NOVEL DUET.

Sure enough, on the afternoon of 2 November the *Nashville* dropped anchor in Limón Bay. There she lay when the *Cartagena* steamed in at midnight.

But independence had not yet been proclaimed, and the *Nashville* could not very well interfere with a landing of Colombian troops on what technically was still Colombian soil. When the Tiradores began to disembark at daybreak without any objection from anyone, the junta went into emergency session. What to do? It was Señora Amador who offered a plan. Quickly the word was passed down the line: play for time while the stage is being set.

After they had seen the last of their men and equipment unloaded, Generals Tovar and Amayo strode into the ticket office and called for immediate transportation for the battalion. Merle Bryan, the clerk, asked innocently where the money for the tickets might be?

"I perceive that you are new on the job," observed General Tovar pleasantly. Then he quoted offhand from the regulations: "Transportation will be furnished to military units upon presentation of a properly signed voucher by the senior officer of the traveling organization."

Bryan hadn't heard about that. He began to leaf painstakingly through his files, but couldn't seem to find anything on it. While the two generals fumed, their soldiers drifted off for a spot of rum and romance down Bottle Alley. Bryan smiled behind his dusty folders; it would take hours to get the men back into ranks.

The morning wore on. At intervals Tovar demanded to see the passenger agent, the general agent, the superintendent, the president, the brakeman, anybody who would know more about it than this thickheaded Yanqui. Bryan was sorry; the big shots were all on the other side that morning, he said as he started laboriously through another sheaf of orders. Please be patient, General; poor Bryan is doing his best.

All this time from the adjoining yards came the usual clang and clatter of coaches being coupled and trains being jerked into motion. The generals did not notice that everything was going out while nothing was coming in. Toward noon the din had subsided, and the hostler-tracks stood deserted. Then a lone train hissed to a stop before the station, and Superintendent J. R. Shaler climbed down from his private coach.

The exasperated dignitaries pounced upon Shaler,

demanding that a special train be furnished immediately and that Bryan be fired. Shaler apologized soothingly for Bryan's incompetence, but pointed out that no delay had been incurred anyway, for all the railroad's rolling stock was at the moment down the line except for his own car and engine. To make amends, he would like to have the two generals and their aides ride across the isthmus in befitting state as his personal guests; the rank and file could follow tomorrow, when plenty of coaches would be available. This flattering gesture restored tempers, and after luncheon (on the railroad) the party pulled out for Panama, leaving Colonel Elisio Torres in command of the troops at Colon.

Three hours later the generals were greeted by a distinguished group as they detrained at Panama, while a band played martial airs. In another twenty minutes they were sitting in a cell under the Sea Wall, with Governor Obaldía (who insisted on being arrested for the sake of appearances) to keep them company.

At 8:00 P.M. the commander of the coalless *Bogotá* sent ashore an ultimatum that the generals must be released within two hours or he would bombard the city. At 10:00 P.M. on the dot he spent his entire supply of ammunition—six shells. One of them killed a Chinese shopkeeper in Sal-Si-Puedes (Get-Out-If-You-Can) Street, and another killed a donkey which was pulling a water cart along Avenida B. The other four went wild. It was the only gunfire and the only bloodshed of the revolt.

Next day at a mass meeting in the cathedral plaza, Bunau-Varilla's manifesto, having been revamped extensively by the junta, was read by Eusebio Morales. It charged, among other things, that the immense revenues which the intersea transit had paid to Bogotá had brought "not a single bridge or road, nor a public building, nor a college" to the Chagres country, and condemned the inaction of the Colombian Congress on the canal treaty. "We separate ourselves from our Colombian brothers," it concluded, "without any hatred and without any joy." It was signed by José Augustín Arango, Federico Boyd, and Tomás Arias, the junta's executive committee.

At 4:00 P.M. the municipal council formally approved the junta's action, and the sovereign Republic of Panama became a going concern. It was 4 November 1903. (But the date of the formal declaration of independence seemed less memorable to the Panameños than that of the first overt act of revolt, when they captured the Colombian field commanders and won the war without even cocking a pistol; so, the national holiday of Panama is 3 Noviembre.)

Simultaneous developments at Colon, in the opinion of the *Nashville's* skipper, Commander John N. Hubbard, "amounted to practically the making of war against the United States."

> At 1 p.m. [he reported to Washington] I was summoned on shore by a preconcerted signal, and on landing met the U.S. consul, vice-consul, and [Superintendent] Shaler. [They] had received notice from . . . Col. Torres [that] if [Tovar and Amayo] were not released by 2 p.m. he, Torres, would open fire on the town . . . and kill every U.S. citizen in the place, and my advice and action were requested.
>
> I advised that all the U.S. citizens should take refuge in the shed of the Panama Railroad Company, a stone building susceptible of being put in a good state for defense, and that I would immediately land . . . a body of men, with extra arms . . . for the citizens . . .

> At 1:30 p.m. [I sent ashore] a party of 42 men under . . . Lt. Comdr. H. M. Witzel [and] Midshipman J. P. Jackson, [with] orders . . . to put [the shed] into the best state of defense possible, and protect the lives of the citizens assembled there, not firing unless fired upon. The women and children took refuge on the German S.S. *Marcomania* and the [Panama Railroad] S.S. *City of Washington*, both ready to haul out from the dock if necessary. The *Nashville* got under way and patrolled along the waterfront close in and ready to use either small arm or shrapnel fire.

Unnoticed by Hubbard—or perhaps considered by him as unworthy of mentioning—the *Cartagena* weighed anchor and streaked out of the harbor when the *Nashville* began to unlimber its big guns.

> The Colombians surrounded the building . . . immediately [and for two hours] their attitude was most threatening, it being seemingly their purpose to provoke an attack. Happily our men were cool and steady, and while the tension was very great, no shot was fired.
>
> At about 3:15 p.m. Col. Torres came into the building for an interview and expressed himself as most friendly to the Americans, and that he would like to send the Alcalde of Colon to Panama to see Gen. Tovar and have him direct the discontinuance of the show of force. A special train was furnished and safe conduct was guaranteed.
>
> At about 5:30 p.m., Col. Torres made the proposition of withdrawing his troops to Monkey Hill if I would withdraw the *Nashville's* forces and leave the town in possession of the police until the return of the Alcalde . . . After an interview with [the consul and Shaler] as to the probability of good faith in the matter, I decided to accept the proposition and brought my men on board, the disparity

> in numbers [ten to one] making me desirous of avoiding a conflict so long as . . . the protection of American citizens was not imperiled.
>
> I am positive that the determined attitude of our men, their coolness and evident intention of standing their ground, had a most salutary and decisive effect . . . and was the initial step in the abandoning of Colon by these troops and their return to Cartagena the following day . . .

But there were other factors in the departure, among them being the arrival of the cruiser *Atlanta* and the transport *Dixie*, which landed a battalion of Marines; it was a bribe of $8,000, handed to Torres by an agent of the junta, that broke up the ball game.

Deserted by the *Cartagena*, Torres took his men aboard the French steam packet *Orinoco*, which had just dropped anchor quietly on the other side of the harbor. On deck he met an excited General Gutierrez, who was headed for Panama carrying Marroquín's commission to relieve Obaldía as governor; when he learned what had happened, the general decided not to land. "JUST A LITTLE TOO LATE," chortled a headline in the *Star & Herald*.

A few days later General Rafael Reyes, who had decided to cast his lot with the independents, arrived from Cartagena. He received a warm welcome, which grew into an ovation when he triumphantly produced and handed over to the treasurer of the junta the $8,000 that had been paid to Torres. How he had come by it, he did not say.

As usual, Bunau-Varilla delivered the goods: Washington recognized the new government on the 6th.

That same day the news of the revolt reached Bogotá.

There were riots, with shouts of "Why didn't the Yanquis take us in also?" One group of partisans stormed the presidential palace, yelling "Down with Marroquín!" while another stoned the American legation. The dictator's soldiers restored order while the cabinet met to ponder the crisis. Marroquín's first move was to send a special plenipotentiary to Panama with an offer of virtual autonomy if the isthmus would remain under titular Colombian sovereignty (the junta advised him on arrival that Panama would receive no one from Bogotá except a minister to an independent republic). His second was to offer to U.S. Minister Beaupre the canal treaty "as signed" with his ratification by decree, if Roosevelt would withdraw his support of the insurrection. But the franchise for the Westward Passage was no longer his to give.

By the 14th the situation on the isthmus had quieted enough for General Huertas to release Tovar and Amayo. To show that there were no hard feelings, they attended a banquet in honor of Huertas, who received the signal homage of having a full case of the finest champagne poured on his head, leaving his bemedaled white uniform a little less than starched. "The General appeared to relish his novel bath," commented the *Star & Herald.*

Exactly two weeks after the formal proclamation of independence, Hay and Bunau-Varilla signed a treaty (quickly ratified by both governments) opening the way for Uncle Sam to build the Westward Passage.

In return for an initial payment of $10 million, and an annuity of $250,000 to begin on the ninth anniversary of the final ratification, Panama granted to the United States "all the rights, power, and authority [which it] would possess and exercise if it were the sovereign" over a zone extending five miles to either side of the still-undetermined center line of the future canal (exempting the cities of Panama and Colon), plus several islands in Panama Bay. The vestigious idea of a renewable lease was dropped; the grant was made "in perpetuity," which, as Chief Justice Melville W. Fuller pointed out, "is a long, long time."

XXXI: PESTHOLE TO PARADISE

If there had been no cleanup of the Chagres country before the Americans loosed their full power upon the building of the Westward Passage, the cost in lives, based on the mortality rates of the French era, would have been no less than 78,000. As it was, the number of canal workers who died of all diseases during the ten construction years was 6,639, and of these two-thirds died during the first three years of Yanqui control, while the change from pesthole to tropical paradise was still under way.

The man who accomplished this latter-day miracle was Colonel William Crawford Gorgas, who had cleaned up Havana after the Spanish-American War—by far the world's greatest achievement in public sanitation up to that time. On the isthmus, Gorgas won a victory over yellow Jack and malaria, and incidentally over governmental red tape and antagonistic superiors, which was in no wise less vital to the cause than the superb work of the construction engineers.

Yellow fever literally had shaped Gorgas's entire life. His father, General Josiah Gorgas of Alabama (West Pointer, chief ordnance officer of the Confederacy, president of the University of the South), met his mother when she fled from her home in Mobile to a nearby military reservation on account of a yellow-fever epidemic in 1853. Dr. J. C. Nott of Mobile, who had advanced an "insect origin" theory of the "black vomit" three decades earlier than Carlos Finlay, attended his birth the following year. One of his patients during an epidemic on the Texas border in 1882 later became his wife. In the same epidemic he contracted the disease, thereby earning the immunity that he needed for a life of war against the great killer of the tropics. He had charge of the army's yellow-fever camp at Siboney during the Cuban campaign, and later assisted Colonel Walter Reed in his dramatic experiments with human volunteers that pinned the guilt finally and exclusively on the female *Aëdes aegypti* mosquito.

In April 1904, Gorgas arrived at Panama, by the same transport which brought General George Davis, first governor of the Canal Zone, to his post. With him came a corps of army, navy, and private physicians, nurses, and sanitation experts. "At last," said Dr. Amador, who had just been elected first presidente of the infant republic, "there will be no more vomito negro on the isthmus."

By treaty, the United States held authority to devise and enforce sanitary measures even in areas outside its zone; after a glimpse at Colon and Panama, Gorgas sent home for all the equipment necessary to build reservoirs, lay mains, install running water, sewer connections, and wire screen in every house, and pave every street in both towns. It was a big order, and the seven-man canal commission in Washington suspected that Gorgas had developed delusions of grandeur. They questioned every item in the requisition; for months nothing was seen of the materials at Panama.

Meanwhile Gorgas went ahead with activities for which he already had supplies. Physicians inspected every house, ordering flower vases, ant guards, and washtubs overturned, supplying covers for cisterns and rain barrels. They sprayed insecticides, fumigated, measured windows for screens, provided nets for acute fever cases so that they would not infect more mosquitoes. Patrolmen cruised the streets with oilcans strapped on their backs, squirting a colorful film on every puddle. Isthmians smiled and shook their heads as the sanitarians plodded behind the water carts, oiling the ruts and the hoofprints, but they objected loudly when their flower beds were turned under to deprive the male *Aëdes* of his food. Other squads carried tampers with which they smashed every fragment of crockery or coco shell that might catch a few drops of rain and provide a mosquito-breeding place. In the first year the exterminators used 120 tons—almost the entire world's output—of pyrethrum powder, 330 tons of sulphur, and 2,600,000 gallons of kerosene.

"The whole isthmus reeks of the stuff," wrote a correspondent of the London *Times*.

The natives, almost without exception, were immune to yellow Jack—not on account of any inherent resistance, but because they had survived infection in babyhood. It was only the constant support of the popular Amador that kept their amused toleration from growing into active antagonism toward the campaign. As they danced the tamborito, the cantadores added an appropriate verse to their endless chain of musical comment, on topics ranging from romance ("Dark-skin, pretty dark-skin, come along with me, but never say I said so") to history ("The devil sent Alzuru to destroy Panama, but God sent Don Tomás"), from politics ("Chiari is a great man; Chiari is my man; he will be president of Panama") to philosophy ("It is easy for a woman to love a poor man until a rich one comes along") and current affairs:

The Gringos invade our houses,
And tell us just what we must do.
The Gringos are the bosses;
Panameños, you're on the spot.
They make us learn to walk the chalk,
Like fence-posts in a row.
They dig and pave and scrub the streets;
They're even cleaning up the jail.
You might suppose that they are mad,
But all Americanos act like that.
OOOPAAA! . . .

The sanitation drive turned some of the Isthmian leaders sour on the whole idea of a canal. Moped *El Diario de Panama* (19 June 1905):

"To excavate thirty million cubic yards of earth on the Isthmus at Culebra is an absolute impossibility; it is an error as great as fumigating all the houses in Panama to destroy mosquitoes, or trying to stamp out yellow fever on the Isthmus. To attempt it is a dream, an illusion, perhaps simply a case of American boasting."

As shiploads of nonimmune laborers and clerks began to pour in at both terminals, Gorgas renewed his plea for supplies. But he received a trickle instead of a flood, and in November yellow fever spread another time across the Chagres valley. While scores of newcomers died, thousands jammed themselves aboard the departing steamers. Work on the canal slowed to a snail's pace. "The shadow of Monkey Hill," wrote Gorgas in his diary, "darkens the whole isthmus."

The commission, headed by Admiral John G. Walker, hurried down from Washington to see what could be done. Gorgas and John F. Wallace, the chief engineer, met the group at Colon, and they stood chatting while a cargo of coffins was being unloaded from the hold of their ship. One of them asked Gorgas:

"Colonel, why those six especially fine caskets in this shipment?"

"Mr. Burr didn't come down with you, you know," replied Gorgas solemnly.

The commission took Gorgas to task for his "lavish" use of supplies, and criticized him especially for demanding such vast quantities of wire screen.

"Screens are not a necessity; they are a luxury," pontificated Walker.

"Do you propose," inserted Commissioner Carl Grunsky, "to make the canal zone into a high-toned resort?"

"I don't want those screens for comfort," replied Gorgas evenly. "They are an absolute necessity if you wish to protect your workers from the mosquitoes that carry the black vomit."

Walker and Grunsky went into gales of laughter, which the others joined. Gorgas then told them bluntly that their penny-pinching policies were "imperiling the whole canal venture for the United States," and later spoke irreverently of Walker as "that old man of the sea." The commission returned to Washington filled with resentment, and demanded that Secretary of War William Howard Taft dismiss Gorgas from his post.

Taft wisely decided to investigate first, and sought the aid of Dr. Charles A. L. Reed of Cincinnati, president of the American Medical Association. Reed journeyed to the isthmus in the guise of a federal land agent, nosed about for several weeks, and returned to Washington without ever disclosing himself.

Gorgas, he said in his report, was "the foremost

authority in the world [on the] problems of [tropical] sanitation," yet he was "subordinate of a whole series of other subordinates who are confessedly ignorant of [them]." For page after page he detailed the commission's "meddling" in technical matters, and vented special scorn on Commissioner Grunsky, concluding every mention of the group with "more especially Mr. Grunsky."

"An instance in point occurred a few days before my departure from Ancon. [An insane] woman was delivered of a child; [she] could not nurse [it]; the nurse [asked] Major LaGarde for a rubber nipple [and] nursing bottle; he had none—the requisition of last September had not been filled; he made out a requisition, took it to . . . Gorgas for indorsement, then to Mr. Tobey, chief of the bureau of materials and supplies, for another indorsement, then to a clerk to have it copied and engrossed; then a messenger was [sent] to a drug store [to] buy a nursing bottle and a nipple, which finally reached the infant [after] two days . . . The articles [cost] thirty cents, but counting the . . . time of the nurse, of . . . La Garde, of his clerical help, of . . . Gorgas, of . . . Tobey, of [his] clerks, of the messenger, the cost to the Government of the United States was in the neighborhood of $6.75—all due to the penny-wise-and-pound-foolish policy of the Commission, more especially of Mr. Grunsky."

When President Roosevelt saw the report, he fired the whole commission.

Under the second commission, which was headed by Theodore P. Shonts of Pennsylvania, conditions improved, but the aftermath of the first group's bumbling had to come. In April 1905, yellow fever broke out again, and once more the workers fled in droves. This time there was trouble at the California and Gulf ports of the United States, where mild epidemics had followed the mass landings of the previous panic. Ships carrying refugees were not allowed to dock; in some cases they were driven from harbors at the point of cannon. They had to steam on to ports farther north, where the disease does not take hold, to unload their passengers.

Gorgas and his men fought doggedly on, but after two months of epidemic, exodus, and disruption of the work, Wallace threw up his job.

The new chief engineer, John Frank Stevens of Maine, accepted the post after an understanding with Roosevelt that "I was not to be hampered or handicapped by anybody high or low, [and that I was giving] no promise to remain until the work was . . . completed, but that I would stay [until] I had made its success certain, or had proved it to be a failure."

Stevens arrived on the isthmus in June, and found "no organization worthy of the name; no answerable head who could delegate authority and [fix] responsibility; no co-operation [between] departments."

While he labored to bring order out of the administrative chaos, Stevens never forgot the morale of the men. Because he always had a long black cigar in his mouth, he became known among them as Big Smoke; and Big Smoke made it a point to be seen frequently in the workers' messes and along the line. He was never too busy to listen to a grievance and render a prompt, impartial decision.

"There are three diseases here," he remarked. "They are yellow fever, malaria, and cold feet. And the greatest of these is cold feet." The men liked that kind of talk; with new respect for their leadership, they went to work with a will.

But the commission still had not decided between a lock-type and a sea-level canal; hence the engineers were largely restricted to digging in Culebra Pass, improving the construction villages, replacing rails (which, Stevens remarked, "could not by the utmost stretch of the imagination be termed railroad tracks"), and laying out a co-ordinated trackage system for handling the future unprecedented quantities of spoil. "As the gift of prophecy is withheld from us in these latter days," opined Big Smoke, "all that we can do now is to make such arrangements as may look proper as far ahead as we can see."

While Stevens did what he could in the face of indecision higher up, Gorgas pushed the battle against *Aëdes* —which would be of value, lock canal, sea-level canal, or no canal at all. Then, on 11 November 1905, the leader called his staff into the autopsy room of Ancon Hospital and gathered them around the body of Jeff Everett, file clerk, from North Carolina.

"Take a good look at this man, boys," Gorgas said softly, "because it is the last case of yellow fever that you will ever see. There will never be any more deaths from this cause on the isthmus."

He was right.

Next Gorgas leveled his spray guns on the malaria-carrying mosquito, the female *Anopheles*. The principles were the same, but the techniques had to be altered, and the extent of operations dwarfed the campaign against the comparatively puny *Aëdes*. The drive against *Aëdes*, Gorgas commented, was like "making war on the family cat," while that against *Anopheles* was more like "fighting all the beasts of the jungle."

Now his men ventured far into the wilds, to set up oil drips at the very headwaters of the creeks and streams that fed the Chagres. More than a hundred square miles of swampland lay within *Anopheles*-flight of the canal strip. To help eliminate this menace, Stevens lent engineers, laborers, and equipment; some of the swamps they filled, others they ditched with concrete and drained with tile. Around every nipa shack they cleared away all growth for a distance of two hundred yards (*Anopheles* dislikes a long nonstop flight), and to the occupants they presented sleeping nets, along with sign-language lectures on the use and care of them. They propagated insect-eating spiders, lizards, frogs, and fish, and released them by the barrelful in the worst mosquito areas. Deaths from malaria dropped steadily, from 7.45 per thousand in 1906 to none in 1914.

Typhoid, cholera, and dysentery diminished as streets were paved, sewers and water mains were laid, filter plants were built, and incinerators were installed. On 4 July 1905, when the water was turned on in Panama, the city regidores decreed a fiesta and passed a resolution of thanks; people in the streets threw flowers at Gorgas's feet; Te Deum was sung in the cathedral.

While he was coaxing up islands of cleanliness out of the muck, Gorgas did not neglect the hospitals themselves. Ancón (later rechristened Gorgas) Hospital was enlarged to 1,500 beds, and the others were proportionately expanded. From them each morning rolled mobile dispensaries, to follow every group of laborers moving along the line, distributing quinine at mealtime and handling emergency cases. A mental hospital was opened at Corozal, quarantine stations were set up at the terminal ports, and a model leper colony was built at Palo Seco.

Gorgas carefully weeded through the roster of army nurses to select those for his hospitals, always insisting on older women with previous experience in the tropics. Once he posted a bulletin in the wards, informing the patients that their nurses knew virtually as much about tropical medicine as most doctors. "Some were with MacArthur in the Philippines," he pointed out, "and some were with Wood in Cuba."

"And some," added a convalescent with a pencil, "were with Washington at Valley Forge."

The annual total of deaths from all causes fell from 39.29 per thousand in 1906 to 5.24 in 1913, when a Missouri-born journalist spent two weeks kicking about in the stables and alleys of Panama in a vain search for a fly. The health record of the isthmus still stands unmatched throughout the Torrid Zone, but even today it requires the work of thousands to maintain it; a veritable dike of DDT holds back from the Yanqui strip the plagues that lurk in the uncharted Chagres jungle. A few brief months of total neglect, say the authorities at Gorgas Hospital, would be enough to bring back the old days.

By the beginning of 1906 the worst of the battle against disease was past, and Gorgas was a hero from Boston to Los Angeles and from London to Singapore as well as from Colon to La Boca. The Chagres country was at last fit to receive the greatest swarm of human bees that had ever attacked a single project of construction since the completion of the Pyramid of Cheops.

All over the United States, editors and orators harped

on variations of the theme: the world has waited long and patiently; the victory over disease has carried it a long mile closer to the realization of its age-old dream, a Westward Passage; at last the road is clear, but the barrier between the oceans yet remains, as adamant as ever; others have failed, but Uncle Sam must not. Then they all joined in on the chorus:

"Now, let's see the dirt fly!"

XXXII: THE DIRT FLIES

Congress enacted, on 29 June 1906, legislation prescribing a lock canal, with a summit level of 85 feet to be reached by three flights of locks on each side, to cost an estimated $140 million. Immediately Stevens set to work installing the appropriate one of the several spoil-disposal systems that he had devised pending a decision, and sent agents in chartered steamers to recruit laborers in all the major population centers of the West Indies and Southern Europe.

The following November, after the final phase of preparation had reached full swing, President Theodore Roosevelt paid a three-day visit to the isthmus, and thereby became the first chief executive to leave the United States while in office. Through ceaseless rain, with the Chagres on its worst rampage in years, he trudged along the line, inspecting installations and questioning everybody. On the last day he stood on the rear platform of his special train, overlooking the turbulent river, and spoke with his usual eloquence to an assemblage of several hundred Americans holding umbrellas.

"You are doing the biggest thing of the kind that has ever been done, and I wanted to see how you are doing it," he said. "As I have seen you at work, seen what you have done and are doing, noted the spirit with which you are approaching the task, I have felt just exactly as I should feel if I saw the picked men of my country engaged in some great war. I am weighing my words when I say that you, here, who do your work well in bringing to completion this great enterprise, will stand exactly as the soldiers of a few, and only a few, of the most famous armies in all the nations stand in history. This is one of the great works of the world. It is a greater work than you, yourselves, at the moment realize. . . . You men here, in the future, each man of you, will have the right to feel, if he has done his duty—and a little more than his duty right up to the handle—in the work here on the isthmus, that he has made his country his debtor, that he has done more than his full share in adding renown to the nation under whose flag this canal is being built."

He acknowledged their cheers with the famous Rooseveltian grin. Then somebody in the crowd noticed, embedded in the opposite bank of the Chagres, a tier of regular white stones, each as high as a man, topped by a fringe of overhanging grass. It was an admirable caricature of the president's teeth and mustache.

"Look," cried the discoverer, pointing, "Roosevelt's mouth!"

Everyone looked and laughed; the president, in great good humor, flashed his grin again to allow a more careful comparison. Thereafter the point was marked on the engineers' maps as Boca de Roosevelt.

On his return to Washington, Roosevelt pronounced himself well satisfied with the state of things at Panama. But he reiterated his contention that "a seven-headed commission [is] a clumsy executive instrument." The canal enterprise, he said, "should have but one commissioner, with such heads of departments and other officers under him as we may find necessary."

Resignations and transfers already had reduced the board to three members; these took the hint and resigned as a group in March. Roosevelt appointed Stevens chairman of the commission as well as chief engineer, and by leaving the other seats vacant achieved his one-man control without going through the tedious process of asking Congress for revised legislation. Then he settled back to watch the dirt fly.

But Stevens was now satisfied that "the work was so well organized . . . that competent engineers . . . could be found to carry it on to a successful completion." So, true to his original agreement with the president, he resigned, effective 1 April 1907.

Tired of the merry-go-round of resignations, Roosevelt decided to place the responsibility on "men who will stay on the job until I get tired of having them there, or till I say they may abandon it." He called on the secretaries of war and the navy to submit the names of their most competent engineers.

The president had had enough of divided authority and uncertain responsibility. Now he rolled all the key positions into one. To be chairman of the commission, chief engineer of the canal, czar of the zone, and president of the Panama Railroad and its subsidiary steamship line, he selected Lieutenant Colonel George Washington Goethals, a native of Brooklyn, whose parents had immigrated from Holland.

Goethals had earned fame among engineers by his work as chief of the Muscle Shoals development, where he designed and built a lock with a record-breaking lift of 26 feet. During the Spanish-American War he had distinguished himself again, by appropriating two Spanish barges for use as an emergency wharf foundation in the harbor of San Juan, Puerto Rico, without troubling to discuss it beforehand with the navy commander who had captured them. The admirals had demanded a court-martial, for unauthorized use of prizes of war. But the War Department, smiling at the navy's righteous wrath, had dragged the matter out until it was forgotten without ever arraigning him.

Roosevelt recognized the invaluable service of Gorgas by giving him a seat on the new commission. Next came two army engineers, Majors David Gaillard (in whose honor Culebra Cut was later designated Gaillard Cut) and William Sibert. From the navy he detached Rear Admiral Harry Rousseau, for the special task of designing and constructing the harbor facilities at the canal terminals. The two remaining seats went to civilians: Jackson Smith, who had served as chief quartermaster of the zone under the previous commission, and former Senator Joseph Blackburn of Kentucky.

As more shiploads of workers arrived, and overloaded the zone's housing facilities, Smith generated the ill will of practically every American by his initiation and rigid enforcement of a complex formula for assigning the available living quarters. Each "Gold" (American) employee received one square foot of floor space for each dollar of his monthly salary; when his wife came down, the allotment was doubled; other adult members of the family got three-fourths of a square foot for each one of the breadwinner's square feet; each child received one square foot for each twenty of the father's for each year of its age; each white adult nonfamily member of the household got space equal to half the master's basic quota. Old Square-Foot Smith, he was known as. After a year of squabbling over the choicer houses, during which Smith was attacked more than once in his office and on the street by umbrella-swinging housewives, Goethals wrote to Roosevelt that he was "convinced of two things: first, of his [Smith's] ability . . . and second, [of] his unpopularity, [which is] so pronounced as to interfere seriously with the efficiency of his department." Smith resigned in June 1908, and Roosevelt gave his seat to Lieutenant Colonel Harry Hodges of the army engineers. Senator Blackburn, the only remaining civilian on the board, continued as Goethals's chief aide in the field of civil affairs.

The president's sweeping changes in the canal organization had given Goethals the authority of an absolute monarch; while he could not inflict the death penalty without due process of law, he could summarily order the deportation of any person from the zone, which for his purposes added up to the same thing. The only appeal from his dispensations was to Roosevelt himself. Joseph B. Bishop, the commission's secretary, characterized him as a "combination of father confessor and Day of Judgment, whose like has rarely if ever been seen since the time of Solomon."

On his arrival Goethals found an organization of civilians who were intensely loyal to Stevens and outspokenly fearful that they would not fit well in a military regime. He reassured them in his first public utterance:

"There will be no more militarism in the future than there has been in the past. I am no longer a commander in the United States Army . . . I am commanding the Army of Panama, and . . . the enemy we are going to combat is the Culebra Cut and the locks and dams . . .

Every man who does his duty will never have any cause to complain . . . of militarism." (The new commander in chief packed away his uniforms when he arrived, and throughout the construction years appeared only in white suit and flat straw hat.) He gave full credit to the accomplishments of his predecessor:

"Mr. Stevens has perfected such an organization . . . that there is nothing left for us to do but to just have the organization continue . . . the good work." In no time the workers were referring to him as "the old man"—the army's own jargon for a commanding officer who is O.K.

But he did not get along well with Gorgas. Goethals felt that the sanitary department was at times unreasonable, as when Gorgas clapped a quarantine on the entire Pacific end of the line, stalling all construction operations south of Culebra for several weeks, because of a single case of bubonic plague at La Boca. And he had little patience with the fever-eradication campaign, which required the constant work of four thousand men.

"Do you know, Gorgas," he remarked at a meeting of the commission, "that every mosquito you kill costs the United States government ten dollars?"

"Yes," Gorgas replied, winking at the others around the conference table, "but suppose one of those ten-dollar mosquitoes were to bite you? Think what a loss to the government that would be." Goethals did not appear to take it in very good spirit, but he offered no rejoinder. Thereafter, Bishop noted, relations between the two were "strictly correct."

It is not likely that Goethals ever attempted to persuade Roosevelt that Gorgas should be removed from the commission, although Mrs. Gorgas suspected him of it;

the engineer, she charged, "carried his passion for dominating everything and everybody to extreme lengths." But Goethals well knew that Gorgas's prestige in Washington—at least until the canal should be completed—was even greater than his own.

To discharge his obligations as the canal zone's last court of appeal, Goethals held informal open house each Sunday morning at his quarters in Culebra. There came the high and the low, knowing that they would get a patient hearing and a prompt dispensation. Even today in the zone clubhouses one can hear many a story of Goethals's Solomonesque decisions "back in the construction days."

Preliminary hearings were held in the waiting rooms, by Secretary Bishop for the English-speakers and by multilingual Giuseppe Garibaldi, grandson of Italy's national hero, for the Latins. They devised a screening system, under which each complainant was told that he would be allowed to "see the old man," but first he must dictate to a stenographer a detailed account of his complaint. In a majority of cases the plaintiff, on being handed his statement for signature, "concluded that he had no grievance," and walked out. A chance to "get it out of his system," Bishop observed, "had been all the relief he needed."

The problems aired in this way were by no means restricted to employer-employee relations. A frequent case was the eternal triangle. When Raquel (or Susan) charged that her Pedro (or Harry) was spending all their money on that moza (or wench) Carmelita (or Jane), Goethals disposed of the matter by deporting all three. The policy raised the moral tone of the Chagres valley, temporarily anyway, a shade above average for the tropics.

Once a Jamaica Negress dragged her husband up, charging that he had confiscated her wages.

"Under English law," the defendant argued, "a man is entitled to his wife's earnings."

"But you are at present under United States law," Goethals pointed out. "Either return her money, or I'll send you back to Jamaica, where you can have all the English law you want." The man shelled out.

On weekdays the chief devoted his mornings to inspection of progress along the line, chugging down the track in a brightly painted open coach, powered by an automobile motor, which the workers called the Yellow Peril or the Brain Wagon. In his hand he always carried (besides a Three Towers cigarette) his timetable of accomplishment, which he consulted as he surveyed the work actually done as of that date.

"Your schedule calls for those forms to be finished by the end of next week," he once said to a foreman. "You are not very far along."

"I know it, colonel," the man replied. "But we are doing our best."

"I don't expect you to just do your best," said Goethals. "I expect you to complete your work on time."

The story was passed along, and the project was finished ahead of schedule.

In and out of Colon harbor bustled the recruiting steamers, delivering hordes of laborers from the West Indies and Southern Europe. As each ship docked, the newcomers were met by white-jacketed medicos brandishing needles; occasionally whole shiploads of Negroes, who had never heard of vaccination, had to be dragged ashore and immunized by force. At the end of 1908 the rolls carried some 25,000 blacks, from Martinique, Barbados, Guadeloupe, and Jamaica, and half as many whites, mostly from Spain, Italy, and Greece. Thereafter the number of workers climbed steadily to a peak of 56,654 in 1913, with United States citizens at all times accounting for about a tenth of the total.

Along the line from village to village rolled a specially built railroad coach, with tellers' cages, bank vaults, and armed guards, disbursing 1,600 pounds of gold and 24 tons of silver to the workers each month. When the pay car rolled up and opened its doors, the men formed lines at windows which were labeled "Gold" (for U.S. citizens) and "Silver" (for all others). This paymaster's system of demarcation in time was extended to the clubhouses, post offices, waiting rooms, and other public places of the zone; newly-arrived visitors always were intrigued by the signs. ("Gold and silver rest rooms? Well I never!") In October 1946 the zone administration ordered all such signs removed, but this step did not herald any change in its adamant policy of segregation. Workers are still listed on distinct Gold and Silver payrolls, and the two classes still use separate housing communities, schools, and other facilities.

Workers in all classifications received pay from a fifth to a half greater than the rates then prevailing elsewhere over the world, plus free quarters and medical attention. For United States citizens, emoluments were added to cover their dependents, and transportation to and from U.S. ports was given to workers free and to their families at $20 a head.

For seven years following the cleanup, the Chagres neck remained one great beehive. An endless chain of barges ferried in sand, gravel, and stone from Porto Bello, Nombre, and several beaches and quarries along the Pacific coast. Batteries of concrete mixers fed strings of dump cars. Explosions, which consumed twenty million tons of dynamite all told, shook the valley continually as the mountains, one after another, crumbled. Steam shovels bit into the slopes of Culebra Pass while train after train of cars hauled away the spoil to build the breakwaters at the ports. Track shifters huffed and steam drills yammered as virtually the entire length of the Panama Railroad was relocated, with heavier rails and a double track throughout. Sledges clanged in the machine shops as 46 pairs of the greatest steel lock gates the world had ever seen, weighing a total of 60 million tons, were tooled and assembled. Across the Chagres bed at Gatún rose a vast earth dam to a height of 105 feet above the sea, filling the saddles between an arc of mountains until its bellied crest spanned a chord of a mile and a half, half a mile thick at the base and 500 feet thick at the surface level of the future lake; so broad it grew that an 18-hole golf course was built on its gentle slopes, and today its outlines, as it stretches away from the three Atlantic-side flights of locks and the Gatún hydroelectric spillway, can hardly be distinguished from the surrounding landscape. At Pedro Miguel, between two flanking dams, rose the highest of the three Pacific-side locks, and at Miraflores a curving dam centered at the two lower flights, every stage consisting of twin concrete basins, each with inside dimensions of 1,000 by 110 feet and a surface level 45 feet above its floor. Inland from Colon churned a fleet of dredges, scooping a sea-level channel to reach the Gatún locks, while a similar flotilla dug a salt-water ditch from La Boca to Miraflores.

The whole world, and especially the United States Congress, watched the news from Panama. When a 250-foot segment of the growing Gatún dam sank 20 feet (November 1908), a special committee hurried down from Capitol Hill. Goethals took the visitors on an inspection tour of the entire valley, and patiently explained the principle of physics by which he assured them that the mishap was insignificant. Once the dam had settled and the water had been released, he said, the lateral force would be slight in proportion to the ponderous thickness of the barrier.

"The pressure of water against the sides of a container increases only in relation to the height of the column, without respect to the area of the surface," the engineer pointed out.

"But," quibbled a congressman, "you say that you are going to create a lake of more than 160 square miles. I don't see how this dam, or any other dam, could hold back such a tremendous volume of water."

"Ah, shut up!" suggested another solon. "How do you suppose the dikes of Holland hold back the Atlantic Ocean?"

As a servant of the government, Goethals could not afford to smile.

The committeemen enjoyed their stay in the luxurious new Washington Hotel at Colon, but they viewed with alarm President Roosevelt's highhanded launching of the United States government into the hostelry business without Congressional authority. One of them mentioned the matter to Goethals at dinner on the terrace.

"I don't believe that it's legal," orated the legislator.

"I doubt the existence of a precedent that would allow you to build and operate a hotel with government funds. I strongly suspect that the whole business is unconstitutional."

"That," replied Goethals, "is not a matter of concern to me. I got an order from my commander in chief to build this hotel, and I built it."

Despite an argument about it at the next session of Congress, the Washington Hotel is still there, and it is still owned and operated by the United States government.

The digging crews in Culebra Pass got used to surprises. As the dynamite gangs blasted away, they occasionally opened fissures which gushed steam and smoke. The first one to be uncovered sent the superstitious Silver workers scurrying. "We have dug down to hell!" they moaned, expecting an indignant Satan to burst forth momentarily. Even the all-wise Yankees took distance, and stood speculating as to whether a volcanic eruption might be imminent. One of the shovel operators, a lanky Texan, broke it up.

"Well, boys," he drawled, "I dunno what it is, but I betcha that Miss Bertha [his 95-ton Bucyrus shovel] and I can dig it out by the roots."

The others said ha-ha, and they all climbed back uneasily into their cabs. Staff geologists arrived shortly and allayed their concern by diagnosing the phenomenon as the result of exposing long-buried pockets of various volatile metallic compounds to the air.

Of course all the diggers kept an eye peeled for gold. In the Y.M.C.A. reading rooms across the valley, there were regular rumors of strikes, but each one turned out

THE LOCKS

AT MIRAFLORES

to be a fluke; apparently the Spanish prospectors had done a thorough job.

Throughout the construction period (and for years afterward) the slides that had harassed the French continued to plague the Americans. In some spots the clayey soil on the steepening banks of the gorge slid sidewise into the cut, while at others the weight of the towering sides pressed directly downward to force the loosened bottom of the newly dug channel up above the surface of the water. One morning the diggers reporting for work near Culebra discovered an island jutting up above the water in the ditch; it had not been there the day before. The geologists were sent for, and they discovered that the displacement was still going on slowly—that the entire village of Culebra, in fact, had sunk several feet, and that fissures along the canalside were widening by the hour. All hands turned to moving the buildings to a less dangerous spot; then, as the shovels and dredges nibbled away at the new island, the bank continued to settle until the old site of Culebra lay at a 45-degree tilt.

The men had a nickname for the most voluminous and persistent one of the slides: La Cucaracha. Whenever the channel south of Gold Hill seemed to be shaping up nicely, The Cockroach could be depended on to spill a few acres of earth across the line, snarling railroad tracks, burying equipment, and blocking traffic.

On Goethals's desk was a calendar pad bearing a printed truism: "Life is just one damn thing after another." One morning an aide discovered that he had marked out "thing" and substituted "slide." And by the time the canal was completed, the slides had added a third to the 85 million cubic yards that the engineers had first expected to remove from Culebra Cut. Of this total, La Cucaracha had been responsible for 12 million. And the end was not yet.

Despite the slides, the original timetable of accomplishment was adhered to. On 10 October 1913, President Woodrow Wilson pressed a button on his desk in the White House and set off a dynamite charge which ruptured the dike across the northern end of Culebra Cut; the Chagres waters rushed into the canyon and surged across the continental divide, spilling at Pedro Miguel into the man-made basin that would grow into Miraflores Lake. Already a larger lake of Chagres water was climbing slowly up the ramps of Gatún Dam, and the orchid pickers were reaping a rich harvest as they paddled their canoes among the tops of a million drowning trees.

The basic construction works were about complete, but the canal would be useless until the Chagres River system could deliver enough water into its revetmented basin to reach the summit level of the highest locks. In the interim the workers concentrated on the slide areas, driving piles into the banks, pouring concrete along the sides, and shoring, in the hope of bringing them to a standstill.

In January 1914, President Wilson signed an executive order setting up a permanent government for the Panama Canal Zone, and the two men who had done most to make the Westward Passage a reality received the honors due them: Goethals was appointed to serve a four-year term as the first governor of the finished canal, with the rank of major general; Gorgas was called to Washington to become the surgeon general of the United States Army.

Using an amalgam of metals salvaged from abandoned French equipment, the Philadelphia mint cast medallions of the Great Seal of the Panama Canal Zone, with a profile of Theodore Roosevelt on the reverse side, to be awarded to all Gold workers of the construction years. The recipients organized themselves into the Society of the Chagres, which today has thinning chapters in the canal towns and in the principal cities of the United States.

In June 1914, the armies of Kaiser Wilhelm crossed the border into Belgium. Two months later, the world was so intent on watching the opening skirmishes of World War I that it gave only a sidewise glance to an event whose roots went far deeper into the past, whose implications would weigh far heavier in future history: the formal opening of the Westward Passage.

XXXIII: THE LAND DIVIDED

THROUGH the construction years the 9,600-ton twin-screw steamer *Ancón*, of the Panama Railroad Company's fleet, had plied between New York and the isthmus, shuttling workers and supplies. Now, as the day of 15 August 1914 dawned cool and clear, she stood to wharf at Cristobal, with new paint, decks scrubbed white, and brass polished like gold; her reward for faithful service was to be the honor of making the inaugural transit of the Panama Canal.

Shortly after daybreak a party of distinguished engineers, army and navy officers, correspondents, photographers, consuls, diplomats, and officials of the governments at Washington and Panama, led by Presidente Belisario Porras, came aboard. At seven o'clock the *Ancón* weighed anchor and moved out of the harbor, between solid ranks of ships waiting to follow her across the Chagres neck. When she reached the three-mile limit (for this passage had to be complete, from the high seas of the Atlantic to the high seas of the Pacific) she put about and, with an exultant scream of her whistle, churned up to full speed. As she recrossed the harbor at the beginning of her historic run, the other ships set up a shrill din. On entering the sea-level channel she settled back to half speed again, in compliance with the safety regulations. All the way to Gatún the banks were lined with construction workers, waving handkerchiefs and flags; the *Ancón*'s whistle peepeeped continually in recognition of their salutes.

An hour later she hove to at the approach wall of Gatún locks, and the passengers cheered as they saw Governor Goethals standing coatless on the lock wall, anxiously puffing a cigarette, with his staff of engineers gathered around. He responded, without taking his eyes off the long-rehearsed movements of the lock gang, by raising his flat straw hat, and the Chagres sun glistened on hair that had turned snow-white during his years on the isthmus.

Along the cog tracks which led down the stairstep-like ramps atop the lock walls, tiny locomotives scurried to meet the *Ancón*. The team of electric mules made fast to her on each side with cables—two engines ahead for pulling, two amidships to prevent sideswiping of the walls, and two astern to guard against ramming the forward gates. Slowly, smoothly they towed the *Ancón* into the first lock. The massive steel plates swung to behind her, the valves in the floor opened, and Chagres water gushed in to raise her 340 inches to the level of the next lock. Then the forward gates parted, and the mules towed her into the intermediate basin.

So it went, with none of the yelling that accompanies the lockage of vessels through the other canals of the world. (Goethals's patient drilling of his men in the use of hand signals began then and there to earn for Panama the characterization that it enjoys today among seamen the earth around as "the silent canal.") A scant 69 minutes after her arrival at the locks, the *Ancón* steamed out under her own power onto the azure expanse of Gatún Lake.

Some two hours later she passed another cheering crowd at Gamboa and entered Culebra Cut. Now she throttled down and proceeded at slow speed, for La Cucaracha was still oozing soft earth into the channel just past Culebra, and a team of dredges was busy attacking it. When the *Ancón* hove into view, the dredges ceased work and pulled to the side. They tootled as the *Ancón* minced carefully past the danger spot; then they swung out and fell upon the obstruction as furiously as before.

At 1:00 P.M. the *Ancón* entered the lock at Pedro Miguel, where Goethals and his aides again were discovered waiting on the lock wall; they had followed in the Yellow Peril, keeping the test ship in sight as much as possible. Down and across little Miraflores Lake, and into Miraflores locks, without incident. Then, in the last stage of the descent to sea level, came the only unexpected delay: when the last pair of gates opened, and the fresh water of the Chagres and the Río Grande mingled with the South Sea's brine, the mixture seethed and churned for half an hour. After the basin had grown quiet, the *Ancón* ventured into the salty channel; thirty minutes later she debouched onto the open sea at La Boca, where another mottle of waiting vessels screeched greetings as she steamed out to deep water at full speed, just as though she were overdue at Hong Kong. More thousands of spectators cheered as she turned back and entered the newly built harbor of Balboa; the ubiquitous Goethals was again on hand, to congratulate Pilots Ralph Osborn and John Constantine.

The *Ancón* had taken 9.6 hours to pass between the American continents from ocean to ocean. The dream of Columbus had come true at last. The Westward Passage was proved.

In its first year of operation, despite occasional minor slides which interrupted traffic for periods of two to seven days, the canal passed 1,058 vessels flying the flags of every maritime nation. They carried 4,888,400 tons of cargo and paid $4,366,747.13 in tolls.

Then, on 18 September 1915, both banks of the gorge near Culebra suddenly collapsed, toppling 20 million cubic yards of debris into the channel. Goethals had tendered his resignation as governor, but he postponed the effective date because of the emergency. It took seven months to clear the cut; consequently, in that year only 724 ships transited. Thereafter business increased steadily up to the peak year of 1929, when tolls amounting to $27,111,125.47 were collected from 6,289 vessels carrying 30,647,768 tons of cargo. The all-time record charge for a single passage was set 23 July 1924, when H.M.S. *Hood* paid $22,400 under the flat rate for warships of 50 cents per displacement ton.

During the world-wide economic recession which began in 1929 the revenues dropped each year, to a low of $19,601,077.17 in 1933. From there they climbed, slowly and erratically, until the outbreak of World War II brought suspension of pleasure cruises and restriction of maritime commerce to war-essential cargoes.

War clouds were gathering again in Europe when, on 15 August 1939, the old-timer *Ancón,* as chipper as ever, re-enacted her memorable transit of a quarter century before. The silver anniversary of the marriage of the oceans was declared a legal holiday throughout the Canal Zone. The original bell from the *Ancón*'s bridge was consigned, with fitting ceremony, to a permanent place of honor in the rotunda of the stately administration building on Balboa Heights. The lions of the day were a small group of white-haired men who carried the medallion of the Society of the Chagres.

When the construction account was closed on 30 June 1921, the canal and all appurtenances (including payments to Panama and to the Compagnie Nouvelle but excluding installations for defense) had cost a total of $386,910,301.04. A subsequent payment of $25 million to Colombia as heart balm (1 March 1922), plus the annual rental to Panama, plus the cost of Madden Dam and other improvements, brought the total nondefense cash outlay at the outbreak of World War II to $464,210,846.71. Income for the same period, less operation and maintenance, totaled $262,940,754.48.

To private financiers that seems a scandalously poor return; it falls far short of yielding a mere 3 per centum per annum of simple interest on the capital. And the picture would look even gloomier if it included the undisclosed millions that have been spent on fortifications.

But there are other ways of looking at it.

If, as eminent naval strategists contend, the Panama Canal virtually doubles the strength of the United States fleets in both oceans, the deficit turns into a staggering profit: a hundred men-o'-war for the price of ten. Since merchantmen of American registry make up a third of the vessels using the canal, the American taxpayer is getting a hidden return on his money through reduced merchant marine subsidies. He receives further benefits in the form of increased business volume and lower retail prices, for a fourth of the cargoes passed are traveling from one U.S. port to another. American commerce gains from every transit of the canal by a foreign ship, since the toll payments build up dollar credits in every seafaring nation around the globe.

No one considers the Lincoln Highway a bad investment, yet it brings in no revenue at all. No one begrudges the outlay for dredging and improving any river or harbor when commercial activity demands it, and the Panama Canal is simply a colossal project of completion and maintenance of a waterway which nature left unfinished. No one begrudges a policeman his pay, and the Panama Canal is the keystone in the defense of the New World. Its indirect dividends are so many and so varied that any cash return whatever is a windfall.

For two decades canal officials had been urging expansion of the facilities when the developments of World War II made it a strategic necessity. The rise of air power, which could hardly have been foreseen a generation before, created a vulnerability in that the locks at each stage stood side by side, offering enemy bombardiers good prospects of double success. Moreover, they were becoming obsolescent in size, for already there were several superliners on the seas, such as the *Queen Mary*, the *Queen Elizabeth*, and the ill-starred *Normandie*, which were too large to transit at Panama.

Accordingly, excavation began 1 July 1940, for the construction of a third set of locks, with basins 1,200 feet long, 140 feet wide, and 45 feet deep—53 per cent larger than those in the original flights. The new locks were sited at some distance from the old ones, to the east of Gatún and to the west of Pedro Miguel and Miraflores; this satisfied military considerations and at the same time achieved the economy of utilizing almost the same diameter of Gatún Lake as is traveled by ships transiting via the smaller locks. The new locks should be "adequate," as Governor Harry Burgess had predicted when he advocated them back in 1931, "for another century."

The Chagres country was transformed, almost overnight, into the most formidable fortress the world has ever seen. Bulldozers swarmed into the jungle, cut away whole mountains, and built secret airfields from which patrolling planes swept the skies in all directions. Coast-artillery pieces, so large that their ammunition must be moved up, round by round, on railroad flatcars, nestled under the tropic foliage, maintaining radio contact with aerial scouts. Cavernous submarine pens, strong points, and bomb shelters were hollowed out of solid rock. Messages crackled in code from vast air-conditioned redoubts which honeycombed the hearts of innocent-looking mountains. Radar eyes scanned the sky and the sea. Torpedo boats and destroyers combed the water approaches. Electronic devices probed every approaching craft for concealed explosives.

Commercial transits fell far below the volume of the worst depression year, while military tonnage reached record heights and kept the canal busy around the clock. Battleships, aircraft carriers, troop transports, and their varied auxiliaries, all in the gray dress of battle, filed silently through the Westward Passage and steamed westward to crush the rising power of the Rising Sun.

XXXIV: VEST-POCKET JUNGLE

THE CHAGRES water, mounting slowly behind Gatún Dam and spreading across the valley, engulfed the lesser hills and subtended the higher peaks as islands. Upon these dry caps clustered the myriad animals of the jungle, imprisoned in a perfect natural setting for what became the laboratory of the Institute for Research in Tropical America.

Barro Colorado keeps the name that it had when Spanish guards along the Gold Road used it for a lookout station, when Morgan's famished men camped there overnight on their march to Panama la Vieja, and when California-bound argonauts paused to drink black coffee at its ranchos. But nowadays it is Gatún Lake's largest island, with an area of 3,609 acres. From its peak, 452 feet above the lake's surface, countless brooklets run down every fold to the inlets and bays which give it a shore line of more than a hundred miles.

For years the island was a bonanza for the natives, who trapped its animals, cut its hardwoods, caught its gorgeous butterflies, and picked its orchids, selling the bounty in Colon at fancy prices to agents of museums, circuses, collectors, and manufacturers. Then Governor Jay J. Morrow, by executive order dated 17 April 1923, set it apart as a natural park and turned it over to the National Research Council. Hunting, trapping, and trespassing were prohibited; the island became a refuge for the specimens of life that its former despoilers had sought. Later some of the smaller adjoining islands were included, and in 1930 a section of the nearby mainland was posted as a forest preserve and made available to the researchers of Barro Colorado.

For the job of curator of the Canal Zone Biological Area, the council selected Dr. James Zetek, entomologist of the U.S. Department of Agriculture, a native of Illinois. He had come to the isthmus in 1911 at the request of Gorgas, who wanted further research into the life habits of the *Anopheles* mosquito. Zetek's studies led Gorgas to make important changes in his authoritative handbook on tropical sanitation. With that mission completed, Zetek suggested the idea of a biological preserve to Dr. Thomas Barbour of the Harvard Museum, chairman of the National Research Council. Patiently the council laid its plans and arranged for institutional support, but they had to wait until the disruptions of World War I had been adjusted for final success.

A dock was built at Frijoles, and then another on the eastern side of Barro Colorado, three miles away. A small area was cleared on the island's steeply rising shore, and a cluster of buildings went up to provide laboratory and library facilities, a mess, and living quarters which can accommodate as many as thirty researchers at a time.

To scientists accredited by the council, the Panama Canal offered the use of its Panama Railroad Company steamers for travel to and from the isthmus, and extended to them the same below-cost rates that are enjoyed by canal employees. It issued passes for their railroad transportation while on the isthmus, and opened its commissaries to them.

Soon the biologists of the world realized that here was the perfect spot for studying the flora and fauna of the tropics, in safety from the hardship and risk of disease and death that hitherto had handicapped their expeditions into the Torrid Zone. Here was the undiluted essence of the jungle world, a natural laboratory of unequaled range, in the back yard of a compound which offered healthful and comfortable accommodations. And the researchers found that the inducements offered by the zone government made it possible to spend a summer or a sabbatical year on Barro Colorado at no greater expense than would be incurred in living at home for the same length of time.

They came in increasing numbers, from the centers of learning in the Old World and the New, and their researches soon began to enrich mankind's knowledge of his habitat. Scientific papers and books published as a result of study on the island have averaged higher than thirty per year, and are still on the increase. They run from popular treatments, such as *A Home-Making Bat, Rainbows on Wings, That Bird the Toucan,* and *Courtship of the Calabatas,* to ponderous expositions like *The Chromosomes of Nautococcus Schraderae Vays., and the Meiotic Division Figure of Male Llaverine Coccids,* and *A Monograph of the Neotropical Mutilid Genus Hoplomutila Ashmead (Hym. Mutilidae).* Since the laboratory is open to scientists of all nations, many of the publications are in the languages of continental Europe.

The island's own unique significance in the scientific world has itself inspired no less than a dozen books and scores of magazine articles. The list of titles is intriguing: *Island Ark, Jungle Island, Tropical Eden, Man-Made Ararat, My Tropical Air Castle, Isle of Upside Down.*

"Here," wrote Carveth Wells, "the zoo is reversed. The scientists work in the laboratories while the animals sit around in the trees outside and look at them."

More than 250 species of birds, from the tiny hummingbird to the giant zopilote and the gawky pelican, have been catalogued, along with at least 53 species of mammals, including the opossum, sloth, anteater, armadillo, deer, peccary, tapir, agouti, squirrel, raccoon, coati, ocelot, cougar, puma, night monkey, capuchin monkey, black howler monkey, marmoset, and several varieties of bats, rats, and mice. The index of insects runs into the thousands: ants, bees, mosquitoes, ticks, lice, wasps, butterflies, moths, fleas, beetles. Reptiles include the crocodile, the alligator, and their less-known cousin the caiman, turtles, tortoises, lizards large and small, and snakes of every size, color, and degree of deadliness, from the tiny coral, whose venom kills in a few minutes, to the giant boa constrictor, whose bone-crushing power is its only weapon. Then there are scorpions, tarantulas, and spiders, and, in the innumerable coves, an endless variety of aquatic plants and animals.

The preserve, which Dr. R. E. Coker called "the embodiment . . . of primeval conditions of life," has not an inch of land, water, or air that is not of interest to some among its visitors. Far beneath the surface run tunnels, leading to the homes of ants, scorpions, tarantulas, spiders, moles, rats, mice, and ground wasps. At ground level are the larger mammals and reptiles, wandering through the undergrowth where swarms of flying insects pursue their varied habits of life. Overhead rise the giants of the rain forest: corotu, black palm, mahogany, cedar, coco, almendro, and the unbelievable maria tree whose wood is so hard that canal engineers use it to make bearings for the lock gates; many of them tower 150 feet above the ground, sending out their lowest branches at fifty feet, from a trunk which at that height is eight feet in diameter. Twining lianas, fungi of both edible and poisonous types, the fabled orchids and other air plants cluster profusely around limb and trunk. Among them scamper the chattering monkeys, and above them dart and soar the birds whose color and song provide an endless enchantment. And around the edges of the island are found tropical fishes, herons, cormorants, algae, and other teeming waterlife.

Even the endless horizons of biology fail to limit the scientific uses of the island. Here goes on a continuing study of the tropical cosmic ray, whose energy potential is believed to be greater by far than that of atomic fission; balloons soar upward from the compound, carrying sensitive instruments with radio broadcasting sets attached, into the stratosphere.

World War II found the island ready for military service no less important in its field than that of the canal itself. Here were conducted definitive experiments in the health and efficiency of soldiers under the conditions of tropical campaign, the deterioration and adequacy of ordnance and combat equipment, and other projects which have not yet been made public.

Here it was that the termite was conquered, after years of experiment with every type of wood and every known or suspected deterrent, repaying the modest investment in the laboratory a million times over in savings to the homeowners of the world. The research continues, and Zetek is confident that the time will come when this greatest destroyer of wooden buildings will be powerless against a single proofing, at nominal cost and effort.

Another of his personal projects has gone far toward halting the ravages of the teredo, the shipworm that riddled the wooden vessels of the early explorers and today poses a problem in the maintenance of piers and wharves in tropical waters.

Over the island spreads a network of trails, each one named, numbered, and marked so that anyone may find his way back to the compound by taking the lower-numbered trail at every junction. Along these paths spread the projects of the scientists: screened bottles, each specially baited to lure and trap a particular variety of insect; fenced-off anthills and beehives; cameras rigged with flash bulbs and trigger releases to capture on film any animal that tampers with the bait; row upon row of wood samples, each treated with a different experimental solution and embedded in the soil to measure relative deterioration.

From their airy cottages around the main building, the wives and children of the scientists assemble to study the butterfly collection, the jars of pickled snakes, the stuffed animals, and the file of microscope slides, or perhaps merely to chat on the veranda while they enjoy frequent concerts by the monkeys in the branches overhead. At mealtime the researchers come in from their vest-pocket jungle, and the Barro Colorado family sits down around a single long dining table.

At the head sits Zetek, presiding over scholarly discussions or the merciless ribbing that each newly arrived scientist gets from the old-timers: "Have you got musserana serum in your snake-bite kit? The ordinary kind won't do you any good here at all, you know. Where's your ammonia pistol? Well, no matter; just stay close to the compound. No need to fear attack from the lions and tigers so long as you can get to a building. You notice that all the doors on Barro Colorado open outward, making it impossible for an animal to push his way in. If you meet a big cat on the trail, don't climb a tree; run for the compound and get a door shut behind you as quick as you can. What! You didn't bring an elephant gun?" And so on. (This deadpan routine has caused more than one tenderfoot to return at an undignified rate of speed from his first venture into the forest.)

Zetek explains to each newcomer the rules of conversation at table: "When the discussion concerns your own specialty," he says, "you have the floor. But when the topic is termites, I'll do the talking."

Every visitor, whether a researcher or not, considers his stay on the island a unique privilege, and the guest book is filled with comments of praise in superlative terms. The wife of Dr. Wendell C. Bennett, assistant curator of anthropology at the American Museum of Natural History (New York), left this testimonial:

Barro Colorado Island Is As Advertised

We declare here and now that the water is just as clear, the Morpho just as blue, the breezes just as soft, the call of the Tinamou just as sad, the Coatis just as mischievous, the Howlers just as uproarious as we have been led to believe.

We have climbed the one hundred and ninety six steps and counted them one by one.

We have sampled Rosa's food most generously and found it good. Her rice is the whitest, lightest, fluffiest rice in the world. Her coffee is delicious and her fried plantain something of which to dream.

Have you heard and possibly doubted tales of Palm Tanagers side by side with the brilliant Summer ones daintily nipping a banana while a Blue Tanager cocks his head from a nearby bush and impatiently awaits his chance?

Have you listened to stories of little white-faced monkeys bounding with incredible leaps from limb to limb, stopping now and again to drain some unknown nectar from the cup of the balsa blossom?

Have you read of the robber Coati who steals shameless the banana left on the food tray for daintier mouths? And who clings tenaciously to the wire as it is pulled and swung, keeping his balance like a trouper until finally, with the last bite in his jaws, he gives up, swings himself around and retreats hand over hand?

Have you heard of bold bright Toucans, just outside the windows, and breath-taking White Hawks winging across the bay? Of stately forest trees and graceful Palms?

Has anyone told you of a fairy island where the air is always sweet—where the sky above and the ground below are filled with strange and fascinating creatures—and where, besides, there are soft beds and good food and cushions and magnificent field glasses and a library?

All this is true—and more—on Barro Colorado.

Signed in good faith, this twenty-fourth day of January, nineteen hundred and thirty eight.

Hope Ranslow Bennett

P.S.: Lest this paradise should seem to be without one flaw, we must add that there is a deplorable lack of archaeological remains.

H. R. B.

Across the mouth of Barro Colorado's harbor, in hailing distance of its guests, steam the ships of the seven seas, flying the flags of all the maritime nations. At the crossroads of the world, our democracy has planted an outpost of pure science, which recognizes no ideologies, no race, no national tongue, no political boundaries.

XXXV: NEW HORIZONS

HERE is more than the greatest engineering feat of all time, more than the world's most important waterway, more than the crux of our military strategy, more even than the proof per se that the tropics can be made pleasantly livable for light-skinned peoples. Here is a department of the United States which is several generations ahead of its own home country in the technique of living.

Its people are United States citizens who, in the service of a great tool of democracy, have submitted to a benevolent dictatorship. Like the residents of the District of Columbia, they have no vote; but, unlike those of the national capital and any other subdivision of American soil, they have no opportunity for private enterprise. They cannot own an inch of ground in the Canal Zone; they cannot operate a business there; they cannot even choose their own living quarters.

It is as though the entire zone were one great military reservation (which it does become during a war). The difference is that the soldier of the Panama Canal in normal times is subject only to civil law, and can terminate his enlistment whenever he sees fit. It is significant, both to the sociologist and to the political theorist, that the turnover of canal employees is very low—so low that it can be assigned almost entirely to other considerations than a worker's dislike of the scheme of things.

The towns of the zone are built all on the same general pattern, with minor variations to fit the lie of the land. The nucleus includes a commissary (where food, clothing, gasoline, furniture, and a complete selection of other personal items are sold at wholesale prices), a dispensary (where medical attention is free), a clubhouse (with cafeteria, laundry station, reading room, soda fountain, movie auditorium, and other recreation facilities), a school, a municipal office (which maintains the buildings and utilities), a Zone Police headquarters, a post office, a firehouse, churches, and a railroad station. Around this center spreads a fringe of dwellings, each looking exactly like its neighbor except for variations in the color of their paint.

The streets and sidewalks are wide, the parkways are green and spacious, the quarters and clubs are airy and inviting, the food is good, the services are efficient, and everything is kept scrupulously clean. There are no skyscrapers, no cramped business districts, no traffic problems, no slums, no unkempt buildings, no eyesores. The architectural monotony (which is the result of economy and not an inherent consequence of the system) is a small price to pay for such advantages. It has, indeed, a beauty all its own.

The lack of business competition and financial risk has not, as some theorists feared that it would, shriveled the spirit of the people; this need, which is said to be basic in human nature, seems to be met by their pride in the efficient operation of the great canal, which itself is not even indirectly a competitive venture. Here is proof that people will strive, for the sheer joy of doing a job well, when their needs are met and when they can comprehend the purposes of the enterprise. A hundred years from now, people all over the world will live as people in the Chagres country live today.

Some of the prophets of the air age foresee within our children's lifetime a world of aerial commerce alone, a world whose seas are barren of ships, whose roads and railways are abandoned, useless strips across the land. If they were right, the future would hold oblivion for the Chagres's great canal. But they disregard some of the basic laws of physics and economics which progress does not change—which, after all, are the levers of progress, through man's increasing efficiency in applying them.

The ton-mile cost of freighting by air is many times the cost by land, which in turn is several times the cost by water. The physicist will confirm that these ratios are independent of technological developments; it is true now and forever that the energy required to propel a mass floating on water is far less than that required to propel it over land, which in turn is far less than that required to hold it aloft against the force of gravity and propel it through the air. An advance in the economy of air transport could hardly fail to bring a proportionate economy in the other two media.

So, until science develops a means of producing and applying energy at a cost so low that it will not affect the final price of goods, the oceans will go on carrying the bulk of the world's trade. This means that the Chagres, for the foreseeable future, will continue to be the world's most valuable river.

Air transport will become an increasingly important factor in world commerce, but this development portends only a deeper entrenchment of our river's importance. Already its new man-made banks are dotted with airfields, which are the hub of the inter-American sky routes. In the coming years, when planes which exist already on drafting boards begin to carry passengers and cargo halfway around the world without a stop, these same fields will fall into their natural place on the axis of Earth's lateral air travel as well.

Beyond the Chagres lies a millennium in which it will continue to see converging at its gates an endless stream of the men and the ships of all the nations, and over them the planes of the shrinking world—sometimes on missions of Peace and Progress, sometimes on missions of Death and Desolation, but always depicting, at this unique scratch on Earth's surface, the frontier of mankind's continuing struggle.

ACKNOWLEDGMENTS

CONTROVERSY is the lone continuing quality, and it characterizes not only the events but the accounts of them. Details differ, often materially, among accepted sources. This is traceable at times to ambiguity, or to an inept translation or transcription from the original, and at others to a writer's higher allegiance to other things than truth. But it weakens a story to acknowledge all its variations. In such cases I weighed the alternatives and selected the version that seemed to me most reliable. Wherever a choice still remained, I chose the best story.

I am grateful to Major General Joseph C. Mehaffey, governor of the Panama Canal, for authority to pursue the project; to Colonel F. H. Wang, executive secretary, for access to official records and to his enviable collection of early Spanish publications; to fellow-Georgian Rufus Hardy, the canal's press representative, for help with research and with problems of quarters and travel in the Zone; to Eleanor D. Burnham, librarian, and her staff of the Panama Canal Library, for special research help, access to the rare-book vault, and the facility of a private study room; to Major A. O. Meyer, chief of the Police and Fire Division, and Zone Policemen James O. Catron and Fred E. Mounts, for transportation and pleasant company on a reconnaissance of the upper Chagres; to G. E.

Matthew, chief of the Hydrographic and Meteorological Section, for maps and enlightening conversations on the river that is his prime official concern and his chief hobby; to Dr. James Zetek, curator of Barro Colorado, for a tour of the island and for access to his records; to Bill Adams, lumber operative, for a woodsman's view of the valley; to Fritz Marti, Fernando Vega, and other old-timers, for firsthand details of past decades; to Evelyn Moore and Sue Core, writers who depict the isthmian scene, for access to unpublished material and permission to draw on their published works; to an officer of the U.S. Air Forces ("Put my name in your book, just because I flew you around? Why in hell should you?") for an air reconnaissance of the Chagres; to Herschel Brickell, of the U.S. Department of State, for a letter of introduction; and to hundreds of others who helped me in various ways to collect my material.

For want of a better word, I have violated my southern raising by the indiscriminate use throughout this book of the word "Yankee" to distinguish United States citizens, irrespective of section, from Latin Americans. "North American" includes too much, and "American" includes still more.

J. E. M.

BIBLIOGRAPHY

Abbot, Henry L., *Problems of the Panama Canal.* New York: The Macmillan Co., 1907.

Abbot, Willis J., *Panama and the Canal.* New York: Dodd, Mead & Co., 1914.

Alba, C., *Etnologia y Poblacion Historica de Panama.* Panama: Imprenta Nacional, 1928.

Ammen, Daniel, *The American Inter-Oceanic Ship Canal Question.* Philadelphia: L. R. Hammersly & Co., 1880.

Andagoya, Pascual de, *Pedrarias Davila.* London: Hakluyt Society, 1865.

Anderson, C. L. G., *Old Panama and Castilla del Oro.* Boston: Page Company, 1914.

Arango, José Augustin, *Datos para la Historia de la Independencia del Istmo.* Panama, 1922.

Arias, Harmodio, *The Panama Canal; a Study in International Law and Diplomacy.* London: P. S. King & Son, 1911.

Arias, Tomás, *Tomás Arias Contestando al Dr. Luiz Martínez Delgado.* Panama: Imprenta Nacional, 1927.

Arosemena, J. D. (ed.), *Panama in 1915.* Panama: Diario de Panama, 1915.

Barrett, John, *Panama Canal; What It Is, What It Means.* Washington: Pan American Union, 1913.

Bates, Lindon W., *The Crisis at Panama.* New York, 1906.

Bell, E. Y., *The Republic of Panama and Its People, with*

Special Reference to the Indians. Washington: Smithsonian Institution Annual Report, 1909.

BELL, HORACE, *On the Old West Coast.* New York: Grosset & Dunlap, 1933.

BENNETT, IRA E., *History of the Panama Canal.* Washington: Historical Publishing Co., 1915.

BENSON, E. F., *Sir Francis Drake.* New York: Harper & Brothers, 1927.

BIGELOW, JOHN, *The Panama Canal.* New York: Press of the Chamber of Commerce, 1886.

BISHOP, FARNHAM, *Panama, Past and Present.* New York: D. Appleton-Century Co., 1916 (rev. ed.).

BISHOP, JOSEPH B., *The Panama Gateway.* New York: Charles Scribner's Sons, 1915 (rev. ed.).

BISHOP, JOSEPH B. AND FARNHAM, *Goethals, Genius of the Panama Canal.* New York: Harper & Brothers, 1930.

BONSAL, STEPHEN, *American Mediterranean.* New York: Moffat, Yard & Co., 1912.

BORTHWICK, J. D., *Three Years in California.* Edinburgh: William Blackwood & Sons, 1857.

BUNAU-VARILIA, PHILIPPE, *The Great Adventure of Panama.* New York: Doubleday, Page & Co., 1920.

———, *Nicaragua or Panama.* New York: Knickerbocker Press, 1901.

———, *Panama: the Creation, Destruction, and Resurrection.* New York: McBride, Nast & Co., 1914.

CARTER, HENRY R., *Yellow Fever.* Baltimore: Williams & Wilkins Co., 1931.

CHATFIELD, MARY, *Light on Dark Places at Panama.* New York: Broadway Publishing Co., 1908.

COLLINS, JOHN O., *Panama Guide.* Panama: Vibert & Dixon, 1912.

CORE, SUE, *Panama Yesterday and Today.* New York: North River Press, 1945.

CORNISH, VAUGHAN, *The Panama Canal and Its Makers.* Boston: Little, Brown & Co., 1909.

COURAU, ROBERT, *Ferdinand de Lesseps.* Paris: Bernard Grasset, 1932.

CROWTHER, SAMUEL, *The Romance and Rise of the American Tropics.* New York: Doubleday, Doran & Co., 1929.

DAMPIER, WILLIAM, *A New Voyage Round the World.* London: Argonaut Press, 1927.

———, *Voyages and Discoveries.* London: Argonaut Press, 1931.

DANSETTE, ADRIEN, *Les Affaires de Panama.* Paris: Perrin, 1934.

DARIEN CANAL COMPANY OF AMERICA, *Prospectus.* New York, 1870.

DELEVANTE, MICHAEL, *Panama Pictures.* New York: Alden Bros., 1907.

DIMOCK, MARSHALL E., *Government-Operated Enterprises in the Panama Canal Zone.* Chicago: University of Chicago Press, 1934.

DULLES, JOHN FOSTER, *The Panama Canal Controversy between Great Britain and the United States.* New York, 1913.

DUVAL, MILES P. JR., *Cadiz to Cathay.* Stanford University: Stanford University Press, 1940.

EXQUEMELIN, ALEXANDRE OLIVIER, *The Buccaneers of America.* New York: E. P. Dutton & Co., 1923.

FABENS, JOSEPH W., *A Story of Life on the Isthmus.* New York: G. P. Putnam & Co., 1853.

FAST, HOWARD, *Goethals and the Panama Canal.* New York: Julian Messner, 1942.

FORBES-LINDSAY, CHARLES H. A., *Panama and the Canal Today*. Boston: L. C. Page & Co., 1926 (rev. ed.).

FRANCK, HARRY A., *Zone Policeman 88*. New York: Century Co., 1913.

FRASER, JOHN FOSTER, *Panama and What It Means*. London: Cassell & Co., 1913.

FRAZER, SIR JAMES GEORGE, *Golden Bough: a Study in Magic and Religion*. New York: The Macmillan Company, 1940.

FREEHOFF, JOSEPH C., *America and the Canal Title*. New York, 1916.

FROUDE, JAMES ANTHONY, *English Seamen in the Sixteenth Century*. New York: Charles Scribner's Sons, 1917.

GAGE, THOMAS, *The English-American*. London: George Routledge & Sons, 1928.

GOETHALS, GEORGE WASHINGTON, *Government of the Canal Zone*. Princeton: Princeton University Press, 1915.

GONZÁLEZ VALENCIA, JOSÉ MARÍA, *Separation of Panama from Colombia*. Washington: Gibson Bros., 1916.

GORGAS, MARIE D., AND BURTON J. HENDRICK, *William Crawford Gorgas*. New York: Doubleday, Page & Co., 1924.

GORGAS, WILLIAM CRAWFORD, *Sanitation in Panama*. New York: D. Appleton & Co., 1915.

GREENE, ELEANOR D., *Panama Sketches*. Boston: Bruce Humphries, 1940.

GREENE, LAURENCE, *The Filibuster*. New York: Bobbs-Merrill Co., 1937.

GREGORY, JOSEPH W. *Gregory's Guide for California Travellers via the Isthmus of Panama*. New York: Nafis & Cornish, 1850.

GRISWOLD, CHAUNCEY D., *The Isthmus of Panama, and*

What I Saw There. New York: Dewitt & Davenport, 1852.

Harris, R. F., *Los Indios de Panama.* Panama: Imprenta Nacional, 1926.

Haskin, Frederic J., *The Panama Canal.* New York: Doubleday, Page & Co., 1914.

Hearn, Lafcadio, *Two Years in the French West Indies.* New York: Harper & Brothers, 1923.

Heilprin, Angelo, *A Defense of the Panama Route.* Philadelphia, 1902.

Henao, J. M., and Gerardo Arrubla, *History of Columbia.* Chapel Hill: University of North Carolina Press, 1938.

Hotchkiss, Charles F., *On the Ebb: a Few Log-Lines from an Old Salt.* New Haven: Tuttle, Morehouse & Taylor, 1878.

Howard, Harry N., *Military Government in the Panama Canal Zone.* Norman, Okla.: University of Oklahoma Press, 1931.

Humphries, F. T., *Indians of Panama: Their History and Culture.* Panama: Editorial la Moderna, 1944.

Irving, Washington, *The Life and Voyages of Christopher Columbus.* New York: G. P. Putnam's Sons, 1902.

———, *Voyages of the Companions of Columbus.* New York: Rimington & Hooper, 1929.

Jefferys, Thomas, *A Description of the Spanish Islands and Settlements on the Coast of the West Indies, Compiled from Authentic Memoirs, Revised by Gentlemen who have Resided Many Years in the Spanish Settlements* . . . London, 1762.

Johnson, Willis F., *Four Centuries of the Panama Canal.* New York: Henry Holt & Co., 1906.

KEMBLE, JOHN HASKELL, *The Panama Route 1848-1869.* Los Angeles: University of California Press, 1943.

KIRKPATRICK, F. A., *Latin America.* New York: The Macmillan Co., 1939.

KNOWER, DANIEL, *The Adventures of a Forty-Niner.* Albany, 1894.

LACHARME, LOUIS DE, *Interoceanic Canal.* New York, 1874.

LAS CASAS, BARTOLOMÉ DE, *An Account of the First Voyages and Discoveries Made by the Spaniards in America, Containing the Most Exact Relation Hitherto Publish'd of Their Unparallel'd Cruelties on the Indians, in the Destruction of Above Forty Millions of People.* London, 1699.

LESSEPS, FERDINAND DE, *Recollections of Forty Years.* New York: D. Appleton & Co., 1888.

LOCKEY, JOSEPH B., *Pan-Americanism: Its Beginnings.* New York: The Macmillan Co., 1920.

LUTZ, OTTO, *Los Habitantes Primitivos de la Republica de la Republica de Panama.* Leipzig: Brandstetter, 1924.

MACGILLIVRAY, W., *The Life, Travels, and Researches of Baron Humboldt.* London: T. Nelson & Sons, 1859.

MACK, GERSTLE, *The Land Divided.* New York: Alfred A. Knopf, 1944.

MAJOR, RICHARD H. (ed.), *Select Letters of Christopher Columbus, with Other Original Documents, Relating to His Four Voyages to the New World.* London: Hakluyt Society, 1870.

MARÉCHAL, HENRI, *Voyage d'un Actionnaire à Panama.* Paris: E. Dentu, 1885.

MARSHALL, LOGAN, *The Story of the Panama Canal.* Philadelphia: J. C. Winston Co., 1913.

MARTYR, PETER (PIETRO MARTIRE D'ANGHIERA), *De Orbe Novo*. New York: G. P. Putnam's Sons, 1912.

MCCAIN, WILLIAM DAVID, *The United States and the Republic of Panama*. Durham, N. C.: Duke University Press, 1937.

MCCOLLUM, WILLIAM S., *California as I Saw It*. Buffalo: George H. Derby & Co., 1850.

MEANS, PHILIP AINSWORTH, *The Spanish Main—Focus of Envy, 1492-1700*. New York: Charles Scribner's Sons, 1935.

MILLS, JOHN SAXON. *The Panama Canal*. London: T. Nelson & Sons, 1913.

MINER, DWIGHT CARROLL, *The Fight for the Panama Route*. New York: Columbia University Press, 1940.

MOORE, DAVID R., *A History of Latin America*. New York: Prentice-Hall, 1938.

MOORE, EVELYN (ed.), *Sancocho; Stories and Sketches of Panama*. Panama: Panama-American Pub. Co., 1938.

MORISON, SAMUEL ELIOT, *Admiral of the Ocean Sea*. Boston: Little, Brown & Co., 1942.

MORROW, JAY J., *The Maintenance and Operation of the Panama Canal*. Mt. Hope: Panama Canal Press, 1923.

NAVARRETE, MARTIN F. DE, *Viajes de Cristobal Colon*. Madrid: Calpe, 1922.

NELSON, WOLFRED, *Five Years at Panama*. New York: Belford Co., 1889.

NIDA, STELLA, *Panama and Its "Bridge of Water."* Chicago: Rand, McNally & Co., 1915.

OTERO, LUIS A., *Panama*. Bogotá: Imprenta Nacional, 1926.

OTIS, F. N., *History of the Panama Railroad*. New York: Harper & Brothers, 1867.

OVIEDO Y VALDES, GONZALO F., *Historia General y Natural*

de las Indias. Madrid: Imprenta de la Real Academia de la Historia, 1853.

PACIFIC MAIL STEAMSHIP COMPANY, *A Sketch of the Route to California, China and Japan, via the Isthmus of Panama.* San Francisco: A. Roman & Co., 1867.

PADELFORD, NORMAN J., *The Panama Canal in Peace and War.* New York: The Macmillan Co., 1942.

PANAMA CANAL RETIREMENT ASSOCIATION, *The Canal Diggers in Panama, 1904 to 1928.* Balboa Heights, 1928.

"The Panama Massacre," *Star & Herald,* Panama, 1857.

PANAMA RAILROAD COMPANY, *Prospectus.* New York, 1849.

———, *Report to Stockholders, April 1, 1872.* New York, 1872.

PATERSON, WILLIAM, *Central America.* London: Trubner & Co., 1857.

PECK, ANNE MERRIMAN, *The Pageant of South American History.* New York: Longmans, Green & Co., 1941.

PEPPERMAN, WALTER L., *Who Built the Panama Canal?* New York: E. P. Dutton & Co., 1915.

PIM, B. C. T., *The Gate of the Pacific.* London: L. Reeve & Co., 1863.

RATCLIFF, SAMUEL, *Considerations on the Subject of a Communication Between the Atlantic and Pacific Oceans, by Means of a Ship Canal Across the Isthmus, which Connects North and South America; and the Best Means of Effecting It, and Permanently Securing Its Benefits for the World at Large.* Georgetown, D. C., 1836.

REED, CHARLES A. L., *Panama Notes.* Cleveland, 1906.

REYES, RAFAEL, *The Two Americas.* New York: Frederick A. Stokes Co., 1914.

Rippy, J. Fred, *The Capitalists and Colombia.* New York: Vanguard Press, 1931.

Robinson, Fayette, *California and Its Gold Regions.* New York: Stringer & Townsend, 1849.

Robinson, Tracy, *Fifty Years at Panama, 1861-1911.* New York: Trow Press, 1911.

Rodrigues, J. Carlos, *The Panama Canal.* New York: Charles Scribner's Sons, 1885.

Roosevelt, Theodore, *An Autobiography.* New York: Charles Scribner's Sons, 1920.

Schonfield, Hugh J., *Ferdinand de Lesseps.* London: Herbert Joseph, 1937.

Scott, William R., *The Americans in Panama.* New York: Statler Publishing Co., 1912.

Scroggs, W. O., *Filibusters and Financiers.* New York: The Macmillan Co., 1916.

Scruggs, William L., *The Colombian and Venezuelan Republics.* Boston: Little, Brown & Co., 1900.

Shelford, Victor E., *Naturalist's Guide to the Americas.* Baltimore: Williams & Wilkins Co., 1926.

Société Civile du Canal du Darien, *Prospectus.* Paris, 1860.

Sosa, Juan B., and Enrique J. Arce, *Compendio de Historia de Panama.* Panama: Diario de Panama, 1911.

Stephens, John Lloyd, *Incidents of Travel in Central America, Chiapas, and Yucatan.* New York: Harper & Brothers, 1841.

Stevens, John Frank, *An Engineer's Recollections.* New York: McGraw-Hill Book Co., 1936.

Stevens, Walter B., *A Trip to Panama.* St. Louis: Lesan-Gould, 1907.

Taylor, Bayard, *Eldorado, or, Adventures in the Path of Empire.* New York: George P. Putnam, 1850.

THOMPSON, G. A., *Hand Book to the Pacific and California.* London: Simpkin & Marshall, 1849.

THOMPSON, RICHARD WIGGINTON, *The Interoceanic Canal at Panama.* Washington: Thomas McGill & Co., 1881.

TOMES, ROBERT, *Panama in 1855.* New York: Harper & Brothers, 1855.

ULLOA, ANTONIO DE, *Relacion Historica del Viaje a la America Meridional.* Madrid: Antonio Marin, 1748.

VAN DYKE, JOHN C., *In the West Indies.* New York: Charles Scribner's Sons, 1932.

VERNON, EDWARD, *Original Papers Relating to the Expedition to Panama.* London: M. Cooper, 1744.

VERRILL, A. HYATT, *Panama of Today.* New York: Dodd, Mead & Co., 1937.

VILLEGAS, SABAS A., *The Republic of Panama.* Panama: Imprenta Nacional, 1924.

WAFER, LIONEL, *A New Voyage and Description of the Isthmus of America.* Oxford: Hakluyt Society, 1934.

WARREN, T. R., *Dust and Foam.* New York: Charles Scribner, 1859.

WEIR, HUGH C., *The Conquest of the Isthmus.* New York: G. P. Putnam's Sons, 1909.

WELLS, CARVETH, *Panamexico.* New York: McBride & Co., 1937.

WILLIAMS, MARY WILHELMINE, *Anglo-American Isthmian Diplomacy, 1815-1915.* Washington: American Historical Association, 1916.

WILSON, CHARLES M., *Ambassadors in White.* New York: Henry Holt & Co., 1942.

WILTSEE, ERNEST A., *Gold Rush Steamers of the Pacific.* San Francisco: Grabhorn Press, 1938.

WINTHROP, THEODORE, *The Canoe and the Saddle.* Boston: James R. Osgood & Co., 1871.

WRIGHT, IRENE ALOHA (ed.), *Documents Concerning English Voyages to the Spanish Main, 1569-1580.* London: Hakluyt Society, 1932.

WYCHERLY, GEORGE, *Buccaneers of the Pacific.* Indianapolis: Bobbs-Merrill Co., 1928.

PERIODICALS

Star & Herald, Panama

Panama American, Panama

Panama Canal Record, Mt. Hope

Bulletin du Canal Interocéanique, Ancon

Annual Reports of the Barro Colorado Island Biological Station, Balboa

Annual Reports of the Governor of the Panama Canal, Washington

Engineering Magazine

National Geographic Magazine

MISCELLANEOUS

The Congressional documents and reports catalogued in the Library of Congress bibliography, *List of References on the Panama Canal and the Panama Canal Zone* (H. H. B. Meyer), 1919, and the file of pamphlets and clippings in the Panama Canal Library, Balboa Heights, known as *The Panama Collection.*

Index